IF THESE WALLS COULD TALK

A CELEBRATION OF THE
SYDNEY CRICKET GROUND

IF THESE WALLS COULD TALK

A CELEBRATION OF THE
SYDNEY CRICKET GROUND

ANDREW WEBSTER

STOKE
HILL
PRESS

First published in 2021

by Stoke Hill Press
c/ 122 Wellbank Street
Concord NSW Australia 2137
www.stokehillpress.com

A catalogue record for this
book is available from the
National Library of Australia

NATIONAL
LIBRARY
OF AUSTRALIA

ISBN: 978-0-6487331-4-0

Cover Design by Luke Causby, Blue Cork
Internal Design & Typesetting by Kirby Jones
Printed in Australia by Ligare Book Printers

'I get a greater thrill playing on the Sydney Cricket Ground than on any other, and I think it is the finest cricket ground in the world on which to play ... It can't be very long before I shall have to put my bat away for good, but it is from the Sydney ground that I shall derive my happiest cricket memories.'

Don Bradman, December 12, 1947

Contents

Foreword

by Anthony Shepherd AO

Trustee No. 136, Chairman No. 14
Sydney Cricket Ground

EVEN WHEN IT'S EMPTY, the Sydney Cricket Ground is alive. It's alive with memories of great athletes and great matches from decades past. Most importantly, it's alive with the memories of the people who sat in the grandstands or watched history play out on the famous field.

Those memories have been captured in print since 1854, when the first report of a cricket match at the Garrison Ground appeared in Sydney's early newspapers.

The written word has since been the constant companion of happenings at the Sydney Cricket Ground, preserving history and taking the tales of victory, defeat and life itself far beyond the grandstands that have ringed the ground.

In *If These Walls Could Talk* Andrew Webster has looked with fresh eyes at some of the most famous moments. His rich and detailed retelling reinforces his standing as one of Australia's finest sportswriters.

Andrew is a personal friend. He is also a great friend of the Sydney Cricket Ground. But, like all the top-tier writers who have come before him — Davis, Corbett, O'Reilly, Goodman, Heads, Gibson — he leaves that friendship at the gates. The ground, its sports and its officials expect no favours. We ask of him and his colleagues honest, fair and expert appraisal. Andrew delivers that and more with a wit that stands him apart from his peers.

The humorous touch that marks the author's writings for the *Sydney Morning Herald* is a recognisable characteristic. It is in no way defining.

The closing chapter, '63 bats', underscores Andrew's skill in storytelling and capturing emotion on personal and collective levels.

All but the bravest authors would avoid finishing with one of the most tragic and saddening moments in our ground's history. Andrew, and his publisher Geoff Armstrong, did not take that easy, comfortable option. The final chapter looks at a moment that united Australia and world cricket in mourning. The fatal injury sustained by Phillip Hughes while batting for South Australia is one of the most singularly shocking moments in Australian sport.

Andrew takes us back to the heartbreak of Phillip's family and friends, the staff who'd watched him mature, the photographers who'd covered his entire career and how grief spread across the nation.

And, as Andrew draws the threads together, he captures how Phillip's memory continues at the Sydney Cricket Ground and gives us a new understanding of those sad days in November 2014.

I was delighted to commission this book as the 14th chairman of Trustees of the Sydney Cricket Ground. I congratulate Andrew for its authorship and Geoff and his team for bringing it to print.

Introduction

By Geoff Armstrong

THE SYDNEY CRICKET GROUND today is much changed from the playing field that was quietly granted to the soldiers of Victoria Barracks in July 1851, and on which a game between the Garrison and Royal Victoria Clubs was played on Wednesday, February 15, 1854. This was the first official cricket match staged at the venue, which is located about four kilometres south-east of Circular Quay. Back then, it was named the Garrison Ground. It would become known as the Military Ground, the Civil and Military Ground, the Association Cricket Ground and, from 1894, the Sydney Cricket Ground or, as we all like to say, the 'SCG'.

Generations on from that low-key beginning, the ground's vista now features six light towers, an almost complete ring of modern grandstands, and electronic scoreboards. But if you have the chance to walk out to the middle of the ground, perhaps during an organised tour, a corporate function or during 'kick-to-kick' after a Sydney Swans AFL game, you can stand on a piece of the playing field and take yourself back to days of old. The stands are new, but that grass you are standing on is exactly where Victor Trumper fielded when 'Tip' Foster made his famous 287 on his Test debut in 1903–04. This is where Douglas Jardine placed his bodyline field when Stan McCabe kept hooking Harold Larwood's lethal bumpers to the pickets. It's where Ron Roberts sprinted over the only piece of reasonably firm turf on a drenched Saturday afternoon in July 1950 to score the try that meant Clive Churchill's Australians regained the rugby league Ashes for the first time in 30 years. It's the ground on which police clashed with protesters during the angry, acrimonious Springbok rugby tour of 1971, almost a century after the local constabulary was called to break up the infamous riot that broke out after NSW captain Billy Murdoch was judged run out by an umpire the locals deemed crooked. They were all convinced the 'ump' was collaborating with the visiting English team led by a crusty autocrat named Lord Harris.

Close your eyes, let your heels sink slowly into the grass, and you're back to any or all of those times. Look out from the middle and it's surprising how close a person sitting in the stands actually is. You can make out their face, their smile or scowl. This is true if a player looks into the upper deck of today's lofty Brewongle Stand as it surely was when he or she looked into the stately old Brewongle Stand that stood on the same territory on the western side of the ground from 1881 to 1978. Look into the Members Pavilion and the experience is as it was any day since 1886, when it was opened amid considerable fanfare. Critics of the day considered it to be an architectural triumph, one that has stood the test of time.

For many young Sydneysiders with a love of sport, a first visit to the SCG remains a rite of passage. For teenagers across the years, the adventure might start with a brisk stroll up Foveaux Street from Central Station and then across Moore Park. Quickly, you realise you are far from alone; like-minded pilgrims are all heading in the same direction and you feel as if you've been conscripted into a privileged club. On my first visit, in the summer of '70–71, when my uncle took me to see Barry Richards bat for South Australia in a Sheffield Shield match, our entry was through the turnstiles at the back of the Sheridan Stand, a task completed with an equal sense of wonder and eager anticipation. Once inside, I skipped on the concrete behind the Sheridan, heading east, not quite knowing what was ahead of me. And then … there it was! … bathed in late morning sunshine: the Hill and, at its summit, the famous scoreboard. To walk out of the shade of the back of the stand into the bright sunlight was to be dazzled by the greenness of it all — the playing surface, the grass on the Hill and the plethora of green-roofed grandstands: the Members Pavilion on the opposite side of the field, the Ladies Stand, the Brewongle, the Sheridan. To the immediate north of the Hill was the 'Bob Stand', its roof just as green, and further along, the 'Paddo hill'. On the field, umpires, the fielding team and then the two batsmen had just emerged from the dressing-rooms in the Pavilion; in winter, third grade might be finishing or the reserves just kicking off. Whenever there is action in the middle, there is a buzz among the spectators. Some patrons are more perceptive than others but all, in their own way, are interesting. The barracking, you quickly learn, is something to behold.

We all have early special memories of the SCG. Australia's most famous bush balladeer, Andrew 'Banjo' Paterson, was 14 when he was an eyewitness to the Lord Harris riot. 'I was sitting by the picket fence, just below where the scoring board is now,' he recalled half a century later. 'We all started to hoot and a chap sitting near me said, "Come on boys, we can't stand this," and he jumped in over the pickets. His feet had hardly touched the ground when there were a thousand men over the fence, all running for the centre of the ground.'

Young Billy McKell, who grew up in Redfern, not far from the ground, knew of an 'adjustable paling' on the Paddington side of the SCG, which he and his mates guarded as secret for several years. 'After squeezing through we would replace the paling,' McKell recalled in 1941, by which time he was NSW Premier and chairman of the SCG Trustees. In 1947, he became Australia's Governor-General and eventually, to the chagrin of many of his old Labor Party comrades, he accepted a knighthood. He never lost his love for the SCG.

'The most thrilling cricket match I saw was the 1903 Test when umpire Crockett gave Clem Hill run out and the crowd jeered him until the match finished,' he told a reporter from the *Daily News*. 'Every person on the ground joined in the demonstration.

'Another feature of that match that I recall was the magnificent knock of Victor Trumper, who compiled 185 not out. Maybe Trumper captured my imagination because I was young, but I rate him the best batsman I have seen.

'The greatest football match was the "Rorke's Drift of rugby league" in 1914, when Harold Wagstaff's English Test side battled on with three men short. That game sticks in my memory,' McKell said, recalling the third Test of a famous series, when the visitors held on to win 14–6, to regain the Ashes.

'Who is the best footballer you have seen?' he was asked.

'Dally Messenger is the greatest footballer to have graced the Cricket Ground.'

Banjo and Bill McKell, like countless others, discovered that the SCG is a stage on which wondrous actors such as Vic and Dally emerge as heroes, and Lord Harris, Bob Crockett and their ilk serve as villains. Every generation provides its own stars, to build on established traditions and to create their own history. Though the ground was commissioned originally as a site for cricket, it has witnessed unforgettable moments across a wide variety of major events, including the British Empire Games, school pageants, religious gatherings and sell-out concerts. Big crowds have watched not just cricket and the football codes, but also cycling, athletics, tennis, baseball and lacrosse. The ground has played an integral part in Sydney's story; its history is as colourful as any of the city's grandest landmarks.

IN JULY 1907, AFTER a crowd first reported at more than 52,000 saw NSW play the New Zealand All Blacks at the SCG, a correspondent from the *Evening News* asked Sydney Fairland, the ground secretary, how the announced attendance figure compared to other events that had taken place at the ground. Fairland replied that the only time it had been exceeded was when 65,000 came for a Jubilee Public Schools sports gathering on June 21, 1897. 'The best cycling attendance,' he continued, 'was when Major Taylor raced here in 1904. The crowd then was 30,000. That was at night, while when [Arthur] Zimmerman competed in November 1895, there were 29,000 persons present on a Saturday afternoon.'

Zimmerman's crowd of cycling enthusiasts was a new ground record. Such was cycling's popularity, the SCG Trustees built a banked asphalt track around the outer edge of the playing field, the top of the track about the same height as the picket fence. From 1898 to the Great War, the track was boldly lit by overhanging acetylene gas lamps and crowds flocked to the night riding in their thousands.

The official crowd figure for the NSW-New Zealand game in 1907 was later reduced to 49,327, after it was found that some spectators had been counted twice. Fairland revealed that contrary to a couple of newspaper reports, the gates had never been closed, so no one was turned away. Indeed, he claimed that 'spectators were sitting down on the terraces [and that] the ground could have held from 5000 to 10,000 more persons'.

This was amply demonstrated on June 5, 1920, when a rugby league crowd officially measured at 65,378 but surely a few thousand more watched England defeat Sydney 27–20 in the opening game of the Lions' Australian tour. A week earlier, 31,064 had seen Easts defeat Wests in a club game, and among them was England manager John Wilson, who told JC Davis, editor of the Sydney sporting weekly *The Referee*, how impressed he was that 'every corner and crevice of the ground' was occupied. 'There'll be 20,000 more here next Saturday if it be a fine day,' said Davis.

An incredulous Wilson couldn't see how, but at 1pm, two hours before kickoff, 50,000 had already found a vantage point, with more and more pouring through the gates. The bike track had recently been removed, which boosted the ground's capacity, but not to this extent. 'Venturesome youths clambered to the dizzy height of the great grandstand roof,' wrote the *Sun*'s Claude Corbett. 'Over the fence and on to the ground went thousands of people who took up positions right on the touchline.' Early on, referee Tom McMahon stopped play because fans were encroaching on the field, and he refused to continue until they were pushed back. At fulltime, wrote Corbett, '10,000 people swarmed over the ground like a colony of ants, running to acclaim their heroes.' Harold Horder, the 'wonder winger' who scored three tries for the home side, was carried shoulder-high from the field.

Nine months later, the crowd at the fifth Ashes Test wasn't as big, but the atmosphere was similarly electric, especially on the final morning when England vice-captain Rockley Wilson clashed with a patron in the Members Pavilion after he was dismissed, and former Australian captain Monty Noble had to dash forward to separate them. Noble is an important figure in the SCG story, whose contribution as one of the greatest all-rounders and captains to play on the ground and as a long-time Trustee (elected as the members' representative) led to the big grandstand built at the northern end in 1936 being named the MA Noble Stand following his death in 1949. Rockley Wilson had denigrated the local barrackers in his match reports of the Sydney Tests in 1920–21 that were published in UK newspapers and then promptly cabled back to Australia, and the fans were quick to let him know that they did not appreciate such a slander.

The clash that prompted Noble's intervention occurred early on day three of the Test; in the crowd for the first two days were a father and son from Bowral in the NSW Southern Highlands — George and Donald Bradman — and the 'privilege' (Don's word) of seeing Charlie Macartney score a superb 170 is said to have helped mould the ambition of 12-year-old Don. Also there was Lou Benaud, a young cricketer from

Penrith, a township situated 50 kilometres west of the SCG, at the foot of the Blue Mountains. Lou's parents had given him a trip to the Test in 1920–21 as a 17th birthday gift. He, too, was transfixed by the great Macartney. 'We are a lucky cricketing set in Sydney to have seen so many wonderful things from Trumper and Macartney,' wrote JC Davis.

'I shall never be satisfied until I play on this ground,' Don Bradman said quietly to his father on their journey home.

Two decades later, Lou Benaud took his nine-year-old son Richie to the SCG for a Sheffield Shield match between South Australia, captained by The Don, who'd moved to Adelaide in 1935, and NSW. 'As it happened, I didn't see much of Bradman because NSW batted almost the whole day, but I did see Clarrie Grimmett bowl and take 6 for 118,' Richie Benaud would recall. 'I went home that evening and started thinking about bowling leg-breaks.'

This reflex of a budding star yearning to be like a current champion he or she had just seen in action at the SCG is common across generations.

Doug Walters, from Dungog in country NSW, was 18 when he saw South Africa's Graeme Pollock score 122 in the third Test at the SCG in January 1964. 'If anything could be said to have fired my personal ambition to play for Australia it was sitting there at the Cricket Ground watching a 19-year-old slaughter the Australian Test attack,' Walters wrote in his book, *Looking for Runs*. During the previous season, Walters had scored 140 not out for NSW Colts against Queensland Colts at the SCG No. 2, famously hitting a six that ended up in Kippax Lake, which is located in Moore Park, across the road from the precinct. In 1965–66, less than a month after his 20th birthday, Walters played his first Test in Sydney. In 1968–69, against the West Indies at the SCG, he became the first man in cricket history to score a double century and single century in the same Test match. In 1974–75, the fans hung a huge banner across the top of the Hill: 'The Doug Walters Stand'.

Walters was a childhood hero of a young lad from south-western Sydney also destined for greatness. 'Many of my favourite cricketing memories revolve around the iconic Sydney Cricket Ground,' Steve Waugh would write in December 2003, on the eve of his 168th and final Test match, against India in Sydney. Waugh was eight years old when his cricket coach introduced him and his team-mates from the Panania-East Hills under-10s to the ground. 'I felt like I'd landed on another planet. Shuffling through the old turnstiles was an experience in itself. We sat on the Hill in our whites eating Four'N Twenty pies, drinking cans of Coke and mimicking the action in front of us.'

Waugh has fond memories of backyard cricket matches, where the driveway at the family home was the SCG pitch and the 'dulcet tones' of Alan McGilvray on the portable transistor provided commentary from a real Test match being played in Sydney or interstate. He and his brothers, including twin Mark, who would also play more than 100 Tests, argued about who would be Australia and who had to be England. 'We wanted to be one of the Chappells or Lillee, Thommo, Dougie Walters or Rod Marsh, never [Tony] Greig or [John] Edrich or [Bob] Willis,' Steve remembers.

What is true of cricket is true of other sports. The famous Wallaby Trevor Allan was 10 years old when he sat with his father among a drenched SCG crowd of 18,000 to see NSW beat South Africa in 1937. Torrential rain created puddles ankle deep on a field that the press said resembled a skating rink, and Allan was 'hooked'. Two years later, he was the star of the Willoughby Public School XV that the *Sun* described as 'one of the finest teams for its years and weight that has played in Sydney — we'll go further — in Australia'. In 1947, just a few days after his 21st birthday, he became Australian captain. Today, alongside Dally Messenger, Richie Benaud, Steve Waugh and a select group of sporting legends, he is honoured with a sculpture as part of the Basil Sellers-SCG Sports Sculptures Project.

Steve Edge sat in the Sheridan Stand with his father and grandfather to see their beloved St George play a succession of big games in the 1960s, including the historic match against Great Britain in 1962 and an epic grand final versus Souths in 1965. Both games attracted colossal crowds. The 57,744 fans who saw the Lions thrash the Dragons 33–5 was a highest attendance for a midweek game at the SCG; the 78,056 who saw the mighty Saints beat the Rabbitohs to win their 10th straight premiership remains the ground record. In fact, there were a few thousand extra squeezed inside, some on grandstand roofs, and more still perched in various high places, including light towers, in the next-door Showground. Some jilted fans loitered outside to catch a little of the atmosphere, or at least to be able to say they were 'there', while others trudged home disappointed, bemoaning the fact that the Trustees' plans in the early '50s to build a 100,000-seat stadium had never come to fruition. The following year's grand final would be an all-ticket affair and, for the first time, would be broadcast live on television. Young Steve Edge told his dad his dream was to play even one game on the ground. He would be involved in 11 grand finals across all grades in 14 seasons, 1971 to 1984, and win five first-grade premierships for St George and Parramatta, four of them as captain.

Edge made his first-grade debut in 1973, the same year the Bradman Stand was built on the site of the old Paddo hill. Four years later, when he led the Dragons to an epic 22–0 win in the rugby league premiership's first grand final replay, the fans in the Brewongle Stand were no longer protected from the elements, as the structure's roof, which had been condemned as dangerous, had been removed. A new, bigger Brewongle Stand, complete with 'corporate boxes', was opened in 1980, four years before the Bob Stand was superseded by a much larger building that was originally known as the Pat Hills Stand, named after the former SCG Trust chairman, and renamed the Bill O'Reilly Stand in 1988. The Hill was concreted and then a brick-and-mortar Doug Walters Stand built in front of the old scoreboard in 1985, the same year the Sheridan Stand was demolished, to make room for the Clive Churchill Stand. More modern stands would emerge in the 21st century: the Victor Trumper Stand on the site of the Hill and new Don Bradman and MA Noble Stands that opened in 2014. Consequently, the ground has lost some of its green, but the Members Pavilion, Ladies Stand and playing field remain largely as they were in the 19th century, as does the SCG's character. A special experience is to be at the ground at night, when there is no one else around except the ghosts of legends past lurking in the shadows, perhaps waiting for you to leave so they can enjoy another game of their own. As true as any baseball park in Iowa, the Sydney Cricket Ground is still a field of dreams.

HOWEVER, THERE IS ONE intrinsic part of the games that are played at the SCG to which we fans are denied access: what is sometimes called the 'inner sanctum'. When HV 'Bert' Evatt, High Court judge, senior member of the John Curtin and Ben Chifley governments, president of the United Nations General Assembly and Labor Party leader, was elected as an SCG Trustee in 1940, his old friend Arthur Mailey, a former Test leg-spinner turned journalist, recalled how 20 years earlier Evatt had 'sat on the Hill and watched Australia play England, [which] inspired in him an ambition — to sit in front of the Trustees' cottage, and watch cricket and football from another angle'. Many fans outside the members reserve look over at the Pavilion and wonder what it would be like to watch the action from that vantage point. Patrons in the 'members' and 'outer' alike can only guess as to what is happening in the dressing-rooms located at the two ends of the Pavilion. Does the view of the SCG change when you become a participant, whether as a player or official?

'As a small boy,' said Sir William McKell, 'I always had the theory that all small boys should see the matches at the Cricket Ground, whether they paid to go in or not. I was greatly embarrassed at a later stage (when he became chairman of the SCG Trustees) when the secretary told me that a lot of trouble was resulting from boys getting over the fence and not paying to go into the ground. He said that something should be done about it.'

Sir William never said whether he did anything about it.

Better than becoming an administrator is, as Steve Edge did so many times, to fulfil the dream of actually playing in a big game on the other side of the boundary fence. Nine years after watching Charlie Macartney make his brilliant hundred against England in 1920–21, Don Bradman scored 452 not out in a Sheffield Shield game against Queensland; three years on from making that then world record score, he was facing Harold Larwood at the SCG during the bodyline series. Doug Walters was in the home dressing-room on the Saturday in February 1971 when another English fast bowler, John Snow flattened Australian No. 9 Terry Jenner with a fierce riser and then clashed, in the manner of Rockley Wilson 50 years before, with a spectator on the fence in front of the Paddo hill. Edge was not a St George fan in the Sheridan but Saints' hooker in the scrums when Graeme Langlands, the mighty 'Chang', a League Immortal, wore white boots on grand final day in 1975 and his team were humbled 38–nil by the Roosters. The Dragons closed ranks after the game and the secrets of what happened in the dressing-room have remained largely silent, one more dramatic tale for the old brick walls of that sacred room to keep to themselves.

This book is not a comprehensive history of the SCG. That was never the intention. Instead, Andrew Webster has focused on 10 of his most memorable moments from the last 60 years of the ground's history, bringing to his stories his twin identities — as a devoted fan and accomplished sportswriter. His subject matter is broad; not just cricket and football, but rock music, too. There is joy and tragedy. The journalist in him meant it was essential he speak to as many key players as he could. His ambition is to find out what *really* happened, to explore part of the SCG's secret history.

When the book was still just an idea, I was fortunate to be invited to a special lunch in the home dressing-room in the Members Pavilion, where Andrew was in conversation with Alan Davidson and Neil Harvey. I was an interloper, happy to stay in the background and listen as these two great men of cricket reminisced about Bradman and Benaud, Ashes and Tied Tests, big hits and brilliant hundreds. I was struck by how much Alan and Neil still cared for each other, as old teammates and lifelong friends, and how much they genuinely loved the ground. They were at their most animated and most passionate when they talked about the camaraderie of the teams they were a part of and the joy of their sport. The strength of their recollection of the moments that mattered to them was extraordinary.

After we bid our farewells and I walked across Moore Park and down Foveaux Street to Central Station, I pondered just what an incredible time I'd enjoyed. I was blessed to have spent time with two sporting legends in a setting that is every sports lover's dream. And I'd had reinforced something that perhaps I'd never fully understood, a lesson that shines again and again through the chapters of this book. From the first time I visited the SCG, I'd always thought it was special because of the history, the atmosphere, the quality of the sport, the stands and the colour, especially the green. And that's all true. The ground provides a glorious, unique setting, and a genuine love for the place gets into your blood when you're a kid and never leaves you. But it's the characters and champions who have emerged from its dressing rooms over the past 170 years who truly set it apart.

CHAPTER 1

Memories Live Longer than Dreams

Alan Davidson and Neil Harvey

IF THESE WALLS COULD TALK, what would they say? Would they tell us all the secrets of the Sydney Cricket Ground?

Would they tell us what's been said, right here, in the home dressing-room of the Members Pavilion, where for more than 130 years giants of sport have risen and fallen; where hard truths have been delivered and quarrelling teammates have pushed and shoved and grabbed each other's throats; where champagne has been necked in triumph or beer solemnly sipped in defeat; where players have converged after the death of one of their own, out there, on the emerald green turf that's supposed to be their playground?

If these walls could talk, what would they tell us?

Would they tell us what Steve Waugh said as he tucked his lucky red rag into his pocket and went out to bat in the final session of the second day of the Fifth Ashes Test in 2003, when he required no less than a century to save his career, with the rest of the country grinding to a standstill to watch and listen as he edged closer to triple figures but also to the last ball of the day?

Would they let us in on the conversation in 1993 when Australian captain Allan Border talked to his bowlers at lunch on day four about how they could dismiss West Indies batsman Brian Lara, who was batting and batting and batting his way to an eventual innings of 277? Or what was said in 2004 as another virtuoso, Sachin Tendulkar, remained unbeaten on 241 in what doubled as Steve Waugh's final Test match?

Would they take us into the corner of the dressing-room in 1992 after a tubby blond right-arm leg-spin bowler, with zinc daubed on the end of his nose, was belted to all parts of the ground in his Test debut against India? Would they tell us about his self-doubt, whether he thought he belonged here, if he figured he'd belong in the club of players who played just one Test? And would they take us back to January 2007, after he played his final Test, this time against England, having captured a world record 708 wickets from 145 matches, when his name, Shane Warne, is written in gold on the honour boards that adorn the walls of the dressing-room?

Would they tell us what it felt like to be sitting on the balcony among the Australian players on New Year's Day in 1996 as Michael Bevan ran his eye along the boundary, requiring four runs from the last ball of the one-day match against the ever-daunting West Indies for victory, with a full house that had *ooh'd* and *ahh'd* every delivery, with all of us at home watching on television because it seemed to mean so much more back then?

Every allowable fieldsman was moved out to the ropes, with towering off-spinner Roger Harper coming in, his arm reaching for the heavens, then leaping into the air before easing out a looping delivery that landed right there, in the slot, for the left-handed Bevan to cannon it straight back down the ground, almost taking off the umpire's head, before it thudded into the gold Benson and Hedges sign in front of the sightscreen. Bill Lawry was up there in the Channel Nine commentary box going absolutely spare as Bevan raised his arms and bat in the air in triumph.

Would the walls tell us about all that?

Maybe.

Maybe they could tell us about other sports, such as the scenes in the dressing-room after Australia's rugby international against New Zealand in 1907, when a short, stocky winger called Herbert Henry Messenger was celebrated after he landed a sideline conversion to secure a last-minute 5–all draw. Maybe they will take us there again, four years later, after the player by then known simply as 'Dally' led NSW to a 35–10 victory over New Zealand in the first game of 'rugby league' played at the ground.

Perhaps the walls will reminisce about all the heroics they've seen, such as Souths captain John Sattler plopping down on the wooden bench after his team's win over Manly in the 1970 grand final, his face bloodied and swollen after rival forward John Bucknall introduced him to his forearm after just three minutes. Or they could tell us about the emotion in the voice of NSW captain Steve Mortimer in 1985, with a can of Toohey's in hand after the Blues had won a State of Origin series against Queensland for the first time. They might speak of the eeriness cast over the ground when word spread through the stands and then out onto the field just minutes before the Centenary Test in 2008 that Jack Gibson, who won five grand finals as a coach at the SCG, had passed away at the age 79.

If you got these walls talking, they might not shut up.

They could talk about the Sydney Swans, the transplanted Australian football team that's made this ground their home since 1982. They could tell us of the flamboyance of full forward Warwick Capper, resplendent with blond mullet, kicking goal after goal, including 10 against Richmond in 1986. They could tell us how Tony Lockett felt after kicking a behind against Essendon in 1996 to send the Swans into their first grand final since their move north. Or when Lockett broke Gordon Coventry's all-time VFL/AFL goalscoring record with his 1300th major, prompting a tide of fans from every stand to jump the fence and charge towards him.

Yes, the sacred red brick and grey mortar of the home dressing-room at the SCG could tell us all these things; about all the pain and excitement and relief and anger it has witnessed. But, regrettably, the walls are issuing a firm 'no comment'. It's a sacred place for a reason. It's giving away nothing.

What's said here, stays here.

And that's fine because here, on a sunny Friday afternoon, two of Australia's greatest cricketers, both now in their early 90s, can talk to us instead. Alan Davidson and Neil Harvey have as deep an affinity with this corner of the ground as any sportsperson can have. On February 20, 1963, at stumps on the final day of the fifth Ashes Test against England, they walked from the field, up the stairs and past standing and applauding members, into this room and into retirement.

Over a long lunch, in the home team's dressing-room, they tell us what the walls will not.

'Memories live longer than dreams,' says Davidson, the boy who went from Lisarow to Lord's and back again, having played 44 Tests, taking 186 wickets and scoring 1328 runs. 'That's the biggest thing about coming back to this place. I can remember every game that I ever played, every incident, every shot.'

Harvey, the left-handed attacking batsman from Victoria who scored 6149 runs in 79 Tests, can similarly remember the times spent on this ground and inside these walls.

'Always do when I come here,' Harvey, says. 'When I got out of the car on Driver Avenue, it all came flooding back — although the ground seems a hell of a lot smaller. You feel closed in now because of the new stands.'

Over the next few hours, sitting in the players' viewing room with its large windows allowing us to look out over the empty sunbathed playing surface, Davidson and Harvey transport us back to another time when the scoreboard didn't run on electricity, nobody was desperate to connect to the WiFi network, and the beer was full strength. It came in a can, not a plastic cup.

'The captain would come out here, into this viewing area, and meet with the journalists after stumps — but they were the only people who came in here,' Davidson recalls, before pointing to a door deeper into the dressing-room. 'Only the players were allowed inside that room. That was our sanctuary. One of the rare times someone else was allowed here was when Robert Menzies came in for a photograph before a match.'

Menzies, it should be pointed out, was the Prime Minister at the time.

'We never really had anyone come in after stumps,' Harvey continues. 'Maybe the opposition players, but nobody from outside. Bradman, after he'd retired and become a selector, would sometimes come in before play started if he was the selector on duty. But outside of him I can't recall anyone other than the players being in this room.'

Davidson waves a finger towards the dressing-room again.

'See those two massage tables in there?' he says. 'Richie and I would sit there and listen when we were the younger players of the team.'

That's Richie Benaud, who went on to captain Australia.

'There was Miller, Lindwall, Morris ...'

Keith Miller. Ray Lindwall. Arthur Morris ...

'Richie and I planted ourselves in that corner and we'd listen, listen, listen. They'd talk over the whole day's play and we learned more in those times than we did in the middle. That's where we learned so much about the game.'

Harvey, who was a 19-year-old in Bradman's 1948 Invincibles side that conquered all opposition when it toured England, was also smart enough to keep his mouth shut and his ears open as he learnt about the art of Test match cricket.

'I would sit there after stumps and not say a word,' he chuckles, indeed an irony for those who know of Harvey's candid views in later years to newspaper reporters about the modern-day game and its players. 'You'd take your boots and socks off and listen to them talk about the game. And that's how I learned, too. The best advice Bradman gave me was to hit the ball along the ground. That way, you could never get caught. Pretty simple.'

The walls won't talk but they do carry the honour boards that list every Australian player to score a century or take five wickets in an innings since the first Test played at this ground in February 1882.

There's Harvey's 190 against South Africa in the Third Test in 1952–53 — an innings that set up Australia's victory by an innings and 38 runs. There had been questions around this time about what was going to happen to Australia's top order after Bradman and others had retired. The answer came in the form of a pocket-sized dynamo, standing at 5 feet 7 inches (170cm), with dark hair slicked back, sleeves rolled up, dispatching Red Kings to all parts of the ground, with every shot in the textbook, played with ferocity or elegance depending on the situation.

'There's your name up there, Davo,' Harvey says. 'What for?'

'I took two five-fors here,' Davidson replies.

Those who saw Davidson bowl will tell you he was poetry in motion when bowling fast-medium. If he was cranky, though, he could be as quick as any other bowler in the world at the time.

'Deadly and devastating,' Keith Miller said of Davidson's fast bowling. 'Lightning fast when the mood took him,' West Indies great Sir Garfield Sobers once offered. And this from former Australian spinner Ashley Mallett: 'Davidson, the cricketer, was a big man with broad shoulders, and he needed them, because for years he carried the Australian pace attack.'

'I was never as fast as Jeff Thomson,' says Davidson, referring to the Australian fast bowler widely considered the quickest of them all. 'But who was?'

Davidson's first five-wicket haul came almost a decade after he made his Test debut, in the third Test against Frank Worrell's West Indies team in 1960–61. He'd already been involved in the frantic scenes at the Gabba in Brisbane earlier in the series when the Test was tied with Davidson scoring 80, with a broken finger, before he was run out late on the fifth day. In Sydney, he took 5–80 in the first innings, including the prized wicket of Sobers, but Australia were still crushed by 222 runs.

Until this point, Davidson had never won a Test at his beloved SCG. He eventually did so two years later, in the third Test against England, and he marked it with a second five-wicket performance.

Davidson and Harvey both announced during the 1962–63 Ashes series that it would be their last. They would retire after the fifth Test, also to be played in Sydney, and when it came time for the two teams to make their way onto the ground at the start of the match, Benaud — who by then was the Australian captain — stopped at the white picket fence and let the two players take the field ahead of anyone else. The skipper started to gently applaud, and the rest of the players followed.

Few people recall with fondness the first day's play that followed as England scratched around after losing early wickets. But they remember that enduring image of 'Davo' and 'Ninna' moving out onto the SCG: Harvey on the left (as the photographers on the field looked at them) with his arm reaching up and around Davidson's broad shoulders, both of them smiling and in step with each other.

'I remember it well,' Davidson smiles. 'We goosestepped out the gate.'

THEY WEREN'T ALWAYS IN step with each other, arm in arm and playing for the same team. They certainly weren't on January 26, 1957, when NSW hosted Victoria in a Sheffield Shield match at the SCG.

In those days, matches between the two states were played with the intensity of a Test match but there was added tension heading into this fixture. A draw would secure NSW the title but, perhaps more than that, Victoria had its nose firmly out of joint after the experienced Harvey, who was 28 at the time, missed out on the Australian captaincy to NSW's 21-year-old skipper Ian Craig.

When the two captains came onto the field for the coin toss, Harvey knew he wanted to bowl, having earlier inspected the pitch.

'We tossed and I lost as usual,' Harvey recalls. 'Ian said, "You can bat." In those days, the wickets were very green. Very grassy. It would seam beautifully."

Losing the toss was bad enough but Harvey's morning became far worse when he returned to the dressing-room, where he was greeted by his great friend and teammate, all-rounder Sam Loxton.

'We've got a problem,' Loxton said.

Opener Colin McDonald had attempted a sweep shot while practising in the nets, missed the ball and taken it square on the nose, which was duly broken. It was so bad that an ambulance was called. McDonald was taken to nearby St Vincent's Hospital.

Bill Lawry was Victoria's 12th man, so they had an obvious replacement to open the batting if NSW and Craig allowed a late change to the team.

'Go down to the other room and tell him what's happened and that you want to change the side,' Loxton advised Harvey. 'I'm sure he'll do it.'

Harvey walked through the members' bar, knocked on the home team's door and politely asked the question.

'You can't do it,' Craig said.

'Bugger you,' Harvey snapped back, the door slamming shut behind him.

Recalls Harvey: 'I stalked back through the members' bar and into our dressing-room and said, "Come on, Lenny [Maddocks]. You and I are opening the batting." It was only the second time I'd opened in first-class cricket in my life.'

Back in the NSW dressing-room, Craig was shaking his head about the audacity of Harvey's request. Both Davidson and Benaud noticed something was troubling him.

"What's happened, Craigy?" Davidson asked.

'Harvey wants to change his team,' Craig said. 'And I told him he can't.'

Davidson and Benaud looked at each other, bewildered.

'You're bloody joking,' they said.

Recalls Davidson: 'We were standing right in this spot where we're eating lunch now. We couldn't believe it. We knew what would happen. He was going to carve us up. When Neil Harvey started to strut, you knew you were in trouble.'

Oh, Harvey strutted. He strutted out into the middle that morning and was still there deep into the second session, strutting up and down the wicket between deliveries as he punished Craig for refusing his request.

'We took the second new ball at 10 minutes past two o'clock that afternoon,' Davidson says. The rules of the day allowed a bowling team to take a second new ball when their opponents' total reached 200. 'One of my secrets was to bowl a perfect delivery with the first ball. I could always pitch my first ball in the right spot. On this day, I bowled the most perfect outswinger; started it on leg and middle stump, and this little bastard just stepped back and went, "Bang!" It hit the fence in front of the Ladies Stand and bounced back about 10 yards into the field of play. I thought, "Oh God." By 5.05pm, he was on 209.'

Harvey was born and bred in the Melbourne industrial suburb of Fitzroy, the fifth of six boys, all of whom played cricket.

But it was at the SCG where the ballad of his epic Test career first started. He made his Sheffield Shield debut for Victoria against NSW at the SCG on January 24, 1947, having played in two first-class matches against Tasmania during the previous December and then been 12th man for a Shield game in Brisbane.

'I was 18 and it was right near the end of the Australian Test season against the Poms,' Harvey recalls. 'I was selected to play for Victoria with only three matches left. We were on the "northern tour" of Queensland and then came here to Sydney.' He laughs, sipping his red wine. 'I made nought in the first innings and then made 49 in the second innings.'

Keith Miller's unbeaten 206 set the home side an unreachable target of 478. NSW fell short by 288 as Victoria claimed the Shield title.

'I then went down to Melbourne and played one match for Victoria against the Poms,' Harvey continues. 'I batted at five and reached 69 before a fellow called Doug Wright — he was like Bill O'Reilly, a big, loping leg-spinner — bowled me a good wrong'un. I nicked it and was out.'

As Harvey trudged from the field, England wicket-keeper Godfrey Evans walked towards him.

'Well, played, son,' Evans said. 'I'll see you in England next year.'

'That's what used to happen on the field in those days,' Harvey says. 'Not the garbage that happens today.'

Davidson was drawn to the SCG sooner because he lived much closer. He was born and raised in Lisarow, on the NSW Central Coast, and they were humble beginnings.

'I was a kid in the bush with no shoes, nothing,' he reflects. 'We lived on the farm, we had an orange orchard and nothing else. They were bloody hard days. I chopped wood because we had no electricity. I missed 12 months of school because I had eye strain because we were doing things under kerosene lamp.'

Davidson had a head full of dreams. Most of them were about cricket and most of them were played out on the stage of the SCG.

He first started bowling on the veranda, pretending Australia's Test wicketkeeper at the time, Don Tallon, was taking the catch for every lethal delivery Davidson sent down. A few years later, he dug out a pitch on the side of the hill of his family's farm. At the age of nine, he was playing second division in the Gosford grade competition against men.

He made his first trip to the SCG as a schoolboy — to play rugby league.

'You talk about dreams,' Davidson continues. 'I played rugby league on this ground as a schoolboy for Gosford High against Randwick. It was a quagmire. The match was decided by a goal kicked from halfway. The player had to scrape the mud away, then form a mound. The ball must've weighed four pound. It's amazing how I can remember those things like it was yesterday ...'

Playing at the SCG for the first time had a profound influence on Davidson's career and life.

'From the moment I played football on this ground,' he says, 'I knew I wanted to play cricket here.'

In January 1940, Davidson was sitting in the old Brewongle Stand, watching NSW take on Victoria.

'Stan McCabe got 49 before he was bowled by Barry Scott,' he says. 'Hit him for six onto the Paddington hill. Sid Barnes came in and was caught in the gully for 17. I was 10 years old.'

The record books reveal that Davidson's recollection is perfect. The Paddington hill was at the northern end of the ground, where the new Bradman Stand is now located.

'Then I wagged school to watch Bradman bat in the Test match here in 1946,' he continues. 'The thing I couldn't get over was his footwork. It was unbelievable. When I watch batsmen today, I watch their feet. If their feet aren't right, they're gone. You are looking for balance and their first movement. Neil will tell you: their first movement needs to be their back foot. Nobody today bats with their back foot first. It's important because it takes you into the line of the ball.'

Then Davidson adds this: 'Only Bradman had better footwork than Neil Harvey. He was something to watch on a bad wicket. No batsman played out of his crease more when playing spin than Neil Harvey, yet he was never stumped in a Test. Best batsman I ever played with.'

Harvey also remembers Bradman batting at the SCG. On November 14, 1947, an Australian XI hosted India in a tour match before the Test series. It was a special fixture. Apart from this being India's first Test tour of Australia, Bradman was on the cusp of history: he was sitting on 99 first-class centuries, having scored exactly 100 for South Australia against Victoria a week earlier.

It might've been a tour match, ahead of the very first Test series between the two countries, but Australia's side was formidable, featuring Bradman, Keith Miller, Sam Loxton, Bill Brown, Bill Johnston and Harvey, who had turned 19 the month before and was yet to make his Test debut.

A moderate crowd was at the ground on day one when India won the toss and batted. It swelled to more than 32,000 on the second day, when it was clear that Bradman would soon be at the crease.

It was always like that with Bradman, says Harvey, from the first match he played with him until the last.

'You couldn't help but sense it,' Harvey says. 'The crowds would flood in. Everybody loved him. And how can you blame them?'

By lunch, with Miller down the other end, Bradman had cautiously eased his way to 11 runs. After the break, he took few risks as he reached his half century in 78 minutes, before surviving a confident appeal for leg before wicket on 80. He kept slowly accelerating and by the last over before tea he had reached 99.

Indian captain Lala Amarnath tossed the ball to Gogumal Kishenchand, who hadn't bowled a single delivery on tour. Now he was being given the task of stopping the game's greatest ever batsman from reaching a rare milestone. Bradman treated him with caution before pushing him to mid-on to race through for the single to reach triple figures.

The crowd roared. Bradman celebrated as Bradman often did: with restraint. He smiled, raised his bat and baggy green and then calmly took up his position at the non-striker's end.

By this stage, he was in the twilight of his career. He had achieved so much at the SCG, from his unfathomable 452 not out for NSW against Queensland in January 1930, when he was chaired from the field by the opposition fieldsmen at the end of his innings, to visions of him during the bodyline series drawing away to the legside and punching England menace Harold Larwood through the covers as spectators on the packed Hill gasped.

A few great batsmen — mostly from England, on account of how much county cricket they play — have scored more first-class centuries than Bradman. However, a closer inspection of the record books reveals a typical Bradman feat: he reached the milestone in 295 innings. England's Denis Compton is the second fastest, taking 552 innings. Another Englishman, Jack Hobbs, has scored the most first-class runs (61,760) and first-class centuries (199). He took 821 innings to reach a hundred hundreds.

After the tea break, Bradman and Miller exploded, scoring runs at will against an inexperienced attack. Miller was eventually dismissed for 86 and then Bradman, finally, for 172.

The term 'following Bradman into bat' has become one of Australian sport's most overused clichés, regardless of the sport. It's applied whenever a rookie replaces a legendary player who has been injured or, most likely, retired.

Neil Harvey was one of those players who really *did* follow Bradman into bat.

'It was better to bat with him than after him,' Harvey smiles.

Harvey made a rapid-fire 32 as Australia established a 54-run first-innings lead, but in the second innings he was trying to save the match as Indian all-rounder Vinoo Mankad destroyed batsmen at the other end.

Early in the innings, Mankad ran out opener Bill Brown in controversial circumstances. Brown had been drifting out of his crease at the non-striker's end as Mankad bowled, trying to pinch singles when he could. Mankad warned him he would run him out if he continued. Then, with Brown on 30, he did. He did the same thing to Brown in the third Test later that summer and the famous cricket term — 'Mankaded' — was born.

In the end, Harvey was left stranded on 56 not out and India won by 47 runs — arguably the greatest result in the country's cricketing history to that point in time. Harvey showed enough poise and maturity in the match to earn selection in the final two Tests of the summer, scoring 153 in the last Test to secure his place in Bradman's team for the Ashes series in England later that year — just as Godfrey Evans had predicted.

By the time Harvey met Davidson and his NSW teammates almost a decade later, in the middle of the SCG as Victoria captain, Bradman had retired and Harvey had established himself as the country's premier batsman, if not the world's.

As he pounded NSW's attack to all parts of the ground, the ball was tossed to Benaud in an attempt to stop the haemorrhaging with his tricky leg-spinners. Harvey played a glorious cover drive, but it was stopped just short of the fence. Next ball, he played the same stroke. It was stopped by the same fieldsman.

The next delivery, he spanked Benaud straight down the ground for four runs.

'Stop that one,' Harvey grumbled as he strutted past Benaud.

Harvey made 209 but the match was eventually drawn, and NSW won the Shield.

'I try not to remember that part,' Harvey says.

NOW THE MEMORIES ARE flooding back …

Davo can see Arthur Morris getting bowled bouncers one day at the SCG. 'He put all three onto the Hill,' he says. 'The fans loved it up there, under the scoreboard. This was before the 1980s, when people just clapped and yelled. You had a feeling they were in the game as much as you were. They came to watch the cricket.'

He can see Bob Simpson also clearing the fence, with England's Colin Cowdrey bowling his leg-spinners. Simpson slogged it towards the stands, where Tom Graveney was fielding.

'Catch it!' yells Cowdrey.

'It went 80 feet over Graveney's head,' Davidson says. 'No chance.'

He can also hear the spectator in the old Bob Stand (which was replaced by the Bill O'Reilly Stand in 1984 and relocated to North Sydney Oval) yelling out to Keith Miller.

'I love ya, Keith! I love ya, Keith! I love ya, Keith!'

Davidson and his teammates know him better as 'Nugget', because he had been dubbed 'The Golden Boy' by the press.

'For Chrissakes,' Miller says to Davidson. 'Tell him that's not my name so he can annoy someone else!'

Now the discussion moves to the fastest bowlers Davidson and Harvey have seen at the SCG.

'They're all too fast when you have a bat in your hand,' Harvey chuckles.

It doesn't take too long for the name of Frank Tyson to find its way into the conversation.

Tyson was 24 years old when he was part of the England team that toured Australia in 1954–55. He certainly wasn't a Test bowler of note when the series started, and was some way off displaying the kind of frightening pace that would prompt both Bradman and Benaud to label him the quickest they ever saw.

If anything, Tyson was an oddity: his enormous run-up seemed self-indulgent — not least because it didn't help him take many wickets.

After Australia won the first Test in Brisbane by an innings and 154 runs — with Tyson taking 1–160 in the first innings — legend has it that Tyson was sharing a beer with Australia's premier fast bowler, Ray Lindwall, and asked for advice.

'How do I bowl the perfect bumper?' Tyson asked.

'When we get to Sydney, watch where I pitch the ball,' Lindwall advised.

Lindwall certainly gave Tyson something to watch when, in the second innings, he sent down a short-pitched thunderbolt to his fellow fast bowler, who had peppered Lindwall with some short-pitched thunderbolts of his own earlier in the match.

Batting at No. 7, Tyson made the catastrophic error of turning away from a bouncer instead of ducking under it. He was struck in the back of the head and as he lay motionless on the turf for the next few minutes the crowd fell silent, fearing the worst. He eventually rose to his feet and was helped from the ground, but when he was laid out on the massage table inside the dressing-room he looked so dazed and confused there were fears he wouldn't be able to continue.

Tyson had already made a strong contribution, shortening his run-up without compromising his speed to take four wickets in Australia's first innings. Still, heading into the fifth day of play, victory for the home team appeared well within reach. They were 2 for 72, needing 151 more runs to win. Most importantly, Harvey was still at the crease, unbeaten on 26. With eight wickets in hand, including a batsman of his calibre and experience, Australia were slight favourites to go two-up in the series.

That morning, England captain Len Hutton scanned the dressing-room and locked his eyes on Tyson. He was no longer dazed and confused. He sensed that 'Typhoon' Tyson was forming off the coast and ready to make landfall.

Bowling from the Randwick end, Tyson conceded four runs from his first over, but his second was pure heat. The first delivery thudded into keeper Godfrey Evans' gloves so hard that he looked at his slips cordon and smiled. They all stepped back a few paces without saying a word.

Tyson thundered in towards Australia's No.3, Jim Burke, and delivered a yorker perfect in placement and impossible to play because of its speed. The off-stump went hurtling backwards before Burke — normally a brickwall in defence — had processed what had happened. Four balls later and another yorker, this time to new batsman Graeme Hole. His leg-stump was knocked over in the same impudent fashion.

Watching all this at the other end was Harvey, who was wrestling against his usual default setting of aggression. At 4 for 77, Australia had lost its grip on the Test — and it had all happened in one over.

At lunch, they were 5 for 118, needing 105 runs with five wickets in hand. Then Tyson bowled Ron Archer and the slide continued. Davidson made a brief appearance but when Brian Statham, Tyson's fellow opening fast bowler, had him caught behind for just 5, it brought Lindwall to the crease.

The crowd stirred. They knew the subplot. They sensed Tyson would seek retribution for the Lindwall bumper the previous day.

'How do you bowl the perfect bumper?' Tyson had asked Lindwall over those cold beers at the Gabba. In Australia's second innings at the SCG, Tyson answered his own question with another question: who cares when you can bowl the perfect yorker?

Lindwall was at the crease for just eight minutes when Tyson knocked his off-stump out of the ground. Australia were now 8 for 136. When Gil Langley was dismissed without scoring, the task at hand for the home team was ominous. They required 78 runs with Harvey — who was now on 64 — and gangly fast bowler Bill Johnston the only two left to steer them to a heroic victory.

Harvey had batted cautiously and carefully, trying to preserve his wicket as much as possible. But now he started to lash out, fighting

Tyson's fire with some of his own. He hooked one of Tyson's short-pitched deliveries with such clarity that it went like a tracer bullet towards the Members Pavilion with patrons diving out of the way.

'Best hook shot I've ever seen,' Davidson recalls. 'It went in under the roof and entered the visitors' dressing-room. It never went higher than this roof.'

The scenario faced at the SCG that afternoon is Test cricket's most fascinating: the gun batsman at one end, a nervous tailender well out of his comfort zone at the other, with a fast bowler stomping in with hellacious pace and accuracy. For the next 41 minutes, the match danced along that knife edge before Johnston finally edged Tyson and was caught behind.

England won the Test by 38 runs with Tyson taking 10 wickets for the match.

'It was bloody hard work,' Harvey, who finished unbeaten on 92, reflects. 'If someone had stayed around, we would've won the game. But Tyson was too quick.'

While the Englishman was lauded for his speed that day, many have claimed it was one of Harvey's greatest innings. Davidson puts it into greater context when he says this: 'The grass was always rolled into the pitch in those days, it was never cut. The wicket we had that day was tough to bat on. They hadn't cross-rolled the pitch, so therefore there were corrugations. It wasn't like the ridge at Lord's. One would hit [the pitch] and come through normal, but the next one might keep a bit low, another one might take off.'

He points at Harvey. 'This bloke was hitting everything in the middle of the bat, but the rest of us couldn't make contact.'

That single Frank Tyson over on the final day of the second Test at the SCG dramatically changed the course of the series. He took nine wickets in the next Test, in Melbourne, with England winning by 128 runs. In the fourth Test, in Adelaide, he took a further six wickets as England won by five wickets to retain the Ashes.

Tyson had retired by the time England toured Australia in 1962–63 for what would be Harvey and Davidson's last series. But Brian Statham was still playing, still charging in and bending his back without complaint. Davidson recalls Statham bowling 20 overs without a break in the third Test at the SCG that summer. After stumps, fellow England quick Freddie Trueman walked into the members' bar, grabbed two slabs of beer, and handed the first bottle to Statham.

But the exhausted fast bowler didn't take a sip.

'He loved a beer, Brian,' Davidson says, 'A tankard wasn't big enough. He'd just taken his boots off and he was just wearing socks — white socks — but there was blood everywhere. He took them off, looked down at his feet and said, "You deserve this more than me."'

Statham then poured the cold amber fluid all over his feet and toes.

'That was one of the most beautiful things I've ever seen,' Davidson says, getting emotional while retelling the story. 'There's a bloke who's bowled his guts out. It would've stung like buggery, but the cold beer would've helped. It's funny, the things you remember.'

Harvey shakes his head and takes another sip of his red wine.

'Today,' he grumbles, 'they wouldn't play for two months.'

ALAN DAVIDSON WALKS ALONG the line of light brown footprints that have been pressed and worn into the SCG turf. They are the unmistakable signs of cricket's crankiest animal: the fast bowler.

He's walked this walk many times — more than 20,000 in Test match cricket, he estimates — but this one has special significance because it's the last time he will do it. The lunch interval is due, and there is no doubt that England captain Ted Dexter will declare during the break.

Davidson walks past umpire Lou Rowan, who smiles. 'Yes, Al,' says Rowan, a Queensland detective when he's doing his real job. 'This is it.'

Davidson walks back to his mark. Fifteen paces. Always fifteen paces. He looks up at the sightscreen and then the rest of the MA Noble Stand behind it. The match is headed towards an inevitable draw, which will see Australia retain the Ashes, but the spectators have come in their thousands to catch one last day, one last session, one last look at Davidson and Harvey playing for Australia.

Can their beloved Davo give them one last wicket with his final delivery? At his home ground? Where he has been coming since he was a boy, first full of dreams and now with a head full of memories?

England wicketkeeper Alan Smith, the batsman facing him, is firmly thinking, 'No.'

Davidson turns and looks at the pitch. He zeroes in on the spot where he wants to land the ball. The plan is to get the ball to move off the wicket, across Smith's body, catch the edge of his bat and then let Australian gloveman Wally Grout take the catch.

That's how Davidson has taken 44 of his 185 Test wickets: c Grout b Davidson. How about one last time? It'd be a nice way to finish.

He moves in. Fifteen paces. Left hand tightens. Index and middle finger grip the seam. Right foot thuds into the turf, the ball firing out of Davidson's hand. Smith moves forward, trying to push it through the off-side.

As planned, the ball moves across his body. And, as planned, it catches the outside edge.

But Smith has got more willow on it than Davidson hoped. It's too wide for Grout, but the catch is child's play for the fieldsman standing at first slip, Bob Simpson. He gobbles it up, the Australians erupt with excitement and emotion.

Smith smiles and walks away without looking at Rowan, whose finger is pointing skywards.

The umpire hands the bowler his baggy green. 'Well done, Davo,' he says to the man who's just underlined his final delivery in Test match cricket with a wicket.

As the Australian players reach the white picket fence in front of the Members Pavilion, captain Richie Benaud stands to the side, just as he had on the first morning of the Test, and lets Davidson and Harvey leave the field ahead of the other players.

The match isn't over but it's drawing towards its inevitable conclusion. Dexter's declaration sets Australia a winning target of 241 in the final two sessions. Given they only need a draw to retain the Ashes, survival is the key and on a benign SCG wicket that should be easily achieved.

Davidson crashes down on the wooden bench inside the dressing-room. He is sitting next to Harvey. Their teammates quickly change, and make their way out for lunch, but these two don't budge. Not yet. They want the memories to last. They sit in silence as they both reflect on their careers, which are now only hours away from coming to an end.

Davidson vividly recalled how he felt in that moment in his autobiography *Fifteen Paces*, released just months after his last Test.

'I seemed to have spent more than a lifetime in this atmosphere, in dressing-rooms with their aroma of liniment and bat oil, tables heaped high with autograph books and cricket bags and gear strewn carelessly in corners,' he wrote. 'Memories flooded back. It had been a rugged road to the top. A fast bowler's life is a tough one. There are moments when every bone in the body aches and you feel that numb legs cannot carry you any farther when the pitch is lifeless and the batsman stubborn and defiant, or openly belligerent.

'But there are sweet memories, too, when the ball flies menacingly from the turf to you, tumbling fieldsmen gather in fine catches and the stumps can be knocked askew. These are moments of rare satisfaction and glory that make it all worthwhile. I have known it all, the triumphs and disappointments, the far-flung horizons of cricket, the roaring, pulsating crowds, the drama and the tensions of Test match battles.'

Given the early start to his career, it was understandable that 34-year-old Harvey was ready to retire.

'I didn't know whether to go for a fifth tour of England,' he says. 'But I thought, "I've done enough." My first wife and I got the chance to become Tupperware distributors. So we gave that a go.'

Davidson was only a year younger than Harvey but he started late in Test match cricket in comparison and was still very much in his prime. Sir Donald Bradman, who was chairman of selectors at the time, believed so.

'It is always sad when the time comes to say, "Au Revoir",' Bradman wrote in the foreword to Davidson's book. 'It is doubly sad when the departing artist is voluntarily retiring whilst still in his prime and when he is a star of the first magnitude ... He could have gone on. Another English tour was virtually certain and many more dazzling performances.'

For Davidson, it was a matter of pure economics.

'I was offered a big promotion at the Commonwealth Bank,' he recalls. 'I was jumping two grades in terms of seniority. It made me seriously think about my future: do I play another year or two or take this opportunity because that's going to be my life? Let's face it: when you were getting two quid a day to play cricket, it was an easy decision. What I got out of the Australian Cricket Board was peanuts compared to what I made at the bank.'

While the retirements of Davidson and Harvey added extra emotion to the series, it turned out to be a fizzer. In the end, the battle for the Ashes developed into an intense grind because of the stubbornness of the two captains, Dexter and Benaud.

After the first Test in Brisbane ended in a draw, England took the ascendancy in the next Test in Melbourne when they won by seven wickets. Heading into the third Test at the SCG, they were well placed to win the urn on foreign soil.

Standing in their way was Davidson, as it had been so many times for Australia. He took four wickets in restricting England to 279 in their first innings. Then, with Australia holding a slender lead, he wrecked them with the new ball in their second innings, taking 5 for 25 as Australia won by eight wickets.

'Alan Davidson led their attack in this and other Tests,' England off-spinner Fred Titmus said in his 2005 autobiography *My Life in Cricket*. 'He had a beautiful action, run-up and delivery and, besides being pretty fast, he made the ball swing into the batsman very late. Often, our batsmen had to make a hurried stroke against him because they thought it would not swing. Then when they got used to the fact that it did, he would send one down that didn't.'

A draw in the fourth Test in Adelaide — with Harvey making 154 in the first innings — set up a live fifth Test back at the SCG. It would be the first time in Australia since the summer of 1936–37 that the final match of the series would determine which team won the Ashes.

Instead of the game being a Test to savour, it was a miserly arm-wrestle on a lifeless pitch. Neither team gave an inch. After winning the toss — and needing to win to claim the Ashes while Australia required a draw — England took almost 10 hours to make 321 in their first innings. Australia posted 349 in response, batting cautiously and carefully. The last day turned into a dawdle. After Dexter closed England's second innings, Benaud wrestled with the idea of going for the runs — even when Simpson was bowled by Fred Trueman without any runs scored. Approaching tea, he told Davidson to pad up: they'd be going for it. Then Australia lost three quick wickets — including Harvey for 28 — and the message sent out to the middle was clear: 'Just stay in.'

That was music to the ears of Bill Lawry, who scratched up 45 runs in four hours. The crowd didn't like it, rattling beer cans, cat-calling and slow-clapping their own player, trying to move things along. Then someone on the Hill remembered the enormity of the occasion. The chant started ...

We want Davo! We want Davo! We want Davo!

'That was the greatest compliment I was ever given: chanting that for the whole of the last session,' Davidson says. 'Because they knew I was retiring.'

Ultimately, he wasn't required, with Australia finishing the Test at 4 for 152. The players left the field to a chorus of booing.

'This deadly dull and absolutely frustrating match left keen cricket followers soured and depressed,' Tom Goodman wrote in the *Sydney Morning Herald*. 'A thoroughly bad match unworthy of the occasion, for was it not in effect a "final" to decide the destination of the Ashes? This Test was a setback to cricket in Australia. Its lack of sparkle and of the element of combat caused a general revulsion of feeling among cricket followers throughout the country, who were influenced to forget what good points the season had brought forth.'

Dexter had promised upon the England team's arrival in Perth that he would play attacking cricket. Winning back the Ashes wasn't enough: he wanted his team to entertain the masses. 'We have to get on with it,' he told reporters.

His tune had changed after the last Test. 'Whoever has got the Ashes is inclined to hang on to them,' he said. 'If there were no Ashes at stake and, say, £1000 a man, then I'm sure the teams would go helter-skelter and there would be a result.'

That line rankled Davidson. It still does. 'That's poor compensation for the paying public to hear from the English captain that the players needed a big cash incentive before they would go all out for a decision,' he says. 'In the closing stages [in 1962–63], the contest had become a duel of personalities, with neither man prepared to take the risk that might expose him to defeat by the other.'

Not that Davidson could ever be too critical of Benaud, who he'd started his Test career alongside a decade earlier after playing against each other as teenagers.

'From the ages of 19 to 34 there was hardly a game we didn't play together for state or country,' Davidson says. 'The bond we had was unbelievable.'

After Davidson's retirement, Australia struggled, winning only one Test series in the four years that followed. As for Harvey, he finished as Australia's second-most prolific Test runscorer and century-maker.

And now, alas, our lunch here in the home dressing-room has also finished. Generations of cricketers and footballers of almost every code have sat in this space, all with their own stories to tell, but few share the depth of experiences of Harvey and Davidson.

The dressing-room is one of the few parts of the SCG that hasn't changed, save for a coat of paint and a flat-screen TV in the corner. When time dictated the Hill be replaced with seating, the old scoreboard where thousands would gather at the bar underneath was taken down. The names of teams and players written on calico are tucked away in the SCG museum, but two were framed. The name 'BRADMAN' is displayed in the members' bar, an unmissable reminder of the ground's history each time you walk in there.

Inside the home dressing-room, just above where we've had lunch on this Friday afternoon, you will find 'DAVIDSON'. Not bad for a kid who grew up with nothing, who came to the SCG as a kid to watch the likes of Bradman and Barnes, who played a game of rugby league here as schoolboy and declared there and then that his next match would be a game of cricket.

'The dream was always to play here,' Davidson says. 'Then I did. Now I am left with the memories.'

CHAPTER 2

The Gladiators

Norm Provan and Arthur Summons

HERE IN THE *SUN-HERALD*'S photographic darkroom, John O'Gready is hunting for page-one gold. Dressed in suit and tie, with the bottom of his trousers splattered with the sanctified mud of the Sydney Cricket Ground, the sweat forms on his top lip as he gathers together a handful of images worthy of selection for the next edition's front-page splash.

Only a few hours earlier, O'Gready had patrolled the sideline as the 1963 rugby league grand final between St George and Western

Suburbs — the third decider in a row between the bitter rivals — played out in front of him on a playing field that looked more like a swamp. In the middle, where the cricket square was used in summer, indistinguishable footballers sloshed around in the famous Bulli soil-turned-mud, with ambulancemen needed to wash the dirt and filth from their eyes. At one stage, early in the second half, St George captain Norm 'Sticks' Provan casually trotted off the field during a break in play, dipped his entire head in a bucket of water and trotted back on. Tough day at the office.

Meanwhile, in the stands and on the Hill, many of the colossal crowd of 69,860 fans huddled beneath umbrellas or positioned the match-day program on their heads to shield themselves from the rain.

Poor old 'Happy Jack' O'Gready was given no such reprieve. He braved the elements in search of the perfect image, just as he had done in every game he'd worked since 1960, when he was appointed Fairfax's chief rugby league photographer. O'Gready could sniff out a good picture from under 10 feet of wet cement, or in this case 10 feet of mud. He'd played the game himself and always seemed to know where the play was headed before any of the other photographers patrolling the sidelines.

As soon as referee Darcy Lawler blew fulltime and the St George players raised their weary arms in celebration for their dour 8–3 victory and eighth successive premiership, O'Gready raced onto the field and fired off as many shots as he could. He then handed five rolls of film to an assistant, who hurried out of the ground to where a car was waiting on Driver Avenue to whisk the cannisters away to the John Fairfax building on Broadway at Ultimo.

Now, back in the darkroom, O'Gready is looking for the money shot. The imposing frame of pictorial editor Graham Wilkinson stands alongside him looking for it, too. O'Gready thinks he's found it: an image of Provan covered in mud, hand on hip, hair tussled, a satisfied smile exposing two gleaming canine teeth that shine through the fading light on a sodden winter's day. The image reveals the quiet satisfaction of a captain who has just won another grand final.

But Wilkinson isn't sold on it. Great picture, he thinks, but not quite what the desk is after for page one. He starts sifting through the reject pile, looking through his thick-rimmed spectacles for the *right* photo.

'I like this one,' he says, picking up a still-wet image.

Later that night, when O'Gready is walking out of the newsroom, no doubt looking for a drink to wash away the taste of the mud and dirt, Wilkinson tells him that the image impressed his superiors, including senior editor Jack Percival, who said it was the second-best picture he'd ever seen. The best, Percival reckoned, was the iconic image of four US Marines lifting up the American flag atop a mountain in Iwo Jima in February 1945. O'Gready smiled and then set off for the nearest boozer.

Imagine his dismay, then, when he picked up the *Sun-Herald* the next morning to discover his image wasn't on the front page. Instead, the editors had decided to run a story about a train accident near Dubbo two days earlier in which 20 people were injured.

O'Gready flicked the page to see his image on three. It was the secondary story, under the headline: 'WHO'S THAT?' It was rare for photographers to receive picture credits in those days, and if they did their names were afforded only a tiny point size. But hadn't this been up there with an iconic American war photo? Didn't matter. O'Gready didn't get his page one and he didn't get his by-line.

Despite its undervalued placement in the paper, the image popped out from the page. Amid the chaos after fulltime, Provan and Wests captain Arthur Summons found each other in the middle of the field. They were almost unrecognisable, each of them looking like they'd been dipped in chocolate.

Provan had already ripped off his jumper, exposing the shoulder pads protecting his square shoulders, and he was ready to swap it with his rival captain, who was still wearing the muddied black-and-white jersey he'd worn with distinction that afternoon.

At 6 foot 3 inches (190.5cm), Provan towered over Summons, who was almost a foot shorter, but that disparity is what made O'Gready's image so strong and symbolic; the towering Adonis and the wily little playmaker with a pug nose that had been broken too many times. It spoke to the belief that rugby league is a game for all shapes and sizes, from the big man to the little big man and everyone in between.

It was a cracking photo, but what chance was there that O'Gready, his editors, devout readers of the *Sun-Herald* and especially Provan and Summons themselves understood the true value of the image on page three that Sunday morning? How could they know it would become the image that defined an entire sport? How could they predict it would be considered in time as the greatest Australian sporting photograph ever taken? Or that it would be cast in bronze two decades later and made into the premiership trophy? Or that it would link Provan and Summons for the rest of their days, the pair of them standing side by side in suits and tuxedos, on grand final stages and even again in the middle of the

SCG half a century later, replicating that very same moment in time? Or that the two former enemies, who hadn't really met outside football until that afternoon, would become great mates because of O'Gready's foresight in the mud and fading light of Saturday, August 24, 1963?

That's the Disney version of the story. Like most scenes in the melodrama of rugby league, not everything is what it seems.

The reason Summons was still wearing his jumper was that he had no intention of swapping it with Provan. Video footage of the brief embrace shows him smiling, but in truth he was furious about the result and, in particular, the performance of referee Lawler. Wests had been on the wrong end of the penalty count, the scrums and two critical decisions: a disallowed try to centre Peter Dimond and the decisive try to Johnny King, Saints' great winger. King had been controversially allowed to get up and run again despite claims he'd been tackled by Magpies fullback Don Parish and despite, according to Wests players, Lawler telling him to 'play it'.

What Summons told Provan as O'Gready pressed the button was a matter of a debate then and remains so decades later.

In Norm Tasker's book, *The Gladiators*, Provan reckoned he never heard Summons 'going crook' about the referee — he just wanted to keep his jumper.

In Gary Lester's history of the Western Suburbs club, *Clouds of Dust, Buckets of Blood*, Summons reckons he said this: 'You were lucky to get away with that. You shouldn't have won it.'

In Philip Derriman's book *Grassy Pitches and Glory Years*, O'Gready remembers Summons simply saying: 'You were lucky to get away with that, Sticks.'

Whatever was said in that moment, Summons believed something more sinister was at play than bad luck. Wests prop Jack Gibson had walked into the dressing-room earlier that day, sat down on the wooden bench in the room next to hooker Noel Kelly, and delivered some disturbing news.

'We can't win today,' Gibson told Kelly. 'Fuckin' Lawler has backed them.'

'Turn it up, Jack,' Kelly laughed. 'It's the grand final!'

'I'm telling you we can't win.'

Gibson, who had worked and played in Sydney's underbelly as a bouncer on the door of illegal casinos and then as an SP bookmaker, had heard a rumour that Lawler had placed a £600 bet on St George to win. As the Wests players left the SCG that night, they were convinced the result stank more than the mud they had just played in.

It was a dramatic final scene in an enthralling, bitter and often violent three-part series that had started in 1961, when Wests tried to halt St George's run of premierships by buying up as many internationals as the rules and their coffers allowed — and then tried to bash Saints into submission.

And it almost worked. For three seasons, Wests were the pebble in St George's sandshoe. A magpie flapping like crazy in their china shop.

'They were the hardest team to play,' Johnny King recalls. 'Man for man, they were the hardest because we knew it would be on *all* day. We knew we could get beaten on the bell — and in the end we almost did.'

EDDIE LUMSDEN AND JOHNNY KING park their cars and then push through the crush of the Moore Park crowd towards the SCG for the 1961 grand final. They are wearing suits and ties. St George secretary Frank Facer insists on his players presenting themselves in respectable attire on most occasions, at most matches, but especially if they are playing at the Cricket Ground and without question for a grand final.

For the past six seasons, the SCG has been like a second home for St George. The match of the round is played here each Saturday and given the side's relentless success under Facer and injured captain-coach Ken 'Killer' Kearney, they feel as much at home here as at Kogarah Oval, their traditional base.

King and Lumsden — the Dragons wingers — walk into the home side's dressing-room in the Members Pavilion and instinctively find their places, take off their suits and ties, and hang them on the peg above where they are sitting. They look around the room and see a constellation of stars: Reg Gasnier, Norm Provan, Bob Bugden, Johnny Raper, Brian Clay, Billy Wilson and Kevin Ryan.

'I'm the youngest in this side,' King says to Lumsden.

'Yeah,' Lumsden says out the corner of his mouth, 'and the highest paid.'

Almost 60 years later, King and Lumsden are sitting next to each other at a tavern in the Lower Hunter Valley, still inseparable. They played together, won premierships together, roomed with each other for club, state and country. In retirement, they both moved to the same area with their families. King played on the left wing and Lumsden on the right. The width of the field was about as far as they ever got away from one another.

'The wing was a great place to be when you played at the Cricket Ground,' Lumsden says. 'The cricket pitch in the middle was too hard.'

Years earlier, also against Wests at the SCG, Kearney devised a play where Lumsden drifted infield and ran off five-eighth Peter Carroll from a scrum. When they first attempted the move, Carroll discovered Lumsden was nowhere to be found — and was subsequently whacked by the defence.

'Where were you?' Carroll berated.

'The ground's too hard,' Lumsden said. 'I wasn't getting tackled on that.'

It was a common complaint from footballers who played at the SCG — then and now. They also complained about the 'poisoned ground'. As a player for Manly in the 1950s, long before he became the boss of the NSW and Australian Rugby Leagues, Ken Arthurson would come from the field, get in the shower and furiously scrub any graze or cut on his body, knowing that if he didn't it would become infected.

And, yes, the SCG also wasn't the greatest place to watch rugby league. Don't worry about fitting a square peg in a round hole; try a rectangular football field on a cricket oval. There's been debate for years about where the best vantage point is to watch football at the venue.

Jack Gibson, when he coached Parramatta to three successive premierships from 1981 to 1983, considered the front row on the upper deck of the Ladies Stand to be ideal because he was sitting side-on to the field. Still, he remained some distance from the action as he sat there in his big fluffy kangaroo fur coat.

Despite all of this, the SCG was rugby league's Mecca. Any player worth his beer money wanted to play there. And any spectator with even a passing interest in their team wanted to be there. Some would stand at the gates at 8 o'clock on grand final morning, with blankets, cut lunch and thermos in their bags, wanting to secure the best seats.

For much of the 1950s and 1960s, the SCG belonged to St George — for their growing band of supporters and an equally growing number of fans getting increasingly tired of watching them win. Western Suburbs did their very best to unsettle the balance of power and they did it in a very un-Wests way: by spending big.

Before they became 'The Fibros' in the 1970s and '80s, Wests were 'The Millionaires'. This is a concept that's hard to fathom for a younger generation who recall a club that represented Sydney's battlers from the outer suburbs. If the city was the heart, the suburbs of the west were the veins and arteries, symbolised by the industrious magpie. They revelled in shoving it up the glamour clubs like Manly and later Easts. For many years from the late '70s they were sponsored by lawn-mower company Victa and it could not have been more appropriate.

In the 1950s, Wests committeemen knew they weren't going to win premierships and thwart a rising St George unless they opened the purse strings. So they did. The club bought internationals Kel O'Shea, Harry Wells, Ian Johnston and Darcy Henry. By the time the 1958 season came around, it had added raw-boned Dapto teenage centre Peter Dimond to a side that also featured the rugged front-rower Nev Charlton and an ageing but still supremely fit halfback Keith Holman.

The faint smell of a premiership wafted through the sheds at Wests' home base at Pratten Park during the mid-1950s. As the '58 season reached its conclusion everyone else could smell it, too.

St George had already won two premierships and were eyeing a third when they met Wests in the major semi-final. Magpies coach

Vic Hey devised a plan to rock Saints, playing Dimond at five-eighth and instructing him to run at Carroll all afternoon. A teenager from the bush with nothing to lose and a body for destruction, Dimond followed the coach's orders to the letter: Wests won 34–10 and Carroll left the field bruised and bloodied.

When the teams met two weeks later in the grand final, Hey employed the same tactic. But instead of Dimond finding Carroll at first receiver from the scrum, he found himself standing opposite an unmoveable little mountain called Brian 'Poppa' Clay, who had been moved out of the scrum to five-eighth.

Although Wests trailed by only a point with 15 minutes remaining, the Dragons triumphed 20–9.

The Millionaires might have showed their hand a game too early, and they might have lost the grand final, but coming so close to the holy grail proved that the investment in new players had been worth it.

So, they spent a little more. Test stars Dick Poole and Ian Moir joined the club in 1959. A year later, they secured the prized signing of Summons, a rugby league junior with Parramatta but a rugby union international with the Wallabies who had rebuffed an offer from Facer to join the Dragons.

Wests went as far as the preliminary final, but at the end of that year, after St George had collected their fifth premiership, they found the man who could give them the extra starch they needed.

Queensland international Noel 'Ned' Kelly had more than a devastating right-hand punch. He could switch between prop and lock, but it was his work at hooker for which he was most famous. His skill and cunning meant his side rarely finished a match behind on the scrums.

He was also a man of his time, perfect for a game in which thuggery was allowed — to a point. He repeatedly recalled over the years how tough it was playing against St George, with their impenetrable straight line of defence and the toughness of forwards such as Kevin Ryan and Billy Wilson. Kelly aligned perfectly with Wests' philosophy of trying to bash St George into submission.

Kearney had a very clear instruction to his players, no matter which team they were playing: don't retaliate and, whatever you do, don't leave the side a man short by getting sent off. But Wests made it difficult.

By the time the two sides reached the 1961 grand final, Kearney figured the best way to counter Wests' tight, physical style was through attacking football. And that's how they won. After just nine minutes, Lumsden was over courtesy of a brilliant no-look flick pass from Poppa Clay. He finished with three tries while King scored another in the 22–0 victory.

'Three grand finals in a row and no tries scored against us is fantastic,' Kearney beamed afterwards, remembering big wins in the previous two grand finals against Manly (20–0 in 1959) and Easts (31–6 in 1960).

Wests had promised in the lead-up to the '61 decider to bash Saints' great centre Reg Gasnier out of the game. It backfired, as the *Sydney Morning Herald*'s Tom Goodman explained: 'Western Suburbs went into the rugby league grand final yesterday with a Gasnier complex. They concentrated on the brilliant centre as the No. 1 menace. They hung off the man with the ball and, as a result, let St George through for two of their first three tries. St George, awake to the Wests' dilemma, shrewdly moved the ball away from Gasnier ... This match ceased to be a contest before the first half was far advanced.'

While the scoreboard suggested an easy win, the carnage in the St George dressing-room revealed how difficult it had been. Several players had carried injures into the game, but none had been more courageous than Raper. He'd played 65 minutes with a suspected fractured chest bone, but instead of leaving the field early he finished it as man of the match.

Afterwards, he was found in a hot bath, his head slumped on his chest, motionless.

'It was agony in the second half,' he told the *Herald*'s Alan Clarkson. 'I thought the match would never end.'

As the St George players completed their lap of honour carrying the JJ Giltinan Shield that afternoon, Holman trudged from the field. This was his last match. It was an inglorious end to a glorious career.

It was also the last in the red and white for St George playmaker Bob Bugden. He'd had a bitter fallout with the club's committeemen earlier in the season and was now heading to Parramatta. That's because it was also the farewell match for Killer Kearney, who had missed most of that season with injury but had tried to edge his way into the grand final side before Facer stepped in. He was going to the Eels to coach them for the 1962 season.

Somewhere in the MA Noble Stand, the wives and partners of the St George players watched their men complete their sixth victory lap in a row. It was a feat that had never been seen in Australian rugby league. Their victory had taken them past the great Souths sides that won five straight from 1925 to 1929.

'It was a home ground to us,' King's wife Sandra recalls. 'Not that we were ever allowed in the Members Stand. All the wives would sit together in the Noble Stand. You don't know how we've suffered over the years!'

Later, as the players mingled in the members' bar with all walks of life, including that afternoon's opponents, their wives and partners waited outside or in the car parked on the fields of Moore Park.

'Ed played in nine grand finals at the SCG and won all nine,' Lumsden's wife, Sylvia, says. 'You just never thought that you would lose.'

Despite Wests' best intentions, nobody really did.

NORM PROVAN LIES ON a bench in the middle of the dressing-room, half-concussed, the deep cut above his left eye closed with eight stitches. Moments earlier, out in the middle of the SCG in the 1962 grand final against Wests, he'd been knocked out cold in an off-the-ball incident and stretchered off the field. The culprit, according to most people that day, including Provan himself, was Magpies back-rower Jim Cody.

Knowing that his afternoon is probably over, Provan looks over at his veteran prop, the international wrecking ball that was Billy Wilson.

'Billy, take over, will you?' he asks him.

Wilson, who is playing his 212th grade game for the Dragons, gathers in his weary players. Playing on a muddy bog, Saints lead 7–2 but Wests are proving far tougher to put away than they were in the previous year's grand final.

The murmurs had already started among the other players about payback, about stiff arms and king hits, about fighting fire with fire.

Wilson knew it was the wrong course of action. Not if they were to win another premiership and extend this magical run to seven.

'I know you blokes are all fired up after what happened to Sticks,' Wilson says. 'But I don't want you to go out there and look to get even with them. This is a grand final and we'll win it for sure if we keep level heads. I don't want to see any of you blokes throwing a punch.'

It's now part of rugby league folklore that immediately after the kick-off for the second half Wilson casually trotted over to Cody, with the ball still in the air, and whacked him so hard that Cody's head almost landed in the Members Stand. Shocked members in suits and ties gasped at the thuggery of it all as Cody fell to the ground as if shot by a sniper. He wouldn't get up for three minutes.

'Best king hit I've ever seen,' Noel Kelly recalled, with a cheeky little laugh.

Elsewhere in the stands, Wests supporters booed and hissed and demanded that Wilson be sent from the field. Referee Jack Bradley obliged, leaving the six-time defending premiers with 11 men. Under the rules of the day, Provan couldn't be replaced.

Wilson walked from the field with the desolation of a man on his way to the electric chair. He showered, changed into his suit and tie, and then sat down and lowered his head. He stayed in that position for the remainder of the game. *What have I done?*

Provan never gave away much but he was under pressure that year after succeeding Kearney as captain-coach. He had a legacy to preserve and a dynasty to continue building. The higher St George climbed, the greater the pressure to keep the party going.

'There were some big differences at training, with more emphasis on speed,' Lumsden says of life under Provan. 'With Killer, we were more defensive through our forwards, because he was a forward. The left and right sides of the field would bet in schooners on who had leaked the most line breaks during a match.'

St George lost their first game of the 1962 season to Balmain at the SCG and while by round 6 they'd assumed their usual position atop the NSW Rugby League ladder, the season became a grind for them in many ways.

On a Wednesday night in the middle of July, an enormous midweek crowd of 57,744 jammed into the SCG to watch St George take on the touring Great Britain side, which featured great players such as halfback Alex Murphy and second-rower Dick Huddart. The result shocked many: a 33–5 hammering delivered by the tourists.

Sure, it was the might of one club versus that of an entire country, but St George's line-up featured many internationals and they took the loss hard. Injuries were biting, too, including Provan suffering concussion after he clunked his head on the hard square of the SCG. Then they suffered late-season losses to Parramatta, Newtown and Easts. They beat Wests 18–10 in the final round but knew they'd be seeing the Magpies again.

The 1963 grand final is remembered for the mud in which it was played, but the 1962 decider was held in barely better conditions. Steady rain greeted both teams when they arrived at the SCG, and the earlier games turned the playing surface into slop. The first 20 minutes were brutal. If Wests' ploy was to target Provan, Saints' was to zero in on Summons. Raper, who was playing five-eighth, was penalised in the early minutes for a late tackle after Summons had kicked downfield.

When Provan was decked late in the first half, most presumed it was Cody. They still do. If you write or hear a mistruth enough times, it becomes fact as the years pass by.

But the Wests players know it was actually their fullback, Ken Bray, who clobbered the Dragons' skipper — and so hard that Provan couldn't address the side at halftime. All he could do was tell Billy Wilson he was now the skipper ...

Should Wilson have been sent off by the referee? Cody has said it was a king hit, pure and simple. So do the other Wests players.

But some of the St George players say Cody had grabbed Wilson by the collar as he raced downfield from the kick-off, and that Wilson had swung his arm to shrug him off but instead clocked him with a left hook. A few observers argued that it was the howls of the Magpies players that convinced Bradley — in his first grand final — to send Wilson off.

Unbelievably, this wasn't the most controversial moment of the match. In fact, there were two more, according to the Magpies players and those who follow them.

Rick Wayde, a long-time Wests official, was sitting on the Hill that afternoon, just near the scoreboard. 'People talk about what happened in 1963,' he says. 'But it's what happened in 1962 that angers many Wests people.'

The first incident came midway through the second half, with St George clinging to a 7–4 lead and Provan back on the field but still dazed and confused, and Wilson ready to 'catch the next train to Darwin', as he confided to Lumsden after the match. Lumsden dropped the ball 30 metres out from his own tryline. Dimond kicked through and chased it downfield like a greyhound. This was it. The try that would give Wests the lead and, most likely, the premiership.

But just as Dimond leaned down to touch the ball as it trickled over the tryline, he was cruelly cut down from behind. It was St George's John Riley.

In the modern era of video referees and endless replays, it would've been a penalty try. At the very least, a penalty. Instead, St George were given the feed into the 10-metre scrum despite Gasnier kicking the ball dead after Riley had cut down Dimond.

'I'm still filthy about that incident today,' Dimond recalls. 'But I laugh with Johnny about it when I see him.'

On the day, he was far more diplomatic. Newspaper articles from the day report that Dimond felt he'd merely been 'bumped' by Riley.

As the game reached its dramatic conclusion, Provan's head cleared and he was seen charging into the teeth of the Wests defence with the ball and then defending St George's try line as if his life depended on it. Dragons fullback Kevin McDonald booted a penalty with two minutes remaining to push the lead out to 9–6 but the game was still there for either side to win.

Another controversial moment came in the final seconds, right on St George's tryline at the Sheridan Stand end, with almost every fan in the ground on their feet, as Wests were presented with their last chance to snatch the premiership.

Riley was tackled with Provan jumping into dummy half. Wests back-rower Garry Russell raked it back as Riley played it. Provan then heeled it back the Dragons' way. The loose ball dribbled into Saints' in-goal. Russell dived on it, believing he'd just stolen the grand final until he heard the shrill of the referee's whistle.

Bradley didn't rule that Russell was offside but that some of his fellow forwards had been. Provan told reporters afterwards that he'd forced the ball first anyway. The fulltime siren sounded just as St George booted the ball into touch.

'There was never any question about Jack Bradley's integrity,' Russell said years later. 'He just happened to pick the grand final to have a bad game. Two bad decisions cost us the premiership.'

Keith Holman, who was writing a column for the Fairfax press in his first year in retirement, reckoned the match was 'the greatest grand final I've ever seen'. Tom Goodman praised the performance of Bradley, despite the complaints from the Wests players who still howl about the result.

What wasn't in dispute was Provan's bravery. As his players chaired him from the field, Billy Wilson was standing to the side, in suit and tie, the most relieved footballer who ever lived.

It was Wilson's last match in the Red V.

FOR MUCH OF 1963, the heavens above Sydney opened up and rain fell — it was one of the wettest years on record. In the moments after Western Suburbs upset St George with a last-minute try in the major semi-final at the SCG, it was raining men's hats. And they mostly belonged to Wests fans.

Noel Kelly had split the Dragons' defensive line right in front of the Members Stand, bursting through before flicking the ball inside to halfback Don Malone. The ball went through the hands, with lock

Kevin Smyth scoring a try that gave Wests a 10–8 lead with 50 seconds left to play. That's when men of all shapes and sizes threw their hats of all shapes and sizes into the air in jubilation.

'My first thought was, "How is everyone going to find their hats again?" recalls Rick Wayde, who was once again standing on the Hill.

His very next thought was shared by many: is this the year St George's run of grand final victories *finally* ends? This was Wests' third win over the seven-time defending premiers that season. Norm Provan's team appeared to be low-hanging fruit.

The Millionaires had stopped spending by the 1963 season. They believed they had the team they needed to knock St George from their lofty perch. Their only real off-season signing was journeyman prop Jack Gibson, who was desperate for a premiership in his final season as a player.

St George, however, had brought two significant players into their first-grade team: fullback Graeme Langlands and centre Billy Smith. They were both 21 years old, and larrikins who loved a drink and joke while chirping up at the senior players. They could back up the smart-arse lines with magical play, sharing an almost telepathic understanding on the field, a connection that ensured St George stayed near the top of the competition table long after the club's glorious run of premierships eventually ended.

Would it be this year? Wests thought so. They could smell it. After St George beat Parramatta in the preliminary final, the Magpies were ordered by coach Jack Fitzgerald to bash St George in the grand final.

The player with the largest target on his back: Reg Gasnier, who had mesmerised Parramatta the week before.

Storms belted Sydney on the Friday night before the match, and then the next day but it didn't stop those 69,860 brave souls pouring into the SCG for the grand final — many of them wanting to see if the Dragons' reign was about to end. The crowd figure posted that afternoon was the largest the SCG had seen for a club match in its history — just 559 short of the ground record.

The rain abated as Darcy Lawler led the players out onto the field, which by 3pm had turned into a quagmire. In crisp white shorts, long-sleeved jersey and well-oiled hair brushed back and parted down the side, Lawler looked immaculate. Whether he was as clean on the inside remains the eternal debate for surviving Wests players and supporters with long memories.

As promised, Wests brutalised Gasnier. His opposite centre, Gil MacDougall — the father of future Knights premiership player Adam — clobbered him whenever the ball threatened to come his way. It was so obvious that King, who was standing outside Gasnier, couldn't recall seeing MacDougall standing onside at any stage throughout the match. At one point, Gasnier clutched at his back after being whacked late and off the ball.

Gasnier was eventually moved out onto Lumsden's right wing for protection before returning to his customary place at left centre for the final 10 minutes.

'They talk about us getting all the calls, but Lawler didn't penalise them for that, did he?' King says. 'What about those controversial moments?'

No, the most controversial moments belong to Wests, just as they did in the previous year's grand final. St George led 5–0 after an early try to halfback George Evans, but the Magpies were certain they had hit back in the 33rd minute when Peter Dimond appeared to have scored from a Summons kick into the in-goal area. Dimond jumped in the air, adamant he had scored, but Lawler ruled he hadn't legally forced the ball over the Dragons' line.

Summons queried the decision.

'Do you want to finish this match in the dressing-room?' Lawler shot back.

Dimond seethed about the moment until his death in April 2021, although it's King's try that generates the most debate.

Wests came roaring back into the match with a MacDougall try to trail 5–3 with 20 minutes remaining. Moments later, the ball came out of a scrum on St George's 25-metre line, finding King down the left.

He spied the only piece of turf that hadn't been churned up and turned into slosh, sprinting down the sideline. He shrugged off one defender, before Wests fullback Don Parish dived to stop him but slipped. Then King slipped. Then Gibson came charging through, barrelling over the top of Parish and knocking him away.

It's at this point that the Wests players insist Lawler gives himself up. They tell you he said, 'Play it'. Backrower John 'Chow' Hayes, who went on to be team manager of Australian teams, is particularly vocal on this point to this day.

But King says he heard nothing. He sprang to his feet and continued downfield, brushing aside weary Wests cover defence to score in the corner.

'The ruling states that if the arm carrying the ball touches the ground, you had to get up and play the ball,' King says. Lumsden, sitting alongside him, is nodding. 'Well it didn't. Donny Parish slid over the sideline and there was nobody there. So I got up and off I went.'

It has also been suggested that the linesman put his flag up because King went out, although that has never been confirmed.

Replays of the incident are inconclusive. Was Parish touching King when the Dragons winger — and his left arm carrying the ball — hit the ground? It's impossible to tell. Did Lawler call 'held'? Only the players and the man himself would ever know.

After the King try was awarded, Wests' frustrations started to bubble over. When Gibson started throwing punches in a scrum, Lawler threatened to send him off.

'Send me off and I'll give you up,' Gibson said. He finished the match, the last of his career, but without a premiership.

There are other elements of that grand final that receive scant mention. A replay of the match shows Lawler constantly penalising Wests at the scrum, which Kelly lost convincingly to St George's international hooker Ian Walsh that afternoon. It's also easily forgotten that Parish failed to convert MacDougall's try from directly in front.

And if you talk to Rick Wayde, there was another moment that everyone seems to have forgotten.

'Peter Dimond scores a try in the first half that isn't anywhere on video,' Wayde recalls. 'It was a set move. Wests won a scrum on the Paddington side, on the 25. Malone fed it, gave it to Summons, and he put it up in the air for Dimond. It was a muddy day, and it landed beautifully just to the left of the uprights in front of the Noble Stand. Peter went straight through. I can still picture him standing up, arms extended in the air. I was on the Hill, in front of the scoreboard, so I had a straight line down the field. Lawler hadn't moved from the scrum base. He ruled no try.'

History remembers John O'Gready's immortal photo of Provan and Summons, but Kelly recalled other moments, such as returning to Wests Leagues Club at Ashfield later that night to find an enormous sketch in the foyer of Provan handing Lawler a bag of money.

Johnny King has retold this story hundreds of times over the years and often with Lumsden by his side, as you would expect. Our discussion about this famous incident eventually drifts to other important matters that day at the SCG — like Lumsden being the only player on the field to leave with a relatively clean jumper. Even Lawler had more mud on him.

'You know why?' Lumsden quips. 'Because they couldn't catch me. When in doubt, step out!'

Six months after I met the two St George wingers for this book, Lumsden suffered a heart attack, was rushed to Royal North Shore Hospital in Sydney, and never recovered. On the morning of the Dragons' annual reunion two days before the 2019 grand final between the Roosters and Canberra, King dropped in to say hello.

King approached his mate, who was unconscious and clinging to life. King grabbed his hand and said hello.

'Hello, Johnny,' Lumsden said, squeezing, before slipping back into unconsciousness. Two days later, on grand final morning, Lumsden passed away. He was 84.

'We were like brothers,' King reflects. 'We played together, we were always roommates, we later owned pubs together.'

And they won premierships together, hard fought and still controversial.

THE FIRST THING YOU notice in Noel Kelly's Collaroy home on Sydney's northern beaches is the pallet of beer sitting in the garage. Yes, a pallet. That's not a typo. He won it at a Men of League golf day.

'Want a beer?' he smiles on the day I visit him. 'Hopefully we'll have enough.'

Kelly's dry sense of humour appealed to Jack Gibson. Gibson's economy of words appealed to Kelly. When they played in the front row for Wests, Jack would utter 'sideswipe' from the corner of his mouth and that was enough. From a short kick-off, the two of them would crunch an opposing player from opposite sides as he caught the ball. 'It was like getting hit by two buses,' Kelly recalls, with fondness.

Kelly shoots straight, just as the late Gibson did, so there's no reason to disbelieve him when he tells you that he knows Darcy Lawler backed St George to win because, three days after the match, Gibson introduced him to the man who put the bet on for him.

'We went for a water-ski on the Tuesday and he introduced me to the bloke who put Lawler's money on,' Kelly says. 'Years later, there was 20 or so of us former Magpies players on a bus on our way out to a match at Campbelltown, and we stopped into Warwick Farm at the races. We had a bet, and I was standing in the enclosure where the bookies are … A bloke came up and said, "Do you remember me?" I said, "No." He said, "I put Darcy's money on." I never had the brains to ask him his name.'

Noel Kelly died only weeks after we met, aged 84, less than a month after the passing of his great teammate Arthur Summons. Few if any footballers have been more popular than these two Magpie warriors. About the only bitter rugby league memories they had were those two grand finals.

The 1963 premiership decider was Darcy Lawler's final match. From 1944 to 1963, he controlled more than 300 first-class games, including eight grand finals — a record bettered only by Bill Harrigan, who finished his career with 10 grand final appearances.

Lawler can't shed any light on the contentious moments of the 1963 grand final. He died in 1994 at the age of 75 following a short illness. He never commented publicly on accusations he fixed the match, or any other match.

'The unfortunate thing is that he cannot defend himself,' Lawler's son, Darcy junior, told me in an interview for the *Daily Telegraph* in 2013. 'Of course, Darce doesn't have a right of reply. The family over the years have let it go. It annoys me that the further it goes on, people are prepared to get out and say he is a cheat, but nobody will speak on Darcy's behalf.'

So Darcy junior did.

'For Gibson and Kelly to say before the game they were off ... Well, it got pretty damned close,' he said. 'It could've gone either way. The penalty count was pretty red-hot, but Darce said they deserved it. I've seen a replay of the 1963 grand final, with Darce, and we've seen Johnny King get tackled on the sideline there, and Darce tells me he didn't yell "held", he wasn't held, he slips out of the tackle. It's very muddy, the Wests players say Lawler said "held". Well, ask the St George players and they'll say no. Darce said he never yelled it. King got up and scored and the rest is history ... It's been going on for such a long time. He used to laugh it off himself when he was alive. He said, "That's life. You cop that."'

Darcy Lawler senior knew that criticism — including accusations of match-fixing — came with the territory. His unpublished, unfinished and handwritten memoirs provide an insight into the pressure he was under.

'I suppose, despite my high stature as an international and Test referee, I was rugby league's most hated man,' Lawler wrote. 'I've been hooted and hated on the field and threatened with my life off it. I've been venomously sworn at by players, have sent them off the field. Even officials have accused me of accepting bribes to "throw" matches, yet they denied all knowledge of their filthy accusations when I challenged them officially.'

In those incomplete memoirs, Lawler sheds light on another two controversial moments of his career — both of them occurring at the SCG.

First, he claims he actually turned down a £300 bribe to ensure England beat Australia in the third Test in 1954.

'I received a letter in the mailbox, no stamp, no post office mark, addressed to me with the offer of £300 for me if England won the deciding Test,' Lawler wrote. 'That was all that was said. This was quite a shock at first, but I finally summed it up as a joke. On arriving at the ground, I was about to go through the members' gate and a gent asked me to sign his autograph book. Upon signing it, he said, "Did you get the letter the other day?"'

Lawler informed league officials. Late in the match, he awarded a try to centre Harry Wells that secured an Australian victory before a crowd of 67,577 people.

'My decision to award a try was the most provocative decision in history,' he wrote. 'But I could easily have copped 300 quid if I didn't.' That a punter so brazenly offered him a bribe to fix a Test match shines a light on the seedy underbelly of the times, and perhaps rugby league.

On July 14, 1962, the Australian team faced the distinct possibility of becoming the first team to lose all three Ashes Tests on home soil. Having lost the first two Tests to Great Britain, they were desperate to save face in Sydney.

With a minute remaining, winger Ken Irvine crossed in the corner but the job wasn't done. Irvine had to kick the sideline conversion to win the match. According to rugby league folklore, after Irvine blessed himself and looked up at the heavens, Lawler whispered to him: 'Not even He's going to help you if you don't straighten up that ball, son.'

Irvine wrote years later that this never happened. Lawler also says as much in his unpublished writings.

'Irvine came back with the ball to take the kick,' Lawler wrote. 'He placed the ball like a real professional but standing 10 yards behind him in a direct line, I could see it was placed too far to the right of the post. If ever I felt like telling a player that he would miss a goal, it was then.

'And then it was like magic. He did not kick the ball. He went back, re-set the ball as if I had telegraphed it to him — and then he kicked the goal and Australia won by a point.'

Not everyone disliked Lawler, according to the man himself. He had his admirers, and sometimes they let him know.

'Often I received amorous letters from adulatory women fans telling me how nice I looked when I ran on to the field in immaculate uniform with hair well-oiled and brushed back,' Lawler wrote. 'The ladies asked me to meet them. Such is fame.'

Darcy junior says his father never accepted those offers, nor did he fix the 1963 grand final to fatten his wallet, as Wests players still insist. What really happened that afternoon, in the sanctified mud of the SCG, will forever be debated. St George won another three premierships, which included the 1965 grand final in which 78,000 or more people jammed into every crevice of the ground, perched along the roofs of the grandstands and then onto the field. It's a record that still stands.

As for Wests, they didn't play in another grand final, let alone win one. It wasn't until they merged with Balmain that the joint-venture Wests Tigers finally won the NRL competition in 2005.

WHAT CAN NEVER BE challenged is John O'Gready's perfect page-three photo. Fifty years after O'Gready took his immortal picture, Provan and Summons stood in the middle of the SCG to re-enact and celebrate the moment. This time, both were dressed in suit and tie and the playing surface looked more like a billiard table than a swamp.

'It's surreal, what happened from that photo being taken,' Summons said that night. 'Our images being used for the premiership trophy … it's beyond my ability to explain it. The mud helped make it, we look like statues and a statue they made from it. We're epitomised for as long as they play for that trophy. We'll be long gone and they'll still be playing for it because it is rugby league.'

Sadly, O'Gready wasn't among them. He died in 1999, aged 62, although he was almost killed in a serious car accident in the 1960s, which cost him the sight in one eye. But that didn't stop him from getting behind the camera lens. The SCG became a second home. He covered 29 grand finals and numerous Test matches, including the deciding 1962 Test match between Australia and Great Britain.

There are two incidents from that match that stood out for O'Gready, as he recalled to colleagues years later. In the second half, Lawler sent off English forward Derek Turner and, as he trudged from the field, O'Gready started firing off shot after shot.

'One more picture and I'll shove that camera up your arse,' Turner barked, as recalled in Philip Derriman's *Grassy Pitches and Glory Years*. Happy Jack kept firing away, unmoved.

The second relates to that moment involving Irvine and Lawler. They might say the referee gave no instructions that day, but O'Gready recalled hearing Lawler tell Irvine, 'A little more to the left' before Irvine then slotted the match-winning conversion.

O'Gready didn't just shoot sport. During the week, he worked the early-morning shift for the *Sun* where 'death knocks' were bread-and-butter stories for the afternoon newspaper. O'Gready had a gruff exterior but a heart of gold, and he had a special knack for putting grieving relatives who had just lost their loved ones at ease — while still getting the photo he needed. He retired from Fairfax in 1988, when they stopped printing the *Sun*.

By then, his image of Provan and Summons had been turned into the Winfield Cup, the premiership trophy until a change in federal laws forbid tobacco companies from sponsoring sport. The Winfield brand was dropped but the statuette remained and it's there, on the winners' podium, handed to the premiership-winning captain on grand final day each year.

Long after taking his grand final picture, O'Gready was in a sports bar in San Francisco when he spied his famous image on the wall.

'See that picture,' he told the barman. 'I took that.'

'Sure,' the barman said. 'Drink up, buddy, and I'll get you another.'

CHAPTER 3

If Only

Ray Baartz

WOULD YOU WANT TO know the identity of the person who nearly killed you? Ray Baartz doesn't. He doesn't know his name. He's tried his best for the best part of half a century to forget him altogether.

He knows only two things about the Uruguayan defender who ended his football career, and almost his life, when the Socceroos played the South American giants in an international friendly on Saturday, April 27, 1974, at the Sydney Cricket Ground.

He remembers what he looks like. 'Big, tall fella … with a moustache,' Baartz says. He also recalls what this man did to him just minutes before halftime that afternoon. 'I was back on our 18-yard line. Uruguay had a corner, but I got possession and cleared it forward. In those days, there was only one television camera covering the game, and it was following the ball. It wasn't following me.'

As Baartz tracked downfield, he felt a rival player loom alongside him, shoulder to shoulder, the proud light blue jumper of Uruguay nudging into Baartz's green and gold of Australia.

The shit was just starting to stir in this match, the second of two 'friendlies' between the two teams ahead of the forthcoming World Cup finals in West Germany later that year. Australia's team of part-time professionals had kept the two-time World Cup champions to a nil–all draw two days earlier at Melbourne's Olympic Park. For passionate Socceroos coach Rale Rasic, that result felt like a win. He knew a heavy defeat would hurt his team's confidence heading to the World Cup finals for the first time.

Now, in the second friendly at the SCG, not only had Uruguay's crack striker, Fernando Morena, squandered two early chances to score, but the visitors were being suffocated in the middle of the park.

And Uruguay, who were seeded fourth for the World Cup, didn't like it. South American teams of this era had a reputation for resorting to dark tactics if things didn't go their way. At the 1966 World Cup in England, the England manager Alf Ramsey had referred to the team from Argentina as 'animals' because, when the home team began to dominate their quarter-final, they dragged the match into the gutter.

So, late in the first half, the big, tall fella with the moustache running alongside Baartz kept to the script. He lashed out in frustration with his right arm.

'That's when he went whack!' Baartz recalls. 'Like a karate chop. And that's when I started choking.'

Almost every person among the 25,708 people at the SCG that afternoon will tell you the Uruguayan player who karate chopped Ray Baartz was Luis Garisto. Almost every single book, news report newspaper article from that period and ever since, says it was Luis Garisto. Even the referee, Donald Campbell, says it was Luis Garisto.

'I do remember Mr Garisto,' Campbell says with a thick Scottish accent. 'He was a filthy bastard.' He then apologises. 'Excuse the expression,' he says. 'That's the Glasgow way of speaking.'

But it wasn't Luis Garisto who hit Baartz late in the first half. Luis Garisto was the Uruguayan defender who attacked Baartz midway through the second half after Baartz had earlier scored a scorching goal from 25 metres out to put the Australians ahead 1–0. Over time, people have merged the two incidents into one.

'And it was an elbow — not a punch,' goalkeeper Jack Reilly says of Garisto's strike in the second half. 'I remember it like it was yesterday. The ball was in my hands and everyone was looking downfield where I was about to kick it.'

Baartz recalls it like this: 'The ball had gone out for a corner and he was having a whinge and carrying on. I tapped him on the shoulder and pointed to the scoreboard. He turned around and went, "BANG!" And knocked me to the ground.'

Whether it was a punch or elbow, Garisto's dirty play ensured the match descended into madness. When Baartz opened his eyes, he peered up to see his teammates crowding over him. 'Stay down!' they ordered. 'Stay down! This bloke will be sent off.'

Campbell was already way ahead of them, promptly producing a red card and flashing it in Garisto's face. Garisto was apoplectic. So, too, his teammates, who surrounded the referee, spitting their disapproval.

Head coach Roberto Porta and other officials rushed onto the SCG, demanding answers from Campbell. For the next five minutes, they followed him all around the field. The problem was Campbell couldn't understand what they were saying. They were speaking Spanish, and rapid and aggressive Spanish at that.

Campbell signalled to FIFA officials on the sideline and an interpreter was located.

'If you keep going,' Campbell told Porta, 'I will abandon the match. How will that look for you when you arrive in West Germany?'

About as bad, the Uruguayans must have figured, as losing to a country they were supposed to be schooling with their South American ball artistry. Down a man, they pushed forward, looking for the equalising goal.

The ball came to Morena, a loaded gun who often found the back of the net when he pulled the trigger. He weaved through several Australian defenders, fired and scored. As his teammates rushed to congratulate him, Campbell ruled that Morena had palmed down the ball before his shot for goal.

As the clock ticked down, the tension built. When Uruguay were awarded a corner on the left with five minutes remaining, every one of their players pushed up into the penalty area. A high, looping cross came in, a pack of players from both sides went up with their foreheads, and when the ball came back to earth it found the feet of the Socceroos player who had been battered more than anyone else.

Baartz had been karate chopped in the throat, and struck in the face, but now the ball was at his feet, right on the penalty spot in Australia's goal. He scanned the field and kicked it long, the ball falling just metres in front of striker Peter Ollerton. Uruguay's goalkeeper, Gustavo Fernández, raced up in a desperate bid to smother the clearance, but Ollerton instead danced around him, raced another 40 metres downfield and gently nudged Australia's second goal into an empty net.

The SCG exploded. So did the Socceroos' dugout. Rasic sprung to his feet and raced to the sideline before leaping into Ollerton's arms, wrapping his legs around him as the rest of the players rushed in.

'That match is the greatest result in Australian soccer history!' Rasic declared soon after.

What nobody in the excited home dressing-room expected was that it would also be the last match Baartz would ever play. That he'd leave the SCG early that night, feeling ill but unaware of the nightmare ahead. That he'd wake up in the middle of the night, completely numb down the left side of his body. That he'd be rushed to Royal North Shore Hospital and be unconscious for two days with his pregnant wife Sue sitting bedside. That it would finally emerge that he almost died because his carotid artery had swelled so much that it went perilously close to bursting.

For the best part of 50 years, most people believed that the person responsible for all this was Garisto.

'But he's not the guy, because it was the incident in the first half that did the damage,' Baartz says. 'Everyone thinks it was Luis Garisto. It wasn't.'

That's because it was the big, tall fella with the moustache.

THAT AFTERNOON IN APRIL 1974 wasn't the first time Baartz had played at the SCG.

Born and raised in Newcastle, he represented the NSW under-14s state schoolboy cricket team alongside a slightly older kid called Doug Walters, a gun batsman from Dungog, also in the Hunter Valley. The following year, when he was 14, Baartz again played at the SCG, this time against a South Australian team that featured Greg Chappell, an elegant young batsman who would go on to captain his country.

'It meant a lot to be playing at the SCG,' Baartz says. 'It was *the* venue.'

At the age of 15, he had to make the choice many abundantly talented young sportspeople face sooner or later: keep playing cricket or pursue his other sporting passion, soccer. He was already playing first grade for Maitland in the Northern NSW competition, making a name for himself as a potent and powerful striker.

'Much to my brother's disgust,' Baartz says, 'I chose soccer.'

It was a prudent move. Two years later, his local club, Adamstown Rosebud, used a contact at Manchester United to send him and teammate Doug Johns to Old Trafford for three months to gain invaluable experience. When their time was up, Johns returned home, but the legendary Manchester United manager Matt Busby was so impressed with Baartz that he invited him to stay another two years.

It was the opportunity of a lifetime. Baartz became mates with United's teenage genius, George Best, and seemed destined to play alongside him in their first team. But he couldn't shake the homesickness that was plaguing him. Best had felt the same way when he arrived in Manchester from Northern Ireland.

One day in 1965, after training, Baartz knocked on the manager's office door.

'I want to go home,' Baartz told Busby.

'But, son, nobody leaves Manchester United,' Busby replied. 'I want you to think about it for a month before I let you go.'

A month later, Baartz knocked on Busby's door. He told him he was heading home and Busby wished him well. He was 18 years old.

A year after arriving back in Newcastle and playing for Adamstown-Rosebud, Baartz's phone rang. It was Frank Lowy, a Sydney businessman who was starting to gain a reputation around town: first, for building shopping centres around the city, and second, for his deep love of football.

Lowy was on the committee at Hakoah Football Club, which had been formed in January 1939 by a small group of Jewish immigrants who had been kicking a ball around a park at Rushcutters Bay in Sydney's eastern suburbs each Sunday. Lowy had grown up in the ghettos of Hungary, watched his father leave the family home when he was 13, spent time in a detention camp in Cyprus, fought in the 1948 Arab-Israeli War and then migrated to Australia in 1952. He had endured a tough start to life but his passion for football helped him through. By 1966, he was starting to find his voice at Hakoah, a portent of bigger things; later, he became Australian football's most dominant figure — and the richest person in the country.

'I was ambitious,' Lowy smiles when I meet him in his office in the Sydney CBD. 'I wasn't [Hakoah] president, but I was on the committee. We wanted Ray Baartz. So we raised the £5000 to sign him. I probably dipped into my pocket, too.'

It was a record fee at the time but the investment made a stunning return: from 1966 to 1974, Baartz scored 211 goals in 236 matches. During that time, he established himself as a mainstay of the Australian national team.

'He had a build and an aggression about him in the midfield, from where most of his goals were scored,' Lowy says. 'He would score them in typical "Baartzy" fashion. He won many games, for both Hakoah and Australia.'

In those days, football was rarely played at the SCG because of the well-preserved cricket pitch in the centre of the field. Most Socceroos matches were played at the nearby Sydney Sports Ground.

'That was the home of the Socceroos,' Baartz says. 'It was a true football pitch; flat and even. It was a fabulous place to play.'

Australia played only one match at the Cricket Ground in the 17 years prior to the 1974 friendly against Uruguay: a friendly versus Greece in 1969, which served as a warm-up for both sides ahead of World Cup qualifiers. Baartz played in that game, won by the Socceroos 1–0.

When Australia failed in December 1969 to qualify for the 1970 World Cup finals in Mexico, following a 2–1 loss over two legs to Israel (the second game being drawn 1–all at the Sports Ground), the

Australian Soccer Federation sacked national team coach Joe Vlasits and appointed Rasic, a 34-year-old from Yugoslavia who was younger than some of his players.

Rasic was something special. He grew up in an orphanage in Belgrade after his parents were killed in World War II. This dire upbringing taught him discipline and made him hungry, and he took those qualities onto the football field, playing for several leading Yugoslav clubs and then for Grenoble in France. An Australian agent spotted him and convinced him to move to Melbourne to play for Footscray JUST (short for 'Footscray Jugoslav United Soccer Team'). He started coaching JUST in 1966, coached Victoria to the state title, and then, in 1970, the orphan and immigrant with the imposing Balkan accent was made Australian head coach.

At the first team dinner after his appointment, he told the chef in the hotel kitchen to cook the steaks rare. When the players complained about their meat being too bloody, the new coach shook his head.

'That's exactly what I want from you in the next four years,' he said. In other words, when you smell blood, go in for the kill.

Rasic had four years to realise the impossible dream for Australian football: to get the Socceroos into the World Cup finals. He calculated the only way that could happen was with a unified team, and that wasn't going to be an easy task.

In many respects, they were a team of professional part-timers. Peter Wilson, the man he would name captain after previous skipper Johnny Warren suffered a serious knee injury, was a car salesman. Defender Col Curran was a truck driver. Baartz was a sales representative with Presto Smallgoods. Equally challenging were the cultural differences in the squad, which featured players with Hungarian, Yugoslav, English, Scottish, German and, of course, Australian backgrounds.

'If you are ashamed of where you come from, if you aren't proud to be called Australian, you are not good enough for me,' Rasic told his players.

There were three players who were fundamental to the style of football Rasic wanted to play, and they all came from Hakoah.

One was Jimmy Mackay. 'An incredible midfield general, who read a game like he was reading a book,' Rasic says. Another was Johnny Watkiss, who was so adaptable that late in his career at club level he'd often play as stopper and striker in the same match. 'That's like Artie Beetson playing fullback and prop,' Rasic says of the former Australian rugby league captain. 'Imagine that.'

And perched between the forward line and the midfielders was Baartz, whose speed allowed him to zip all over the field, wherever required. His pace and agility were crucial, but it was his deadly range in front of goal that appealed most to Rasic.

'Because of Ray's incredible power, he had a shooting distance of 30 to 40 metres,' Rasic says. 'We employed a so-called "deep formation". We could play cautious football at the back simply because of Ray's ability to score from *any* distance. His volleying technique … outstanding. His kicking technique … incredible. And don't forget this: it was with his bloody left *and* right foot. He could score goals with the left, too. A devastating shot.'

It took time for that formation to take hold, but by the time the World Cup qualifiers came around in 1973, Rasic had his side playing the football he wanted. One team from Asia and Oceania would earn the right to go to West Germany. Now known as the 'Socceroos' following a marketing initiative by the Australian Soccer Federation in 1972, the Australians progressed through their first round of qualifiers against New Zealand, Indonesia and Iraq undefeated. After beating Iran 3–0 at the Sydney Sports Ground in the first leg of the second round of qualifying, they travelled to Tehran, where they met the home team before 80,000 in stifling heat. They conceded two goals after just 31 minutes but held on to win on aggregate and reach the final qualifying round against South Korea.

A nil-all draw in the first leg in Sydney, then a 2–all draw in the second leg in Seoul, meant a decider had to be played at a neutral venue: the Government Stadium in Hong Kong (now known as Hong Kong Stadium). After 70 minutes, there had been no goals. The tension was palpable. Then, after the South Koreans cleared a free kick, Mackay unleashed a thunderbolt from 30 metres out to score the match-winner and send the Socceroos to the World Cup finals.

Baartz didn't score the defining goal but he had established himself as the Socceroos' best player.

'I played like the No. 10 role you find now — but it hadn't really been invented yet,' Baartz says. 'Rale said the hardest role for him was to find someone to play that position. A role that was quite demanding. You had to be back defending, then up attacking, and then score goals. You weren't a striker or midfielder; you were back and down, back and down. But it seemed to be working for us.'

'He's too modest,' Rasic says. 'He won't mention this to you, but Ray Baartz was a player you could not compare with anyone else.

I'd never seen a player who had an impact on his team as much as he did for the Socceroos.'

DRESSED IN GOLD-COLOURED tracksuit pants and a dark green Adidas team hoodie with three gold stripes down each sleeve, Rasic patrols the sideline, getting louder and angrier and more animated as he watches his players being massacred in the middle of the SCG.

The second friendly against Uruguay is starting to get ugly.

'Rale was absolutely doing his charlie,' recalls referee Donald Campbell. 'When Australia got in front, it became less of a game of football as a game of brutality. Two or three yellow cards didn't make any difference. When Ray had the ball, they just butchered him.'

It hadn't been like this in the first match in Melbourne, although there was plenty on the line for Rasic and his team. He'd mapped out a tough campaign in preparation for the World Cup finals, so much so that Uruguay coach Roberto Porta had publicly questioned the strategy when they touched down in Australia. Since the start of 1973, the Socceroos had met some of the best sides from Asia, plus the Bulgarian national team and the crack Hungarian club side, Ferencváros, but playing Uruguay, one of the favourites for the World Cup, was an entirely different proposition.

Because the Socceroos would play Chile in one of their group matches in West Germany, Rasic wanted experience against another South American team even if he knew it was a risk. 'So close to the World Cup, if they beat us by five or six goals it would be very difficult for us to recover mentally,' Rasic says. 'There was a lot of pressure on us.'

So, when the Socceroos dug out a scoreless draw, it felt like a win. 'This is a football miracle!' iconic Melbourne sports broadcaster Tony Charlton boomed at Rasic when he bumped into him after fulltime.

While Rasic recalls the Melbourne game being played cleanly — 'It wasn't a dirty match at all' — Baartz and his teammates sensed they had poked the bear. 'They thought they could just push it around and lairise, and we took it to them,' Baartz says. 'Not physically but competitively.'

The tabloids certainly had a whiff of drama for the second match at the SCG. The *Daily Mirror*'s understated back-page headline on match-day was 'BLOODBATH FEAR!'

'The scene is set for one of the bloodiest clashes in the history of Australian soccer,' wrote Tom Anderson, the *Mirror*'s football correspondent. Anderson quoted Porta, who was convinced *his* team were the victims in Melbourne. 'They tackled very, very hard and this upset our players,' Porta said. 'Maybe in Sydney we will play much harder and it will be very interesting.'

Rasic had wanted blood when he took over as coach and now, according to the *Mirror*, he was going to get it.

Drizzling rain was falling when the teams walked onto the SCG, finally easing as prime minister Gough Whitlam and NSW premier Sir Robert Askin shook hands with the players and coaches at the pre-match presentation. Whitlam had a special bond with the Socceroos because he had a special bond with Rasic. There had been much debate at this time about whether *Advance Australia Fair* should be the national anthem, and when the Socceroos became one of the first teams to start singing it before matches, Rasic had a friend and ally for life in the prime minister.

As the anthem was sung on this afternoon, Rasic noticed tears in Whitlam's eyes.

'You hear this national anthem sometimes four or five times a day,' Rasic said to him.

'Rale,' Whitlam replied, 'The tears are not embarrassing.'

The first half, according to newspaper match reports, belonged to Uruguay, with Morena blowing a handful of chances.

The Sun's soccer reporter David Jack had the unenviable job of filing his story at halftime, such was the deadline of the afternoon newspaper he was working for. 'AUSSIE GETS SOCCER LESSON' screamed the headline when the paper hit the streets. The last paragraph read: 'Despite worries this might be a vicious match, players on both sides behaved like perfect gentlemen in the first half and referee Donald Campbell of Adelaide virtually had nothing to do.'

Jack, along with those alongside him in the press box, didn't see the crafty kung-fu chop on Baartz late in the half. Neither did Campbell, or Rasic, or most of the Socceroos. Almost everyone at the SCG on this afternoon was following the play downfield.

But Frank Lowy saw it. He was now the president of Hakoah and Baartz was his most prized player.

'I was in the timber stands, sitting on the timber seats, and it happened right in front of my eyes,' Lowy, 89, says. 'He was running towards the opposing goal, in full flight, and he was chopped — and mercilessly. Those of us who knew him were immediately concerned. It was a terrible challenge.

'Ever since that day, whenever I see a player running like that, whether for Hakoah or Sydney FC or Australia, I picture that incident.'

Who was it, Frank? Who karate chopped your beloved Ray Baartz, a player you would describe in later years as the 'best Socceroos player I ever saw'? We're all dying to know …

'I have no idea,' Lowy shrugs. 'It was a long time ago.'

As Baartz walked from the field at halftime, he sensed something wasn't right. The first person he went looking for in the dressing-room was team doctor Brian Corrigan.

Corrigan was a legend. He'd been with the Socceroos since 1967, but also worked with national and state teams from many other sports, including cricket and rugby league. He was a team doctor for the Australian Olympic team at the 1968 Games in Mexico City, and the first to rush onto the track after Ron Clarke collapsed over the finish line in the 10,000 metres. He found Clarke close to death because of severe altitude sickness.

'I've got a stinking headache, Brian,' Baartz told him.

'Here you go, Baartzy,' Corrigan said. 'Have a couple of Aspros. You'll be right.'

Rasic also knew something was amiss with his star midfielder because one of his teammates had whispered to him, 'Ray isn't well.'

'I'm all right,' Baartz told the coach, batting him away as the team made their way out for the second half.

'That's how Australian sportspeople are,' Rasic recalls. 'South American players would be out for three months. Baartzy just walked back out.'

Frustrated at failing to score in the first half, embarrassed that a minnow like Australia was showing up a South American heavyweight with a proud football history, the butchering from Uruguay began from the opening whistle.

Australia's defence stiffened, and the midfield of Jimmy Rooney, Jimmy Mackay and Dave Harding started to find space. 'The frustration brought a slide in the Uruguayan play, and the second half became a rapid series of fouls and sheer dirty football as they attempted to hold the Australians, rapidly gaining in confidence,' wrote Brian Mossop in the *Sun-Herald*.

In the 57th minute, Rooney put a laser-sharp pass at Baartz's feet. Australia had barely given Uruguayan keeper Gustavo Fernández anything to do thus far, but then Baartz steadied, swung back his lethal right leg, and pulled the trigger …

'Fernández was rated one of the best keepers in world football,' Rasic recalls enthusiastically. 'But he didn't move. He didn't see it rocket into the roof of the net. Believe me, great goalkeepers go for it. But Ray did not allow him to even think about it.'

With typical self-effacement, Baartz simply says this: 'Yeah, I got onto it.'

From the moment the goal was scored, according to Campbell, the match descended into a street fight. It took a lot to shock the experienced whistleblower, who grew up in Glasgow, watching the traditionally violent clashes between Rangers and Celtic. 'But that was baby talk compared to this,' he told the *Mirror* days after the match.

Campbell was 20 metres away from the play when Garisto struck Baartz in the 76th minute. His linesman rushed onto the field and broke into the pack of Uruguayan players who had crowded around Campbell.

'It was No. 3, wasn't it?' Campbell asked.

'Yes,' said the linesman.

Campbell dispatched Garisto from the field and then issued his warning: he would abandon the match if the Uruguayan players and coaching staff didn't back away. Play resumed, but as Socceroos winger Atti Abonyi worked the ball back downfield on the right, Porta came back out on the pitch, mindlessly wandering about his players, barking instructions. They were crazy scenes befitting a crazy match.

The Uruguay coach eventually returned to the dugout and watched in bewilderment as his side eventually suffered a defeat that would reverberate around the football world. In newsrooms around the globe, the reports filtered through that the football backwater of Australia had beaten the fourth seeds for the upcoming World Cup. It was such a shock that it was immediately assumed the score had been misreported.

'The story was queried,' Baartz recalls. 'The world press didn't believe it. They thought it was a typo. *Surely you mean it's the other way around?* That's how much of an upset it was.'

In the jubilant Australian dressing-room, Rasic offered a simple explanation: 'When they lost their tempers, they lost the match.'

With deadlines looming, reporters walked through a packed members' bar to the away dressing-room to get Porta's reaction. He waved them away, grumbling: 'If the Australians had played football, we could've played football.'

Soon after, Australian Soccer Federation president Sir Arthur George came into the Socceroos dressing-room, alongside premier Askin. Whitlam was already there, standing next to Rasic.

'Sir Robert,' George said, trademark cigar in hand, 'can I introduce you to the best coach of all time — and the greatest son of a bitch?'

'Yes,' Rasic fired back, 'and being introduced by another son of a bitch.'

'Well done,' George said. 'Very well done. Now I need 22 names for the final squad for the World Cup.'

'I nominated 27,' Rasic said.

'I need 22.'

'I nominated 27.'

'I demand 22! I employ you!'

'No bastard employs me!'

And with that, Rasic ordered George from the dressing-room. Askin, according to Rasic, was laughing and shaking his head at the madness of it all.

After they had showered and dressed, the players started to slowly drift into the members' bar to enjoy a well-earned beer. Baartz found his wife Sue and then he was introduced to Reg Date, another gifted footballer from Newcastle. From 1937 to 1953, Date scored 664 goals in a senior career that saw him labelled the 'Don Bradman of Football'.

Then Baartz bumped into Campbell and they shared a quiet drink. Campbell didn't sense anything was wrong. 'I thought everything was all good,' Campbell recalls. 'I never realised how injured he was.'

Nobody did. Nobody expected what was to come. After a few beers, Baartz said to Sue: 'I don't feel too good. We'd better go.'

When Baartz's head hit the pillow that night, he was thinking about a famous Australian victory. At 3am, he stirred and woke up. There was no feeling in his left arm or leg. He asked Sue to turn him over, thinking it was nothing more than pins and needles after sleeping on his side. He drifted off to sleep but woke up and the numbness was still there. Perhaps it was a pinched nerve.

He immediately phoned Brian Corrigan.

'Baartzy, it's 7 o'clock, Sunday morning,' the doctor said.

'I've got a problem, Brian,' Baartz said. 'I can't feel my left arm or left leg.'

Corrigan ordered him to immediately make his way to Royal North Shore Hospital. They met in the carpark. Corrigan took one look at the star Socceroo and knew this was far more serious than a pinched nerve.

'Get me the neurosurgeon!' Corrigan barked at the first nurse he saw. 'Now!'

THE CAROTID ARTERIES ARE the freeways that deliver blood to the brain, neck and face. There are two of them: one on the left side of the neck and the other on the right. People can die from a blockage of a carotid artery, but it's very rare for someone to die from 'blunt trauma' to one of them. It can happen.

When cricketer Phillip Hughes was struck in the neck by a bouncer while batting for South Australia against NSW at the SCG in November 2014, Baartz called Corrigan.

'I know what you're ringing me about,' Corrigan said.

'Phillip Hughes,' Baartz said.

'Where the ball hit him is exactly where you were hit,' Corrigan explained. 'The difference between you and him is that your artery swelled. His swelled and burst.'

Hughes' life support was turned off two days after he was struck, plunging the cricket community — indeed, much of the nation — into grief and mourning. It was subsequently revealed that the damage was in the nearby vertebral artery, not the carotid artery; the fact that two sportspeople could be felled with very similar injuries, on the same ground, 40 years apart, is deeply unsettling.

For two days, Baartz lay unconscious in a hospital bed in the emergency ward, with pregnant wife Sue holding his hand and praying that he would wake up and be OK. Don't worry about going to the World Cup. Don't worry about playing again. The concern was whether he would survive.

'They didn't know if I was going to make it,' Baartz says. 'Or if I would have all my faculties. They did an angiogram through the groin. I haemorrhaged from that. Because the arteries swelled and didn't burst, it [only] reduced the flow of blood, and that's why I wasn't affected immediately.'

While no reporters had picked up on the incident that caused the calamity during or after the match, by mid-morning on Sunday the news had filtered through to every newsroom in the city.

The *Daily Mirror*'s back page on the Monday screamed about the seriousness of the situation: 'STROKE FEAR ON BAARTZ: Karate chop victim!'

'Socceroos wife blasts "thuggery",' said the *Sun*.

'I didn't think such a thing could happen in a game,' Sue told journalist Roy Miller.

'I had the TV and radio stations calling me,' Rale Rasic recalls. They were telling him that he had lost his best player.

'I'd just got out of bed. I knew that something had been wrong with him [at halftime] but we didn't take it seriously.'

Corrigan made the call quickly. There was no possible way Baartz could play in the World Cup finals, which were only six weeks away. He wouldn't be able to train for months, let alone play. Rumours about retirement swirled, although Socceroos teammate Johnny Warren was adamant he would not. 'Retire? I doubt it,' Warren said.

But the brutal reality was that Baartz's career was over. After the swelling went down, and Baartz regained consciousness, Corrigan visited him in hospital.

'You are very lucky,' he told him. 'I am advising you to never play again. You have had one angiogram; we can't do any more tests to see if the artery has healed or not. But another blow could be fatal.'

Baartz was philosophical. 'I'd turned 27 a few months before the game,' he says. 'When Brian told me how close I'd come to death, I accepted it straight away.'

So that was it. Forty-eight full internationals for the Socceroos, scoring 18 goals — the most of any player to that time. But it was all over because of one single moment, that few saw, from a player nobody can remember.

Lowy remains furious about what had happened to his star player. 'Neither he nor his family will want for anything,' Lowy said at the time. 'We will make sure that he receives the best of everything. His injury was a disgrace to soccer and we hope that the Australian Soccer Federation will make a full inquiry and take appropriate action. If they fail to do this, we certainly will.'

Rasic also wanted justice. But nobody knew who had delivered the karate chop, and the coach was also fighting battles with his own administrators. He had just come out of a fight over the national federation's refusal to raise the players' daily allowance at the World Cup from a miserly $16.50 to $20. However, his biggest argument with Sir Arthur George in his four years in charge of the Socceroos was over Baartz.

'Ray Baartz will come with us to the World Cup,' Rasic demanded. 'If not, I will include him in the 22-man squad.'

'Not on my life,' George replied.

Days later, he backflipped. 'Baartz has done so much for Australian soccer,' George told the *Mirror*. 'We will have no hesitation in taking him along with us.'

Said Rasic: 'With this wonderful gesture by Sir Arthur George and the ASF in including Baartz in the party, I will not include him in the 22 players in the playing squad.'

AUSTRALIA WERE DRAWN IN Group One for the World Cup finals, along with hosts West Germany, East Germany and Chile. Rasic was confident of a draw in the opening match against the East Germans, not least because of a conversation with acting England manager Joe Mercer, whose side had played the Socceroos' first-up opponents in a friendly just two weeks before the tournament began.

'Son, shut the gate, park the bus, hope for the best,' said Mercer, who was looking after the English side following their failure to qualify for the World Cup finals under Sir Alf Ramsey. 'They are robots. It was 1–all and if the match had gone another 15 minutes there would've been a funeral.'

Baartz didn't travel to West Germany with his teammates, arriving soon after in Hamburg with the officials. Only then did the enormity of what had happened — his injury, his forced retirement, that he wasn't going to be part of Australia's first appearance on football's biggest stage — dawn on him.

'Being with the team in Germany was harder than when I was told

I wouldn't play again,' he says. 'I'd always been in the team. I'd never been substituted; I'd never been on the bench. I stayed in the camp with the boys and when Rale was going through the tactics for East Germany, and going through everyone's role, I was sitting there and when he didn't mention me it hit me: *Shit, I'm not playing.*'

The Socceroos lost to East Germany 2–0. Four days later, they were beaten 3–0 by West Germany. They fought out a scoreless draw against Chile in Berlin in their final match.

To this day, Rasic is adamant Baartz would have made a significant difference. 'We would cause a World Cup upset!' he booms. 'If he was there, we would not have lost to East Germany. Against Chile, on a wet ground, Baartzy would have shot from 40 to 50 metres … A player like Ray Baartz is irreplaceable.'

Soon after arriving back in Australia, Baartz and his young family moved back to Newcastle, where he opened a sports store, popular with generations of local sportspeople for the next 35 years until Baartz retired. He sold the store and it was replaced by a Hungry Jack's restaurant.

No action was ever taken against Uruguay, no inquiry ever launched. And the identity of the big fella with the moustache was never revealed. Baartz hasn't tried to find out who he was, let alone find justice. He was lucky, he says, to get out of the situation with his life.

'I was in hospital for two weeks,' he says, 'but it took me two years to get over it.'

THE SECRETS OF THE past can be found in the underground bottom floor of the NSW State Library. Giggly university students sit alongside researchers with furrowed brows, winding through more than a century of microfilm, the scratchy noise of the film on the green plastic reel sounding like fingernails down a blackboard.

Could the newspapers of the day reveal the secret of who nearly killed Ray Baartz? Alas, they do not.

But then, after hours of searching and reading, you come to the *Daily Telegraph* for Monday, April 29, 1974. The lead story on the front page is about a 'sudden and mysterious credit squeeze' rocking the Whitlam government's re-election campaign. Other stories include an exclusive report about The Seekers making a comeback. A photo of Rolling Stones lead singer Mick Jagger, bare-chested and wearing a white jumpsuit, points to an inside story revealing his affair with Marianne Faithfull.

At the bottom of the page, a small story jumps out at you. 'Socceroo hero paralysed' reads the headline. Beneath it is a small headshot of Baartz. The story is written by John Taylor, in those days a fresh-faced reporter who had recently come onto the soccer round having previously covered his preferred sport of rugby league.

'Ray Baartz, Australia's hero in Saturday's Soccer international against Uruguay at the SCG, is paralysed,' reads the opening paragraph.

But it's the seventh par that stands out: 'The incident that caused Baartz's injury occurred in the first half when he was hit by Uruguayan defender Alberto Cardaccio ...'

Alberto Cardaccio.

Is that him? Is that the guy we've been looking for?

You race out of the library and up onto Macquarie Street and get Baartz on the phone. He's on his way to a primary school in Newcastle to pick up his grandchildren. He does the 3pm run most weekdays.

Who needs to be the best Socceroo in history when you can be the best grandfather?

You tell Baartz that you might've discovered the identity of the man who almost killed him. It's not Luis Garisto, although he already knew that. It's another player. Another defender.

Alberto Cardaccio.

'Mate, I wouldn't know,' Baartz says. 'I said a lot of things to a lot of people at that time. I was fighting for my life … What does he look like?'

The magic of *Google* allows you to easily find the photo of Cardaccio in the program for the 1974 World Cup. There he is: big, tall fella — with a moustache.

After a pause, Baartz speaks. 'That's him. There you go.'

Baartz has tried his best to forget the big, tall fella with the moustache and what happened that day. For Donald Campbell, the memory actually still hurts.

'If you talk to Ray, please give him my deepest sympathies,' he says. 'I want to apologise to him. I've never had anything like that in a game before. I was a FIFA referee for 25 years and I never officiated a match with that much bad temper. It was the toughest game I've ever refereed. The Australian Soccer Federation wrote to me to congratulate me on how I controlled it, because it could've really got out of hand. I'm just apologising to Ray as a mark of respect. I felt terrible because it happened in a game that I was involved in. I hope the truth comes out and the offenders get punished.'

Neither Garisto nor Cardaccio can defend themselves, or even give their side of the story. Garisto died on November 21, 2017, aged 71. Alberto Victor Cardaccio Traversa, who was actually more midfielder than defender and made one substitute appearance at the 1974 World Cup, died on January 28, 2015. He was 65.

Baartz has been back to the SCG several times since 1974, mostly for cricket. In November 2017, he and some of his former teammates gathered at the ground, invited by the SCG Trust to commemorate the 50th anniversary of the Quoc Khanh Cup (also known as the South Vietnam National Day tournament), a friendly competition that involved South Korea, Singapore, Malaysia, Australia and host nation South Vietnam. It was conducted while the Vietnam War was raging. The players recalled how they ate Spam with soldiers in the mess tent, and trained and played on nondescript fields, next to paddocks full of land mines, with mortar fire blasting in the background. Despite the oppressive heat, the Socceroos won five straight games, including a 3–2 victory over South Korea in the final in front of 30,000 fans at Cong Hoa Stadium in Saigon. It was the Australian team's first piece of international silverware, but the madness of the war meant the achievement barely caused a ripple back home.

The luncheon was held in the members' bar, where Baartz had felt the first signs in 1974 that something wasn't right. Former Socceroos striker Robbie Slater presented the players with jumpers and then they all moved out on to the emerald turf for a team photo.

As the players chatted among themselves, Baartz eyed a patch of turf he hadn't walked on for 43 years. It was the exact spot where the big, tall fella with the moustache had karate chopped him. He walked over, stared down at the ground.

'I thought: *If only*,' he says. 'If it hadn't have happened, I wonder where my career would've gone.'

CHAPTER 4

C'mon Aussie, C'mon!

Kerry Packer and The Don

THE LETTER ARRIVED IN Arthur Morris' letterbox in early July 1977. He instantly recognised the handwriting.

It was Sir Donald.

'Amidst all of this it has been told to me that the Trustees of the SCG are seriously considering an offer from Packer to lease the ground for matches,' Bradman wrote in a letter dated June 29, 1977. 'I can't believe it. If the Trustees rat on the Board and the NSWCA and if Packer wins, the great Trust and heritage you helped to build will crumble to dust.'

Morris had been one of the key men in Bradman's team on the 1948 Ashes tour of England. Determined to return home undefeated, Bradman had made Morris, the NSW captain, part of his inner sanctum. Heaven knows they'd shared enough time at the crease over the years, and especially in '48 as the team became the Invincibles. On the final day of the fourth Test, at Headingley in Leeds, Bradman and Morris helped the Australians to a famous victory, tearing into the English bowling attack as they hunted down 404 — a record successful fourth-innings run chase.

Bradman was judicious with his praise of players — of anything, it seems — but in the years that followed he was effusive about Morris and his cricketing abilities, marvelling at the power he generated in his wrists and forearms, describing him as the 'ideal' left-handed opening batsman.

They still had a close relationship when Bradman's letter arrived some 29 years later.

By then, Morris was 55 years old and working in public relations for security group Wormald International. He was also an SCG Trustee, having been appointed in 1965. He would hold that role for 22 years, eight of them as deputy chairman.

Bradman was 68, and still casting an imposing shadow over cricket and all who played it. He'd served twice as chairman of the Australian Cricket Board, dealing with issues such as illegal bowling actions and a cancelled tour of Australia by South Africa because of the South African government's policy of apartheid. By the middle of 1977, however, The Don was grappling with an entirely different matter. He was no longer ACB chairman, but he was a member of the Board's 'emergency committee' to deal with a new opponent.

The opponent wasn't an English fast bowler, nor a tricky pitch. This time it was Kerry Francis Bullmore Packer, the 39-year-old media proprietor and businessman who was bankrolling 'World Series Cricket'.

'Total control of Australian cricket must remain with the Board and the states, and not be sacrificed for a handful of silver,' Bradman continued in his letter to Morris. 'Surely money cannot buy such a principle.'

Bradman's letter is one of several in previously private correspondence between Bradman and Morris. It forms part of the SCG's Arthur Morris Collection. The letters — some typed, some handwritten — have never been published until now. They are a portal into the inner thoughts of Australia's greatest cricketer at the time of Australian cricket's greatest upheaval.

Countless words have been written or spoken since 1977 about World Series Cricket, but for our purposes let's focus on the afternoon and evening of Tuesday, November 28, 1978, the first big match of the second season of Packer's rebel competition, when Australia played the West Indies.

This was a night not easily forgotten by all those who saw it; by the 50,000-plus fans crammed into the stands, on the Hill and even in the pile of rubble where the demolished Brewongle Stand once stood; by the cricketers, who were playing on the sacred turf of the SCG under lights — the ground illuminated by six enormous and newly erected towers — for the first time; by the mixture of celebrities and officials in the executive room sipping champagne and chardonnay as *C'mon Aussie, C'mon* blared from the speakers; by the women who were walking through the Members Stand for the first time, decades of tradition having been cast aside by Packer himself; by the World Series Cricket and Channel Nine employees who had either survived Packer's cull after the lukewarm success of the first season, or those who had been hired to change the public's perception of the venture; and, perhaps mostly, by the multitudes watching at home — because that's what this whole thing was about, wasn't it?

This was a night that ended with Packer sitting on his own, in the dark, in the top tier of the Members Stand, looking over the floodlit SCG and out to Moore Park as people streamed out happy, content, drunk. 'It's been an encouraging start,' was all he would say when asked by the press for comment before politely ending the interview.

It was a rare sign of restraint on a night when Sydney indulged itself. This was the night, really, that changed cricket forever. The night Kerry Packer won the war.

IT'S BEEN NEARLY 45 years since Australian journalists Peter McFarline and Alan Shiell broke the story about Packer's clandestine plans to form a breakaway competition, yet it still captivates each time it's rehashed, regurgitated or retold.

Its appeal lies in the rich, larger-than-life characters involved: Packer, the frightening, volatile media baron trying to live up to his late father Sir Frank's legend after inheriting two television stations, five radio stations and the country's largest magazine publishing company; John Cornell, the business partner of comedian Paul Hogan, who first sold the idea to Packer; and the moustachioed heroes of the day, Australian captain Ian Chappell, his brother Greg, swashbuckling wicketkeeper Rodney Marsh and, of course, Dennis Lillee.

Packer established World Series Cricket when the ACB rebuffed his offer to take Test cricket from the ABC and broadcast it exclusively on his flagship television network, Channel Nine. He did so with the promise of creating better conditions for the game's underpaid and undervalued stars.

Ian Chappell had twice fronted the ACB asking for better pay when he was captain. Twice, he was refused. Twice, by Bradman. He recalled, in the 2020 documentary *A Glorious Life*, one such meeting. 'Points five and six were to do with finance,' he said. 'Bradman sat back in his chair for the first four points. When it got to the fifth, he sat up and said, "No, son, we can't do that." And away he went. I didn't have a relationship with him before, but once I became captain any relationship went downhill to the point when it wasn't a very good relationship at all.'

If the players were the pawns in this game of chess, the board on which it was being played were the iconic cricket grounds of the world. In England, it was Lord's, the home of cricket, which had banned the breakaway players. In Australia, it was the Sydney and Melbourne cricket grounds. When Packer launched World Series Cricket in May 1977, he was asked whether the NSW and Victorian governments should allow access to the country's two most iconic venues.

'They were built by governments for the use of the people,' he replied. 'If the people are angry enough, and want the grounds enough, I'm sure the governments will come to some arrangement.'

In NSW, where Labor's Neville Wran was the premier of the day, they most certainly did.

The SCG Trust had a long-standing contractual agreement with the NSW Cricket Association, which had priority for the use of the ground as set out in legislation that had been in place for 100 years. The Trust wrote to Packer on July 25, 1977, and informed him that no World Series Cricket match — whether it was a Supertest or a 50-over International Cup game — would be played at the ground.

Upon hearing the news, Bradman sent Morris a letter of approval.

'First, my congratulations to the SCG Trustees for having the courage to resist the tempting Packer offer,' he wrote. 'I presume and hope they saw the issue as the survival of Test cricket as we know it, or capitulation to a Packer monopoly. For mine, I place principle before money, but not everyone does. In the end, principle will win, albeit through a long and costly process.'

Bradman knew that Packer and his deep pockets weren't going away.

'I see the ICC Test countries had the guts to confront Packer but what will happen next?' he continued in his letter. 'The legal aspect is worrying. It is unbelievable that one man because of a lust for power can throw into the melting pot the growth of over 100 years.'

What Bradman and the rest of the cricket establishment perhaps underestimated was just how far Packer's power extended. Within 24 hours of the SCG Trust rejecting the bid to use the ground, the government performed a stunning about-face, dissolving the Trust. When it came to appointing 12 new Trustees, only three of the old incumbents remained: chairman Pat Hills, NSW Country Rugby League secretary John O'Toole and Morris. Hills was a senior minister in Wran's cabinet.

In his weighty Packer biography, *The Rise and Rise of Kerry Packer*, author Paul Barry wondered if the dramatic change had come about because 'Neville Wran had seen political advantage in giving one of the state's biggest media proprietors a hand'. It's an easy line to draw. Speaking to the *Sydney Morning Herald*, Packer was delighted that Wran had listened to the people of NSW. 'I give Mr Wran full marks for this,' he said. 'He is a very shrewd politician, and I would have thought he would have seen the public groundswell against the existing situation.'

The NSW Cricket Association dug in, taking the matter to court. A few days before the hearing, which began in October 1977, Bradman fired off another letter — not to his friend Arthur Morris, but to John Wood, the secretary of the Trust since 1974.

'I have been deeply disturbed at what I have read in the press concerning the SCG and the Packer circus,' Bradman wrote on October 12. 'Originally, I understood the Trustees had stood firm and refused him the use of the ground. Is it true that this decision has been reversed? I find it difficult to believe that the Trustees would think temporary financial reward of more value than the less tangible but nevertheless real values which people like myself cherish so much.'

Wood's reply, which is also part of Morris' collection, exposes how the Trust was being pulled in different directions by Packer, Bradman, the ACB and mostly the Wran Government, which could appoint and sack Trustees as it saw fit.

'Your letter was placed before the full Trust meeting in October and noted with due concern,' Wood replied to Bradman. 'The original application of World Series Cricket was declined by the Trust in July 1977. A further application was received from World Series Cricket in September submitting a new set of dates. Conferences were held by the Trust separately with both NSW Cricket Association Executive

Committee and representatives of World Series Cricket and finally the application was put to a vote of Trustees and carried by a majority in favour.

'Thereupon the Trust's decision was notified to NSW Cricket Association, who in turn commenced an action against World Series Cricket and the Trustees as joint defendants, in the Supreme Court (Equity) to restrain the use of Sydney Cricket Ground for World Series Cricket matches. The hearing took place from October 27 to November 1, and I was hoping to give you the judgment so handed down in my reply to you, hence the delayed time factor, but the Court has reserved its decision and to date it has not been received by us.

'However, I thought you should know these facts without further delay, and I will be in a better position to tell you in more detail when the matter is resolved in the Court.'

The court eventually ruled in favour of the Association, but the Wran Government responded by repealing the legislation relating to the Trust and introducing a new Bill that did not include any reference to a special relationship between the Association and the ground. The Liberal Opposition delayed the Bill in the Legislative Council until April 1978, an impasse that denied Packer use of the SCG for his first season. Instead, WSC matches in Sydney were played at the adjacent Sydney Showground, which wasn't under the Trust's jurisdiction.

In some strange way, the stubbornness of ground officials in Australia's major cities led to a series of events from which day-night cricket was born. Needing a venue in Melbourne for that first season because the Melbourne Cricket Ground remained loyal to the cricket establishment, Packer and Cornell focused on VFL Park. After attending a game of Australian football under lights, they decided to try a limited-over cricket match starting in the afternoon and finishing under floodlights.

The relative success of those matches provided a glimmer of hope for Packer heading into World Series Cricket's second season, which had until that point been a money bonfire for his company. Deputy chairman and mentor Harry Chester, otherwise known as 'The Axe', was regularly on his case, according to Ian Chappell. Day-night cricket emerged as a potential saviour because it allowed people to attend — or, more importantly as far as Packer was concerned, watch on television — after they knocked off work.

The revamped SCG Trust cleared the path for Packer to finally use the famous ground, as he'd wanted all along. But he had one more favour to ask Neville Wran: he needed lights if he was going to play day-night matches in Sydney. Instead of installing lights at the Showground, Packer wanted towering floodlights erected at the SCG. On May 1, 1978, Pat Hills announced that six light towers, at a cost of $1.3 million, would be installed.

Over the decades, a myth that Packer paid for the light towers has been perpetuated. While Basil Sellers' sculptures around the ground celebrate the likes of Gasnier, Benaud, Messenger and Cuthbert, the six towering beams in some respects honour Packer and his influence on the ground and the game.

'Did Kerry pay for them?' a curious Ian Chappell inquired during an interview for this book.

He did not. Pat Hills revealed that Packer did offer to fund the project, but 'as the SCG is Crown land, it could not be done'. Two-thirds of the bill was paid for by SCG members, many of whom were aligned to the establishment and not Packer. The other third was covered by the NSW taxpayer, at the urging of Hills, according to Philip Derriman in *Grassy Pitches and Glory Years*.

The erection of the lights captured Sydney's attention. Soon enough, like a scene from HG Wells' *The War of the Worlds*, the towers emerged from holes in the ground to take their place around the SCG like death machines ready to exterminate the cricket conformists trying to block Packer and the millions of dollars he wanted to extract from the sport.

When they were completed, each tower stood 80 metres tall. A total of 576 lights generating 1.9 million watts didn't just light up the SCG but also the surrounding suburbs. Complaints started flooding in. A woman who lived 15 kilometres away at Balgowlah Heights claimed that the glare was so strong it 'hurt the back of my eyes'. Said one Moore Park resident: 'We turned off every light in the flat and could still read the newspaper by the lights on the ground.'

Sir Donald Bradman had been watching all of this from afar, in Adelaide, with revulsion. He'd been talking to the Trust about donating a large portion of his memorabilia — 'cricketana' as he curiously called it — but after hearing a deal had been struck with Packer, he changed his mind.

'Before the Packer episode, approaches were made to me by the Trustees of the SCG concerning the possible acquisition by them of my cricketana,' he wrote in a letter to Morris on June 5, 1978. 'Some preliminary inquiries were made and then, when the big turnaround in the use of the SCG was made known, I engaged in some delaying correspondence with John Wood ... However, on reflection, perhaps I should pursue the matter with an open mind and not be dissuaded by my prejudices. If I do, it would need to be on a business basis, because I am certainly no longer interested in making a donation of anything to the SCG. They are making plenty of money from a business venture not associated with traditional cricket.'

In other words, if Packer was profiting from the SCG, why shouldn't Bradman?

Was all this going to be worth it? For Packer's bottom line? For the credibility of the SCG? For anyone?

SCG members were angry. NSW taxpayers frustrated. Big unsightly light towers glowing like the moon were getting up the nose and in the eyes of residents. And then there was Sir Donald himself, so cranky that he was now asking for top dollar for his weathered bats and sweat-stained old gloves.

One thing was clear. As day turned to night in the twilight of November 28, 1978, one side was going to emerge triumphant.

PERHAPS THE EVER DIMINISHING space on the Hill gave it away as swarms of young men carrying eskies of KB Lager cans fought for their patch of grass. They wore terry-towelling hats and skin-tight t-shirts brandishing World Series Cricket's new catchcry, 'Big Boys Play at Night'.

The stands were filling up, too, all part of a growing tide of people flooding the SCG for Australia's International Cup match against Clive Lloyd's West Indies. The only docile place was the Members Stand, even if it was being opened for the first time to women — an initiative of the hirer, Kerry Packer.

What was clear that afternoon at the SCG was that the public's perception of World Series Cricket had dramatically changed. This wasn't lost on the Australian players as Ian Chappell led them onto the ground just before 2.30pm, the official start time. As the players walked from the dressing-room, down the steps of the Members Stand, and then trotted out onto the field, Rod Marsh took one look around the well-patronised ground, drank it all in and turned to the skipper.

'We're back!' he said.

Chappell felt it, too. Various reports from the day say about 5000 people were there for the first ball. What nobody had predicted was the mass of people who hadn't yet arrived. Packer had a figure of 25,000 in his head but a quick survey of the scene outside suggested that was going to easily surpassed. As the Australian fieldsmen threw giveaway white cricket balls to those who had arrived early, enormous lines snaked in all directions down Driver Avenue.

What mostly surprised Ian Chappell were the number of people singing the theme song, *C'mon Aussie, C'mon*, the new siren sound of World Series Cricket that was seared into the minds of every fan's head because it had been played so many times on radio stations and, of course, Packer's various media platforms. John Cornell had approached industry titans Allan Johnston and Alan Morris at Sydney advertising firm Mojo to come up with a jingle that eulogised and lauded the stars of the day. And it worked.

'Lillee's pounding down like a machine,' the song begins. The second line features another fiery paceman, Len Pascoe, 'making divots in the green'.

'Marshy's taking wickets ... Hookesy's clearing pickets ... and the Chappells' eyes have got that killer gleam.'

And then the chorus, which Australian cricket fans of the late '70s will always remember ...

Come on Aussie

Come on, come on!

'That was the first time I'd heard the song and to hear everyone singing it said to me the public now saw us as the Australian team,' Ian Chappell recalls. 'I thought it was pretty important because we had a big crowd there. If we'd lost, it would've been a bit of a downer.'

He'd been appointed captain two years earlier after being summoned to Packer's office, fronting in a denim jacket and check shirt.

'What are you? Some fucking cowboy?' Packer, in signature pose with bare feet on his desk, grumbled. 'Who do you want in your team?'

'I'm not captain of Australia any longer, Kerry,' Chappell said firmly. 'Greg is.'

'What do you think this is? A democracy?'

Ian phoned brother Greg for permission to captain Packer's new Australian side.

'It's a bastard of a job,' the younger Chappell said. 'You can have it.'

Along with others in Packer's rebel side, the Chappells had enjoyed famous wins at the SCG.

'It was always my favourite ground,' Ian Chappell says. 'I didn't have a lot of success there, but to me it was a perfect size. The fact you were changing in the same dressing-room where Keith Miller and Bill

113

O'Reilly had once been was always an attraction. Not that I'm a great sentimentalist, but to me that was important.'

While Ian averaged 17.47 runs in Test matches at the SCG, Greg Chappell thrived at the ground with both bat and ball. He scored four hundreds in 12 Tests, including 204 in Australia's innings victory against India on a good batting wicket in 1980–81, although he still rates his unbeaten 182 against the West Indies in 1975–76, in his first series as captain, as one of his finest.

'Oh, I loved playing there,' Greg oozes, even now. 'It's a cricket ground. The Melbourne Cricket Ground is a stadium. It's more a football ground than a cricket ground. The SCG is a cricket ground. It was the most consistently good wicket because it gave everyone a chance. If you were a good quick bowler, you got something out of it. Good spinner, you got something out of it. And, if you got in with the bat, you got value for your shots.'

In the home dressing-room, victories were celebrated and losses dissected over beers from the cellar room located beneath them. 'Doug Walters would sit on a chair near the ice chest, where all the drinks were,' Ian recalls. 'He'd bang on the floor with his bat and that signalled to the cellarman to bring up another dozen beers.'

Would the Australians be banging the floorboards in celebration at the end of this night? Dennis Lillee took his place at the top of his mark in readiness to deliver the first delivery of World Series Cricket at a traditional venue — with a white ball!

His hair was shorter and thinning slightly from the days earlier in the '70s when he and Jeff Thomson had terrorised overseas batting orders, and his action was slightly altered, his arms and shoulders more controlled. But it was still unmistakable that it was 'DK' charging in for the first over. His second delivery was a wide but come the fourth over he'd found his rhythm, trapping opening batsman Richard Austin on the back foot to have him judged lbw. Three balls later, Lillee had the prized wicket of Viv Richards, who miscalculated a hook shot and watched on as the ball dropped onto the stumps. Lloyd's decision to bat first denied the crowd the opportunity to watch Lillee with the white ball under lights. He was determined to put on a show nonetheless.

The great fast bowler had been critical to all this happening in the first place. The first kernels of World Series Cricket were planted two years earlier in a Perth hotel room, where Lillee was telling Cornell and businessman Austin Robertson about the lack of respect — and money — the Australian team was being shown by cricket authorities. Robertson proposed a one-off match involving the game's best players, all of whom would receive a share of the revenue. Cornell's ears pricked; he said he knew of someone who might be interested in bankrolling and broadcasting such a match. He took the idea to Packer, who at the same time was being roundly dismissed by the ACB whenever he asked about broadcasting rights.

Two years later, as Lillee charged in, Packer was standing over the turnstiles, watching the fans flood into the SCG. The West Indies had rested players for this match, perhaps with an eye to the many matches they'd be playing before the season was through, and the haemorrhaging of the top order only stopped when Gordon Greenidge (41) and Lloyd (21) shared a 34-run fourth-wicket partnership. But they, too, fell to Lillee, who finished the innings with 4–13 from nine overs.

Greg Chappell tells me he only remembers the occasion, not the match, forgetting that he took 5–19 with his deceptive medium pace as the West Indies were dismissed for 128 in the 48th over.

'I loved bowling with the white ball in Sydney because the seam was always a little more prominent than the red ball,' he says. 'They kept saying it was the same ball and I would say, "Bullshit." The seam was very prominent on the white ball and not so the red ball. There was always a bit of nibble if you wanted to pitch it up.'

Sitting in the commentary box was David Hill, the executive producer of Nine's cricket coverage, who had been at the forefront of the network's innovative approach to its broadcasts, including stump microphones, in World Series Cricket's first season. At the tea break, he was making his way down the steps when he bumped into director Brian Morelli, who'd been stationed in the production trucks behind the stands.

They surveyed the scene before them. The lights had been turned on, illuminating the grassy stage. A red sun was sinking in the west, visible in the gap where the Brewongle Stand once stood. The Hill was heaving with fans and every stand was almost full. Hill and Morelli looked at each other and burst into tears.

'It's worked!' they said in unison before hugging and making their way down to the dining room.

'That moment is seared in my memory,' Hill recalls. 'Anyone connected with World Series Cricket had become a pariah. I was called a prostitute. My friends boycotted me. That first year, we all travelled with the players and we knew and felt the pressure they were under. We all knew the pressure that Kerry was under. We knew he'd put everything on the line. We all felt we were partly responsible for it not working. Heading into that first match under lights in Sydney, we all felt the pressure.'

At the start of the tea break, *National Times* journalist Adrian McGregor was standing at the door to the executive room on the second level of the Members Stand, trying to convince the doorman to let him in. A flash of his police press pass did the trick.

The scene before him provided the perfect metaphor for his story that would run in a fortnight's time. The walls were lined with images of cricket's greatest players, including Bradman after he reached his century of centuries, looking down upon celebrities clinking champagne glasses. John Cornell and his wife Delvene Delaney chatted with Paul Hogan, celebrity agent Harry M. Miller and Bruce Gyngell, the first man on Australian television. At one point, Lillee made a brief appearance. He took one look at the scene and chuckled. 'I never made it up here when I was with the Cricket Board,' he told McGregor.

Packer showed his face and mingled briefly before making his way downstairs and then out to the front of the stand. That's where he found Rod Marsh and Greg Chappell, who'd finished dinner and were about to head back to the dressing-room before play resumed. The vantage point allowed all three men to look directly across the ground at the gaping hole left by the demolished Brewongle Stand.

'People were running across Moore Park to get into the ground,' Greg recalls. 'They were streaming in.' Marsh uttered the same line to Greg as he had to Ian at the start of the day: 'We're back!'

What happened next is part of Australian sporting folklore. Upon hearing that the gates had been shut for security reasons, Packer raced down the stairs and out to the main entrance. Precisely 44,377 people had come through the turnstiles. Packer ordered the gates to be re-opened, allowing the masses to flow into the ground free of charge. He even manned a gate on his own to ease congestion.

Mayhem followed. The crowd swelled like an angry river, rising to 50,000 people, maybe more. The Members Reserve had been relatively unoccupied, but Packer opened that up, too. Some 'interlopers' made their way into the Members Pavilion itself. Why waste empty seats? The vacant benches outside the press box reserved for journalists were also quickly commandeered by spectators.

It's not as if the benches were being used by hard-working members of the cricketing press. A grand total of three local reporters — Phil Wilkins from the *Australian* and two from wire agencies — had been sent to cover the match. A few of the British media contingent in Australia for the traditional Ashes series that was about to begin in Brisbane were also in attendance, as was Bill O'Reilly, the *Sydney Morning Herald*'s cricket columnist. But the contrast with the scene three days later at the Gabba, where no less than 40 cricket writers were covering the first Test between Graham Yallop's Australian team and Mike Brearley's England, was stark. At one point, Cornell rushed in to report the enormous crowd figure. 'These people have found truth!' he announced.

Alan Lee, who was following both the Ashes tour and WSC for the *Evening News* and the *Sunday Telegraph* in London, was at the SCG that night and cornered Packer for a rare interview. 'English cricket writers and I are like oil and water,' Packer told him. 'They attack me because they won't attack the establishment.'

Right: Neil Harvey (left) and Alan Davidson lead the Australians out, with captain Richie Benaud following, at the start of their farewell Test, the final match of the 1962–63 Ashes series at the Sydney Cricket Ground.

Below: Harvey and Davidson, two legends of Australian sport, back in a space they came to know so well: the home dressing room at the SCG.

Alan Davidson in the SCG nets (left) and opening the bowling to England's David Sheppard in the fifth Ashes Test in 1962–63. The Australian slip cordon is (from left) Peter Burge, Richie Benaud, Graham McKenzie, Bob Simpson and keeper Wally Grout. The batsman at the non-striker's end is Colin Cowdrey.

Above left: Neil Harvey's trademark cover drive. Above right: Harvey sweeps during his farewell Test innings.

Below: St George's Norm Provan tackles Wests' Fred Norden early in the 1962 rugby league grand final. Saints' Reg Gasnier (obscuring referee Jack Bradley), Billy Wilson and Monty Porter, and Wests' Jim Cody (on ground) and John Hayes (far right) are close by.

John O'Gready's epic photograph of 'The Gladiators', Norm Provan and Arthur Summons.

Above: The Socceroos team that started in both matches against Iran and the first leg against South Korea in the qualifying games for the 1974 World Cup finals. Back (from left): Ray Baartz, Ray Richards, John Watkiss, Peter Wilson (captain), Adrian Alston, Doug Utjesenovic, Johnny Warren. Front: Jim Mackay, Col Curran, Rale Rasic (coach), Jim Fraser, Atti Abonyi.

Left: Ray Baartz lies prostrate on the SCG turf after the infamous 'karate chop' incident against Uruguay in 1974.

Below: Robbie Slater, who played 28 full internationals for Australia from 1988 to 1997, with Baartz in the Members Pavilion in November 2017, when the Socceroos of 1967 gathered to celebrate the 50th anniversary of their historic victory in the Quoc Khanh Cup in South Vietnam.

Above: The new SCG floodlights are switched on for the first time, the night before World Series Cricket made its debut at the ground on November 28, 1978.

Below: The Australians celebrate the dismissal of the West Indies' Viv Richards, bowled by Dennis Lillee for a duck, in the early overs of the landmark game. From left: Bruce Laird (with back to camera), David Hookes, Richards, Gary Gilmour, Rod Marsh and Ian Chappell.

Left: As the sun sets over Sydney and the floodlights take over on the evening of World Series Cricket's debut at the SCG, every vantage point on the Hill and in the Sheridan Stand is taken.

Below: Ian Chappell hooks at the start of the Australian innings.

Above: The All Blacks perform their haka prior to the kick-off of the Bledisloe Cup Test at the SCG in 1979.

Below: Captain Mark Loane (right) and Paul McLean begin the Wallabies' lap of honour after their famous win. Coach Dave Brockhoff is at the back of the group, the proudest man at the SCG.

Lee asked Packer how long he intended to invest money into the World Series Cricket experiment. 'It depends whether we are bull-headed or not,' he said. 'Perhaps stupidity is a more accurate description of what I have been involved in. It became a matter of principle with me. We will never make a big profit out of this.'

Whether the profit was big or small, fundamental to the concept's success was a successful Australian team. In the first season, they had won just five matches: two Supertests and three International Cup games. It was clear, however, in this first important match of the new season that Ian Chappell's side was taking a more professional approach.

Greg Chappell and Bruce Laird opened the run chase and began cautiously. The matches played under lights at VFL Park during the previous summer had been tricky because of the 'drop-in' pitches that were used. While the Australians were comfortable playing on the truer wicket of the SCG, this was still a match at night with a white ball.

In those early experimental years, one ball was used throughout the 50 overs of an innings. The white paint dulled after 20 overs, often making it the same colour as the pitch itself. If the pitch was green, the ball also became green.

'I could tell you every time where a red ball landed as it pitched,' Greg Chappell says. 'You didn't have that with the white ball initially. It was still harder to play and the lighting wasn't as good as it is now. With six banks of lights, the ball looks smaller at night. Instead of having one light source, the sun, you had six with a shadow around the ball. It didn't look as small as a golf ball but it was smaller than a cricket ball. Batting under lights was challenging but twilight was even

119

more difficult, especially at the SCG when the Brewongle Stand was missing and the western sun got in your eyes. The early overs of the evening sessions were challenging.'

Nevertheless, in this match, he and Laird put on 40 for the first wicket. Before long, Australia needed just 34 from the final 20 overs. One of Channel Nine's cameras zoomed in on the moon, prompting Caribbean commentator Tony Cozier to break into a version of the ballad *Blue Moon*.

After just one season, Nine's commentary team had become celebrities in their own right. There was Richie Benaud, of course, fronting the coverage in his signature beige jacket. Victorian Bill Lawry had been a dour opening batsman for his country and state, but now he was part of the Packer stable, chuckling when he saw a large, white sheet on the Hill emblazoned with the words: 'BILL LAWRY'S HANKY'.

As the Australians closed in on the target, the crowd bubbled with enthusiasm, aided no doubt by the oceans of alcohol that had been swilled over the preceding seven hours. Reports from the day describe scuffles that broke out and empty beer cans raining upon some officials. One male patron kept exposing his bare buttocks to sections of the Members Stand.

When Ian Davis and Rodney Marsh guided the home team to victory just after 9.20pm, with five wickets and 13 overs to spare, thousands of spectators jumped the fence and charged towards the middle. As this happened, Alan Lee was sitting next to Tony Greig, the former England captain who was now an outcast at Lord's because of his allegiance to Packer. Greig had missed the West Indies' innings because he was flying back from Perth after attending to business interests.

'I had to fight back tears when I saw this,' Greig said. 'It's taken a long time, with a lot of setbacks, and it's hard to explain what it means to me to see it come right.'

Greg Chappell invited McGregor to the home dressing-room after the match. Lloyd and Packer were also there.

'Got you at last, you old bastard,' Packer said to Lloyd, according to McGregor. 'It's been a long wait.'

'Pleased?' Lloyd asked.

'Of course,' Packer said. 'What do you think I am? A sadist?'

'I expected 60,000,' Rod Marsh joked, prompting laughs from all in earshot.

The masses oozed out of the SCG, into Moore Park and the surrounding suburbs, and the scene was utter chaos. Cars slowly angled their way out of the choked carparks as the mob moved towards Central Station or the next pub where they could continue to drink and sing the ubiquitous *C'mon Aussie, C'mon*.

The executive room was still in full swing, including Richie Benaud and his wife Daphne. Both had been an important part of the WSC machine since the day Packer had bumped into Richie at a lunch in April 1977, which quickly led to a more formal meeting in Packer's office.

'Richie,' Packer began, as recalled by former Nine sports boss Steve Crawley in the *Women's Weekly*. 'What we are about to discuss, you can tell no one.'

'I'm sorry, Mr Packer, I can't agree to that.'

'What? This is confidential … you can't tell anyone.'

'Well, should I leave now?'

'Just who do you have to tell, Richie?'

'Daphne.'

'Why do you have to tell Daphne?'

'She knows I've come here at short notice to see you and the first thing she'll ask when I get home is what did Mr Packer want?'

'Okay, you can tell Daphne … but no one else.'

Packer understood that securing Benaud was pivotal to his cause. The former Australian captain turned highly respected journalist and commentator brought respect and gravitas when others were dismissing World Series Cricket with unflattering monikers like 'The Circus' and 'Packerball'. Richie was the bridge between cricket's storied past and its exciting future.

'That night, at the SCG, the gates were opened by Kerry Packer, rather than closed by the ground authorities, as 52,000 people swarmed in,' Benaud wrote years later. 'They were captivated by the spectacle of cricket being played under lights. Nothing has been the same since. It was all a tremendous blow to those who claimed that if God had meant for cricket to be played with a white ball, he wouldn't have made cricket balls red, conveniently forgetting that all cricket balls are white before they're dyed red.'

The Benauds would have noticed that, as the executive room grew louder in triumph, Packer was nowhere to be seen. Instead, he was sitting in the stands, on his own until Greig joined him.

'This is it,' Greig said to him.

'Yes,' Packer replied softly. 'I think you're right.'

The morning after the night before revealed the carnage. There were piles of rubbish both inside and outside the ground, quickly swept up and removed by casual employees because the Australian team had another match that night, against the World XI, who were captained by Greig.

With the hangover still running strong, a crowd of 20,134 turned up. Restrictions placed on the amount of alcohol allowed into the ground meant the natives weren't as restless this time, although they were in full voice just before 9pm when they booed Greig as he made his way into the middle to face Lillee under lights. Alas, a storm blew in soon after, forcing the players from the field. Australia were declared winners because of their superior run rate.

In the decades that have followed, that night of November 28, 1978, is considered the turning point that led to Packer winning the so-called 'cricket war'. Over the next 12 months, the masses gravitated towards World Series Cricket and away from the 'official' Australian Test side. Crowds often swelled above 30,000. Greig was the villain, playing it up for the crowd, while Lillee was the hero, striking his helmet with a short-pitched delivery. The people loved it.

'There was an incredible sense of occasion,' McGregor tells me now. 'The floodlit scene, the famous personalities revelling at their own exclusivity; the whole room universally joyful at witnessing 50,000 people changing the face of sport. And Kerry's expansive triumphalism at this fatal salient into the ACB. In terms of cricket history, that evening could rank alongside bodyline, perhaps, and in terms of national significance, behind only the America's Cup win five years later.'

While the perception from the outside was that Packer was highly stressed during the two seasons of World Series Cricket, both Chappells say they felt the big man was at ease with the money he was sinking into a concept that might never have borne fruit. Throughout the first season and at the start of the second, rival media organisations essentially ignored the WSC competition, as evidenced by how few covered it that first night at the SCG.

Indeed, most outlets except Packer's Channel Nine, the *Bulletin* and *Women's Weekly* talked it down. Channel Seven held the broadcast rights to the summer of tennis in Australia, which was in competition with Packer's cricket matches. One advertisement on Seven focused on images from VFL Park with a small handful of fans looking on from bays of vacant seats. 'These are some of the people who aren't watching the Australian Open on Channel Seven,' the voiceover said. Ouch.

Greg Chappell lunched with Packer a few days after those advertisements were first aired. He asked Packer if he was concerned about the adverse publicity, the limited press coverage, the money he was burning through.

'Son, they don't know what they're talking about,' Packer replied. 'I've got to have 60 per cent Australian content on my station. The cheapest television is live sport. A soapie would cost three times as much and earn me less money.'

'I don't think he was feeling the pressure as much as everyone else thought, but that night at the SCG was the turning point for WSC nonetheless,' Greg says now. 'Until that point, many people were willing it to fail. But that shut everyone up. From then on, it gathered momentum and people took notice, not least the Australian Cricket Board. It realised Packer was a serious competitor.'

World Series Cricket might have been crass to the cricketing establishment, especially when night games were eventually played in garish coloured clothing, the 12th man ferrying refreshments to the players in drinks breaks on golf carts, or, on one infamous and short-lived occasion, with the aid of Playboy Bunnies. But Packer understood his audience and understood that cricket was like every other sport: it was entertainment, something for the public to watch and enjoy.

'He understood the punter better than anyone else,' Greg continues. 'He understood the power of live sport. They wanted sport, colour, something to do after work. He gave it to them.'

Ian Chappell reflects on that night at the SCG this way: 'Day-night cricket would have been invented at some point, you'd think, but Kerry brought it forward. Cricket administrators aren't ultra-progressive unless there's a dollar involved. They still aren't.'

KERRY PACKER USUALLY WAITED for nobody, but he was waiting patiently for John Quayle on the footpath outside Packer's offices at 54 Park Street in Sydney's CBD on the morning of Friday, October 8, 1993. Quayle, the general manager of the Australian Rugby League, had convinced Packer to attend a media conference in the middle of the SCG to announce Nine's seven-year deal worth $70 million to broadcast all rugby league in Australia, including the Winfield Cup, State of Origin and internationals.

By now, Packer was 55 and the richest man in the country. He looked about as good as his bank balance. Three years earlier, he'd suffered a massive heart attack while playing polo at Warwick Farm and stared at the other side for six or seven minutes while his heart stopped beating. When he discovered there was nothing there, he decided to return to the land of the living. A new diet allowed him to drop 22 kilograms from his enormous frame.

Still, Packer was no longer comfortable making public appearances, unlike the days of the hard sell during World Series Cricket. When Quayle asked him to attend the media launch, he flatly refused.

'Nope,' he grunted. 'I won't be doing that.'

Quayle called again two days later and assured him he wouldn't have to talk, take questions, do anything he didn't want to do.

'I'll even pick you up, Kerry,' Quayle promised.

Quayle drove through the gates of the SCG off Moore Park Road and parked under the Bradman Stand, near the service entry to the ground. The function was to be held in front of the Doug Walters Stand, which had been built in front of the old Hill scoreboard. Nine's Ken Sutcliffe was the MC.

As Quayle and Packer made their way out into the middle, Packer abruptly stopped.

'Just a minute,' he said. 'Come over here.'

Packer started trudging towards the roped-off centre square and pitch. He was in awe, according to Quayle.

'You know, I've never been out here,' Packer revealed to him.

Quayle was stunned. The SCG had been one of the most important battlegrounds for World Series Cricket. That night, Packer had been everywhere, from the gates out the front, to the commentary box, almost every single part of the venue. But not the middle. He'd never been in the middle.

With the media waiting over near the stage, Sutcliffe politely intervened.

'Come on Mr Packer,' he said. 'We've got a deadline to get started.'

'Listen, son,' Packer barked back, 'I'll be there when I get there.'

That's when he started rattling off all the records of individual teams and players at the ground. Quayle recalls Packer best remembered Bradman's statistics. For someone who wasn't going to answer questions, Packer answered a lot of questions, all in good humour, including one from the *Daily Telegraph-Mirror*'s legendary chief rugby league reporter Peter Frilingos.

'The Sunday game is a 6pm replay and cut down to 40 minutes of play shown,' Frilingos started.

'Who are you?' Packer smiled. 'Oh, you work for Mr Murdoch, don't you? Well, if you don't like it, turn it off. And when you own a TV station, you can do what you like.'

Packer's mood changed when he was asked if he should've brought his cricket bat.

'That would have been the big thing in my life,' Packer said wistfully. 'To do anything here, anything.'

'Here we were to launch rugby league,' recalls Quayle, 'but his passion was clearly cricket.'

On that point, Ian Chappell disagrees.

'His two loves were cricket and rugby league,' he says. 'He understood the people who watched them. When Nine had just got the [league] rights, he was talking to David Hill and he said of rugby league: "Just fucking remember, son, it's a game played by wharfies, watched by wharfies and administered by fucking wharfies."'

Quayle wasn't a wharfie but the son of an Anglican priest who had first played on the SCG in 1968, when he played rugby league for Eastern Suburbs under Jack Gibson. After the formalities at the SCG that day in 1993, Quayle dropped Packer as promised back at his Park Street bunker.

'Thanks, son, I must say I really enjoyed that,' Packer said as he got out of the car. 'Especially being at the pitch.'

Packer died on the evening of December 26, 2005, nine days after his 68th birthday. Australian and South African cricketers held a minute's silence before play on the second day of the Boxing Day Test match at the MCG. Sir Donald Bradman had died nearly five years earlier, on February 25, 2001, at the age of 92.

These titans of Australian sport and life met on two occasions. The second time was in 1996 after Packer had met with Bradman to negotiate Bradman's final television interview. Ray Martin was pencilled in to do the interview. As recalled in his memoir, *Stories of My Life*, Martin asked Packer how the meeting went.

'I loved it, son,' Packer replied. 'It was truly one of the greatest days of my life. He had answers for everything. Now listen, son. I promised him, when the show is cut and before we put it on air, he can have a look at it. I told him that if he doesn't like it, for any reason, then we'll burn the bastard. Okay? So don't fuck it up, son.'

The first meeting between Bradman and Packer isn't as well known and wasn't revealed until 2016 in a long-form piece in *The Cricket Monthly* from Daniel Brettig. On February 13, 1979, Packer flew to Adelaide in his private jet to finally end the war between World Series Cricket and the Australian Cricket Board.

Instead of finding a combative Bradman, Packer and his people were greeted by a pragmatic one, looking for compromise.

'I don't care what we have to give away to get this deal done,' Bradman told them. 'I want it done.'

It was clear to those with access to the Board's finances that it might not survive if the war continued. On May 30, it was announced that the exclusive broadcast rights had been handed to Packer's Channel Nine, just as he had wanted all along. Nine held the rights for the next 40 years.

Bradman might have been responsible for this peace, but he didn't necessarily like it. In his final letter to Arthur Morris on the matter, dated July 10, 1979, Sir Donald wondered out loud to an old friend if the game's fresh dawn, under the glare of the new lights at the SCG, was for the better.

'As for the lights, I remain somewhat sceptical about the agreement with Packer, one-day games, lights and so on,' he wrote. 'Only time can answer these questions, but I feel that the Packer interlude has damaged the whole structure of cricket more than anyone yet realises.'

In fact, The Don was being overly pessimistic, as he would concede himself in *Wisden* in 1986, when he contributed a story under the heading 'Whither Cricket Now?'. Sir Donald wrote of the 'great stadiums of Sydney and Melbourne [that] now display huge electronic scoreboards costing millions of dollars and giving a wealth of information to the spectators, [and] the enormous electric light towers [that] turn night into day at the flick of a switch'.

'Despite my deep feeling for the traditional game, and my conviction that a vast majority of players and public still regard Test cricket as the supreme contest, we must accept that we live in a new era,' he continued. 'I am satisfied that one-day cricket, especially day/night cricket, is here to stay.'

One can picture Kerry Packer reading The Don's essay and allowing himself a contented smile. This would have been especially true when he got to the final paragraph, which closed with a message that seemed straight from the World Series Cricket playbook.

'It remains for players and administrators to accept the challenge to keep cricket alive and vibrant,' Sir Donald wrote, 'and not to shrink from the decisions needed to ensure that end.'

CHAPTER 5

Rugby Crazy

Dave Brockhoff and the Bledisloe Cup

WITH HEADS BOWED AND hearts heavy, the All Blacks trudged up the steps of the Members Pavilion towards the sanctuary of their dressing-room. They'd been laughing just a few hours earlier about how much space there was in their lockers, which usually housed cricket bats and pads. They'd carefully put blazers and trousers away, and pulled on their iconic black jumpers, brimming with confidence. They always were, this all-conquering rugby union superpower. Now they were grimly making their way through the delirious members, the studs of their boots, covered in dirt and grass and even some Wallaby skin, offering a solemn clickety-clack on the concrete.

Inside the dressing-room, the enormity of what had just happened started to hit home. This try-less 12–6 defeat to the Wallabies marked their first Bledisloe Cup loss in 30 years — and their first defeat in a Test on Australian soil in 45. The All Blacks didn't want to play this match, but the New Zealand Rugby Union had agreed to do so to help the financially stricken Australian Rugby Union, which was in danger of collapsing.

Now, Australian rugby smelt a little better. This result had the potential to change everything.

Soon enough, the All Blacks players realised the crowd of nearly 33,000 wasn't leaving. They made their way over to the large windows at the front of the dressing-room and couldn't believe what they were seeing: Australia's players were embarking on a lap of honour. At the front of the pack were captain Mark Loane and fullback Paul McLean, each holding a handle of the enormous silver trophy known as the Bledisloe Cup. Not far behind them was Wallabies coach Dave Brockhoff, dressed in dark green blazer and tie, arms held aloft in triumph.

'What are they doing?' All Blacks winger Stu Wilson asked with a chuckle. 'Do they think they've won Lotto?'

Towering second-rower Andy Haden pushed his way to the front of the pack, pressed his nose against the glass window and turned to his teammates.

'Remember that image,' he said. 'When we come back next year, we're going to take that trophy back home.'

When the Wallabies returned to their dressing-room, and the enormous lid came off the Bledisloe Cup so it could be filled with cold beer, Haden pushed his way through the packed members' bar and knocked on the home team's door. He wanted to see Brockhoff. He had something for him.

'I've got to give this to you, Brock,' Haden said, handing him his sweat and blood-soaked jumper. 'I've never seen an Australian team take the ball off the All Blacks like that.'

Brockhoff recalled the gesture in *Wallaby Gold*, Peter Jenkins' comprehensive history of Australia in Test rugby. 'I can see it still,' he told Jenkins. 'Haden said to me it must have been 13 rucks and mauls we won in a row at one stage. We had taken them on, we had beaten them at their game. We had a low, vicious, marauding pack and they were, that day, magnificent. We didn't have the pretty backs, but everyone played it perfectly. This was what I had always wanted to present to the Australian rugby public.'

The Australian rugby public had been waiting for that moment to be presented to them, too. It came on a Saturday in the winter of 1979, an afternoon so unseasonably warm that All Blacks players asked for sunscreen at halftime. It was the culmination of five years of hard work; of trying to create a mindset within Australian teams that they weren't going to be bullied by anyone, including and especially the All Blacks, who had lowered their guard against Australia to lose Test matches just a handful of times since the two countries first met in 1903.

THE ARU HAD PLEADED with their counterparts in New Zealand to agree to this one-off Test. When the NZRU agreed, Australian officials asked if the Bledisloe Cup could be dispatched ahead of them for promotional purposes. The request was met with confusion at the NZRU offices in Wellington. The All Blacks had held the trophy for so long, most had forgotten it even existed, let alone knew where it was.

'They found it in a cleaning cupboard,' Stu Wilson explains. 'It's the size of Mount Everest but the players didn't know what it looked like. We didn't know what we had half the time. We didn't show trophies on a little table with pieces of blue satin over the top of it. In the old days, you got changed after matches and then had a beer and got on with it.'

The NZRU put the Cup on a plane to Australia then sent an audacious telex to Qantas informing the airline of the precious cargo: 'One large black box containing Bledisloe Cup stop Australian Rugby Union requires for promotional purposes during New Zealand All Blacks' annihilation of Wallabies on Saturday stop Please contact rugby union and liaise with terminal duty controller stop Obtain delivery/ publicity etc stop Cup will return to New Zealand stop.'

What the All Blacks hadn't expected on the afternoon of July 28, 1979, was a Wallabies side capable of producing a first half of rugby perfection and a second of desperation that only comes when history beckons. They hadn't counted on the pilfering ability of flankers Loane and Andy Stewart, plunging into breakdowns as if they were diving for pearls. They hadn't counted on the poise of fullback McLean, who some Sydney scribes wanted dumped for the game, as he defused bombs at one end of the field and clinically slotted three penalty goals at the other. They hadn't counted on the control of 19-year-old five-eighth Tony Melrose, or the coolness of rookie halfback Peter Carson, or the way squat prop Chris 'Buddha' Handy, with blood streaming down his face, continually annoyed Haden in lineouts and scrums despite a dramatic discrepancy between the two in height.

And mostly, they hadn't counted on what victory truly meant for Dave Brockhoff, who was one of the last known people in Australian rugby to have had his hands on the Bledisloe Cup, having been a part of the Wallabies side that defeated the All Blacks in Wellington and Auckland in 1949 while playing alongside greats such as Trevor Allan, Nick Shehadie and Rex Mossop.

'It's so heavy, the plane was nearly touching the water on the flight back home,' he recalled for his players on the morning of the 1979 match.

He then informed them that the Bledisloe Cup would be on display at the SCG before kick-off later that afternoon. If they won the match, they could keep the silverware. How good would that be?

'That's great, Brock,' Loane said to him. 'What does it look like again?'

As the players came together in front of the Members Stand after their victory, Brockhoff jumped the fence and made a dash for the mighty trophy.

'There it is!' Brockhoff declared. 'Let's get hold of it.'

He wanted to show his players, and the people who had watched that afternoon, what the Bledisloe Cup meant.

Not to him — he already knew that — but to them.

IF AUSTRALIAN RUGBY FELT a little lighter that sunny afternoon in 1979, it's probably because it had been lugging around almost a century of heavy baggage thanks to our New Zealand compadres.

From the very beginning of rugby on these shores, they've seemed to have our measure. Many battles had been fought at the SCG, almost all of them were lost.

First, a quick history lesson. The first intercolonial game between the Northern (Queensland) and Southern (NSW) rugby unions took place at the Association Ground in 1882. The *Sydney Morning Herald* wrote that the home side won a 'fast and exciting' game decisively, four or five tries (two match descriptions in the paper disagree as to how many tries were scored) and four goals to one goal. The attendance was reported at 4000. A few weeks later, the Southern Rugby Football Union sent a team to New Zealand for the first time. A New Zealand team first toured Australia in 1884.

The writing was on the wall even then. 'Rugby isn't our game,' declared an editorial in the *Sydney Morning Herald* in 1884. 'We'll always court defeat if we play the New Zealanders.'

But Australia wouldn't be deterred from playing the 15-man code. On June 24, 1899, four days after a referendum had ruled in favour of a federation, more than 28,000 people jammed into the SCG for the nation's first ever Test match, as Australia beat Great Britain 13–3. The first Test between Australia and New Zealand was also held at the SCG, on August 15, 1903, when more than 30,000 witnessed a comprehensive 22–3 victory to the tourists. In 1905, the New Zealanders set sail for the UK. This was when they adopted their famous name, first coined by an English journalist: the 'All Blacks'.

That 1903 series in Australia launched years — nay *decades* — of pain at the hands of our Trans-Tasman rivals. The concept of the Bledisloe Cup, named after Lord Bledisloe, the Governor-General of New Zealand from 1930 to 1935, as the trophy to be awarded to the winning team was introduced in 1931, when the All Blacks won 20–13. On the eve of the match, the Press Association reported that the idea of a trophy had been 'accepted' by officials in New Zealand and Australia. 'The design of the Cup will be decided upon later,' the wire service continued. 'It will be symbolical of both countries.' Sure enough, a striking piece of silverware materialised prior to the start of the following year's series, as the *New Zealand Herald* of June 29, 1932, explained:

The cup presented by the Governor-General, Lord Bledisloe, as a trophy for Test rugby matches between New Zealand and Australia, has arrived in Auckland from England and is now on exhibition in the windows of Milne and Choyce, Limited.

The cup is one of the most handsome presented in New Zealand. It is of sterling silver and is surmounted by a silver rugby football. The chasing on the lid is an interweaving of New Zealand fern and Australian gum nuts and leaves in high relief. Engraved on the front of the cup are the arms of New Zealand, the arms of Australia being on the reverse side. The chasing around the base is an intermingling of Australian wattle flowers and New Zealand kowhai flowers in relief.

The height of the cup, irrespective of the plinth, is 28 inches. It is 25 inches in width and weighs 290oz [8.2kg]. The substantial oak plinth is surrounded by 25 shields for the names of the winning country in each series of games. The cup is to be known as the 'Bledisloe Cup' and is engraved: 'Presented by Lord Bledisloe, Governor-General of New Zealand, 1931.'

The two countries now officially had a trophy to play for: an enormous cup that often required two men to carry it. The All Blacks lost the opening Test in Sydney in 1932, but recovered to win the three-match series. Two years later, the Wallabies got their hands on the Bledisloe Cup for the first time, winning 25–11 at the SCG in the opening Test of a two-game series and then clawing their way to a draw at the same venue two weeks later. The side was captained by fullback Alec Ross, otherwise known as the 'Ross of Gibraltar'. In the forwards was Edward 'Weary' Dunlop, destined for a distinguished life as a surgeon and soldier, renowned for his selfless actions while a prisoner of war on the Burma-Thailand railway, and his subsequent work in the community and advocacy for war veterans. Dunlop would be knighted in 1969, for his services to medicine, and be named Australian of the Year in 1976.

As far as the Bledisloe Cup was concerned, things truly faded to black for Australia after 1934. The New Zealanders won the next nine matches played, from 1936 to 1947. In 1949, the Wallabies gained some respite when the New Zealand Maoris toured Australia, the two teams squaring a three-game series in June, with two of the matches being staged at the SCG.

Later that year, the Wallabies were presented with an opportunity to end their Bledisloe drought, thanks mostly to All Blacks hubris. The NZRU sent 30 of their best players to South Africa for a tour that included four Tests. Because of South Africa's strict apartheid regime, no player with more than one-eighth Maori blood was allowed to enter the Republic. The remaining All Blacks were scheduled to play a two-Test series against the Wallabies, in Wellington and then Auckland, but they were still expected to win. One young Australian flanker, though, was determined to ensure that didn't happen.

DAVE BROCKHOFF WAS THE son of a flour miller whose business was on Glebe Point Road, Glebe, within walking distance of Sydney University. His day job provided him with the perfect physique for rugby: he was tall, strong, agile and barrel-chested as a result of lugging heavy bags of flour to bakeries all across Sydney's inner-west. He'd arrive at training for University, where he was studying science but majoring in rugby, covered in flour. 'I'd walk through the place looking like a ghost,' he often quipped later in life.

Brockhoff quickly made a name for himself as a player, forcing his way into University's first XV, and then touring New Zealand with the Combined Australian Universities team as a breakaway in 1949. The season suddenly became busy. He received a phone call during that tour, asking him to come home to play for Australia in their two Tests against the Maoris. He kept his place for the two Tests in New Zealand against the All Blacks.

On September 3, 1949, New Zealand rugby set itself a monumental task: beating Australia and South Africa on either side of the world in the space of 24 hours. The All Blacks team that played Trevor Allan's Wallabies team that day in Wellington has often been described as a 'third-string outfit'. But you can only beat what's in front of you and that's what Australia did, winning 11–6 thanks in no small part to Brockhoff launching himself at the New Zealand halves all afternoon. 'We missiled them all day,' he told rugby historian Spiro Zavos years later. 'Never gave them a sniff.' The All Blacks rarely lost at all, let alone twice in the space of a day, but a few hours later they lost 'again' — 9–3 against South Africa in Durban.

In the second Bledisloe Cup Test, at Eden Park, Australia dominated the lineout and refused to be outmuscled by their fearsome All Blacks rivals, triumphing 16–9 to claim the silverware for just the second time. Brockhoff was in awe of small front-rower Jack Baxter that day — and throughout that tour. He recalled in *Wallaby Gold* one moment against Canterbury: 'They hit him [Baxter] with everything, and his eyebrow came off. It was twitching on the ground, the whole eyebrow, you've never seen anything so ugly. Of course, I vomited out of sheer disgust. But he smacks me on the jaw, this tough guy who'd been through the war in the navy, and says, "Listen you, put it back on or you're off!" So, I've grabbed the eyebrow and slapped it back on his face and went down in the next scrum sick with fight and terror. That was Baxter.'

That was Brockhoff, an eccentric character and storyteller who played a total of eight Tests, his last in 1951. When he finished playing, he slipped instantly into coaching, his passion and knowledge infusing every player who came within his orbit.

As Brockhoff was making a name for himself coaching club rugby at University and Eastern Suburbs in the Sydney grade competition, the Wallabies struggled on the international stage. The sport suffered for it, unable to maintain relevance up against the heathen code of rugby league. Tests were played in front of dwindling crowds. There were brave victories here and there, but Australian teams mostly seemed cursed. Wallabies captain Ken Catchpole's career ended when, in a Test at the SCG in 1968, he dived into a maul only for All Blacks great

Colin Meads to recklessly yank his leg, tearing groin ligaments from the champion halfback's bone. New Zealand won 27–11.

Sometimes the drama wasn't isolated to the field. On July 17, 1971, thousands of anti-apartheid campaigners converged on the SCG, clashing with police and fans alike as the Wallabies played the opening Test of a series against an all-white South Africa. In extraordinary scenes, barbed wire and a heavy police presence encircled the playing arena. More than 2500 protesters gathered on the Hill, blowing whistles and singing anthems before pelting the hallowed turf with flares and fireworks. An orange mist greeted the players as they made their way out into the middle. Then it became really nasty. Some activists threw golf balls and beer cans at police; others pegged balloons full of tacks and sharp metal.

Amid the chaos, Meredith Burgmann and her sister Verity stood quietly on the fence, disguised as Springboks supporters in wigs and white cable-knit coats. When the opportunity presented itself, they charged onto the field.

'Once among the players, we didn't have a clue what to do next,' Meredith Burgmann told author Larry Writer in his book *Pitched Battle: in the frontline of the 1971 Springbok tour of Australia*. 'It had never occurred to us that we'd ever get that far. So, as the game continued around us, I sat down on the grass, which seemed the obvious thing to do. Verity, however, was more adventurous. She grabbed the rugby ball and kicked it as hard as she could. *The Bulletin* called it the best kick of the match. Our invasion actually brought the game to a halt. I'm glad of that …

'Then the police got us. They were nasty, angry that we'd slipped through their cordon. They dragged me roughly hundreds of metres around the perimeter fence. They wouldn't let me stand up. My metal watchband cut into my wrist and drew blood. All the rugger buggers ran down to the fence and screamed abuse and spat on me as I was being hauled past. I saw pure hatred in their faces. Coming between these blokes and their sport was the most dangerous thing I ever did.'

Burgmann went onto to become a Member of the Legislative Council in the NSW Parliament. The next time she rushed onto the SCG was 28 years later when Tony Lockett kicked his 1300th career goal, breaking Gordon Coventry's longstanding record.

As for the match, the Wallabies lost 19–11, something that was becoming a common theme in Australia rugby, something Brockhoff simply could not stomach. While the Wallabies were wandering about in the wilderness, he was searching for new methods to turn them into an international force — and that included going to New Zealand.

When he returned, Brockhoff was convinced the only way to beat the All Blacks was to mimic them. 'His philosophy, inspired primarily by New Zealand coach Vic Cavanagh, involved embracing the powerful rucking game, which relied upon organising a fierce, dominant pack and making them brutal at the breakdown and scrum,' offered the late *Herald* chief rugby writer Greg Growden. 'To match New Zealand, you similarly had to be mongrel dogs.'

By the time Brockhoff was appointed Australian coach in 1975, the Wallabies had played 36 Tests against New Zealand since the Second World War and won just six of them, none of them at home. He brought not just a new voice but a new policy: a relentless forward-based game that would give the backs the freedom to play. The 'Step Forward' policy would change the way Australian rugby was played, he argued, and what better way to try it out then a two-Test series against England at the SCG and Ballymore?

There was another call adopted early into Brockhoff's tenure, as explained in *Wallaby Gold*. Whenever players heard 'Bondi Beach', it didn't conjure images of lazing about on Sydney's most famous stretch of sand. It was a war cry, only to be used for retaliation if a teammate was getting worked over by the opposition. If 'Bondi Beach' was called, every Wallaby player was obliged to fight fire with fire.

Prop Steve Finnane, who'd been selected to make his Test debut, didn't need much encouragement. In the first Test at the SCG, Australia's unheralded pack put the much-fancied England forwards firmly back in their box. 'Finnane's right hand served to draw a deep line in the sand after years of intimidation by All Blacks and Springboks alike, where brute force was as important as technical expertise,' wrote Phil Wilkins in the *Herald*. Australia won 16–9 with Brockhoff excitedly telling reporters afterwards: 'The controlled possession by the forwards was the best I've seen from an Australian pack since the war.'

An ankle injury ruled Finnane out of the second Test, which would degenerate into a match that would become known as 'The Battle of Ballymore', such was the mayhem that played out that afternoon. Australia won the game and the fight, which started from the opening whistle. The result prompted condemnation from the rugby establishment in the United Kingdom and forced ARU officials to gag Brockhoff from talking to the press on the end-of-season tour of Europe and the United States.

The following year, after three Test-match victories against Fiji, Brockhoff stood down because business commitments prevented him from travelling. In just two seasons, he'd turned Australian rugby on its head with nine wins from 12 Tests, including seven straight victories at home. There were fears he wouldn't return. Little did they know he was just getting started.

The Wallabies enjoyed further success in his absence, under the coaching of Daryl Haberecht, who had made his name as an innovative and successful coach of NSW Country. After playing no internationals in 1977, they secured a series win over Grand Slam champions Wales with a brutal 19–17 victory at the SCG in front of a near-capacity crowd. Finnane, nicknamed 'The Gunfighter' by his teammates by this stage, plonked his right hand on the prodigious chin of Welsh prop Graham Price, breaking his jaw. 'I belted him,' Finnane admitted. 'But I didn't mean to hurt him like that.'

Australia were fast gaining respect at international level, but victory still seemed all too easy for the All Blacks. The Wallabies toured New Zealand in late 1978, losing the first two matches and therefore the Bledisloe Cup — again — before saving face with a 30–16 win at Eden Park. They'd been inspired in that final match by the hospitalisation of Haberecht, who had suffered a heart attack in Wanganui in the days after the Bledisloe Cup was lost.

For 27 years, from 1951 to 1978, New Zealand won the Cup 12 times, with legendary figures such as Fred Allen, Don Clarke and Graham Mourie always having the measure of their Australian counterparts. 'No one ever bothered about the Bledisloe Cup,' Wilson Whinerary, All Blacks skipper from 1958 to 1965, once said. 'It just sat in someone's office.'

Occasionally, it wasn't even important enough for an office. Instead, it spent time in a cleaner's cupboard. But it hadn't always been so redundant.

After the Wallabies won the trophy in 1949, coach Bill Cerutti patiently waited down at the wharves in Sydney. The 'first string' All Blacks team would be docking there soon enough as they made their way back to New Zealand following their failed tour of South Africa. When they arrived, Cerutti showed it to them.

'Here it is!' he bellowed. 'We've got it now.'

Come 1979, Dave Brockhoff thought it was time to take possession of it once more.

THE FIRST THING STU WILSON noticed when he walked onto the SCG that afternoon was the sun stretching across the turf. As he and his All Blacks teammates lined up in front of the Members Pavilion, facing their Wallabies combatants and preparing to shake hands with the assembled dignitaries, he felt the firm surface beneath his long studs.

'When it was winter in New Zealand, you played in mud,' Wilson offers. 'Wingers never saw the ball because it stayed in the forwards. Suddenly, you're playing a warm-up match in Brisbane in 25-degree weather, then on to Sydney, playing on this rock-hard surface. You'd skid a bit at the SCG, so you'd wear those nice long sprigs, which were quite good for tearing off a bit of Wallaby skin in the rucks.'

With the formalities over, Wilson made his way over to the far side of the ground and, as the shrill of referee Dick Byers whistle's neared, a sense of history fell over him. 'Where was Dennis Lillee when he came out to bowl?' Wilson pondered. 'Which Englishman's head did he take off? Where was Doug Walters having that cigarette in the tea break?'

Then Wilson noticed something else: he could barely see the outside backs on the other side of the field. 'Because the cricket square was in the way,' he says in reference to the SCG's famed slope. 'It was like a speed hump. You'd look over at the other winger and you could only see him from the knees up. That was unusual.'

Wallabies great Paul McLean understood and appreciated the nuances of the SCG, too. He played ten Tests there — including his first and last, which were both in mud. He found it a happy hunting place. 'Once you put it in perspective, of having a rectangular field in an oval shape, I enjoyed it,' he says. 'It always seemed more open there, for whatever reason.'

McLean was a controversial selection for that one-off Test in the eyes of some critics, including McLean himself. He'd played at five-eighth in a two-Test series loss against Ireland earlier that year. The Wallabies lost the first in Brisbane 27–12 and the second at the SCG 19–3. 'I was dreadfully disappointed with my form against Ireland,' McLean told his biographer, Malcolm McGregor, in 1985. 'I fully expected to be dropped from the side to play New Zealand.'

Instead, McLean was moved to fullback with Tony Melrose slipping into the No. 10 jersey. Another key selection was Peter Carson at scrum half. For the past decade, Carson had lived in the shadow of the great John Hipwell.

The Sydney press were divided about McLean's selection. The *Daily Telegraph*'s Jim Woodward questioned why Easts' Geoff Richards, who was also an excellent goalkicker, wasn't selected at fullback and McLean dispatched to the bench. This from the highly regarded Parramatta club coach Peter Fenton: 'Both Tony Melrose and Mark Ella are better players than McLean. I think McLean has lost his confidence.' And this from Phil Wilkins: 'Whatever Queenslanders think, McLean is a better fullback, where he has time to move, just as Melrose is a better five-eighth than centre.'

McLean wasn't concerned about the criticism then, nor now. It reveals a lot about the changing relationship between player and reporter when he says: 'It helped if you didn't read the press — it made life a lot simpler. But that's how it was. Those guys were good blokes. They'd been on tour with us. We'd had plenty of beers over the years. They were just writing their opinion, so that's fine. If the criticism wasn't coming from a selector, it didn't matter.'

There were other changes for the Wallabies. Following the loss to Ireland, Tony Shaw lost the captaincy to Mark Loane, although he wasn't dropped and instead moved into the second-row. Brockhoff said it wasn't his call to take the captaincy from Shaw. Experienced centre Geoff Shaw, who hadn't been available for the series against Ireland, was included after showing his desperation to take on the All Blacks. 'I knew what a competitive lot of blokes these guys were,' he said. 'I wanted to be part of it, take another crack at the Blacks before I retired and died.'

Few anticipated an Australian win, however. The series loss to Ireland was the Wallabies' first at home in five years. There was also a feeling the All Blacks would be hell-bent on avenging their defeat by the Wallabies in the third Test of the previous year. They'd had the better of a two-Test series at home against France, one of the best sides in the world, losing narrowly at Eden Park but winning decisively in Christchurch. Their confidence was high.

In the dressing-room just before kick-off, Brockhoff gathered his players in. No time for war stories. No time for riddles. He gave it to them straight.

'It's up to our tight five,' he told them. 'It'll be total war up front, and if our forwards hold them, we'll be smelling like roses. And if they overrun us there, the Test is theirs.'

The tight five comprised props Chris Handy and fearsome fellow Queenslander Stan Pilecki, hooker Peter Horton and locks Tony Shaw and Peter McLean.

As predicted, it was an intense struggle. As predicted, the All Blacks put Paul McLean under immense pressure at fullback, peppering him with 'up and unders'. He'd seen it coming and asked Melrose at training to send a deluge of kicks his way. 'That gave me confidence,' said McLean, who time and time again latched onto the ball, despite a wall of black jumpers converging on him, before roosting it back downfield and turning defence into counterattack.

It was a point not lost on the *Sunday Telegraph*'s Dick Tucker, who was sitting in the press box in the Noble Stand alongside his 19-year-old son, Jim, frantically writing 'go last' — body copy that would run 'last' in match reports — for the next day's paper. 'McLean's towering kicks were the signal for wave upon wave of gold attacks,' Dick wrote.

The match quickly developed into an arm wrestle. Melrose, still a teenager, handled the pressure with aplomb, his boot as accurate as McLean's. It was 6–all at halftime, but the Wallabies were considered the better team.

'I knew the game wouldn't explode into a high-scoring game, which we normally came to expect against the Wallabies, because they were always pretty slick and skilful in the backs and held their own in the forwards,' Wilson recalls. 'They had some good thugs in the forward pack. As the game meandered on, we knew it was going to be a tight one. Who was going to hold on the best? Would the Wallabies panic in the dogfight?'

In the second half, the kicking of McLean and Melrose was decisive as the Wallabies clung to a 12–6 lead. Geoff Shaw came within inches of scoring but couldn't. Meanwhile, Handy was terrorising the All Blacks, a square cube of white flesh knocking over Kiwis who were double his size with abandon. At one point, blood streamed down his face from a deep cut above his right eye, providing photographers with the perfect image of an exhausted prop panting, sweating, bleeding for the cause. The 'Legend of Buddha' was born in this match. He's spent a lifetime trying to live it down.

'I might have won something of a reputation as a hit man, but the real story was that I couldn't fight,' Handy said in the book *Well I'll Be Ruggered!*, which he co-authored with Jeff Sayle and John Lambie. 'I got belted all the time. I was the beltee, not the belter. But the "bloodied hero" photographs littered the pages of the sports dailies … The legend of the toughness and fighting abilities of the Buddha were created out of that time. It was ridiculous, really. My mashed-up and multi-broken hand and the blood all over my face attested to the fact that, yes, I could certainly step forward. But I was more stupid than capable as a pugilist.'

Geoff Shaw reckons Handy is selling himself short. He was getting under the All Blacks' skin, so much so their forwards were constantly complaining to referee Byers. This wasn't the All Blacks way. This was a team that played clean and were respectful to the opposition, to the point that they swept out the dressing-room before they left at the end of the day. 'We were invited to your home,' Wilson says. 'That's how we did things.'

But on *this* afternoon the Wallabies drew a line in the hardened surface of the centre wicket. 'What I remember of that game is how much whingeing the All Blacks did,' Shaw told Peter Jenkins in *Wallaby Gold*. 'Traditionally, they were always intimidating you, because they had the ascendancy. Not this time. I remember the way Buddha Handy was climbing into them, how all the forwards were just so committed. It was a huge confidence booster for the backs to look ahead and see these guys on top.'

The question as the minutes ticked down ... would it be enough? There's something unique about the final minutes of a closely contested rugby match as each side holds its nerve, knowing that momentum can be so difficult to halt. As fulltime neared, with the Wallabies clinging to their six-point lead, the mighty All Blacks continually surged towards the line.

'They were lifting like they were the one creature,' Loane recalls. 'Right through to the end, they were close to breaking through. New Zealand is always dangerous in that last part of the first and second half. They were lifting themselves — but we lifted with them.'

Few lifted as much as the skipper himself. He wasn't losing this one. All Blacks centre Bruce Robertson broke through the line, streaming downfield, only for Loane to rustle him up in cover.

It took time for the Wallabies to realise what they'd achieved when the final whistle sounded. Carson didn't know when he'd be playing his next Test, so he instinctively souvenired one of the leather match balls and swapped jumpers with his opposing No. 9, Mark Donaldson. 'We gave it to them that day,' Carson told the *Courier-Mail* years later. 'It was one of the turning points in Australian rugby.'

Players from both sides mulled around the front of the Members Stand. Nobody was really thinking about the presentation of the Bledisloe Cup until Brockhoff jumped the fence, his eyes fixed on the trophy. 'He almost tore a hamstring jumping the fence onto the SCG,' Loane laughs. 'Security didn't know who he was, but he was too quick for them anyway.'

That's when Brockhoff urged McLean and Loane to take the Cup on their lap of honour. The other photograph seared on the memory from that afternoon is of McLean and Loane taking their first strides. With McLean on the left and Loane on the right, they are both smiling like the cats that got the cream. Their Wallabies teammates are behind them. In the background, thousands of fans in the grandstands are standing, looking on. In the middle of the shot, standing on his own at the back surveying the scene, is Brock, the most satisfied man in the SCG — maybe in the world — that afternoon.

The man who took the image was News Limited's Ian Mainsbridge, who had become close to some of the Wallabies players after covering the tour of New Zealand the previous year. 'Good photographers get in the right place at the right time,' McLean recalls. 'Ian knew exactly where to be.'

As the players made their way around the ground, ABC-TV commentator Norman May joked how Handy wouldn't be fit enough to complete a lap of honour. Pilecki revealed in his book *Stan The Man* that he was the one who couldn't muster the energy to get around the field, but replays show he joined in for at least 100 metres.

While Wilson and the rest of the All Blacks watched the festivities from the dressing-room, almost everyone in the stands and on the

Hill remained. 'The good thing about that lap of honour was that nobody left, even the New Zealanders in the crowd,' Wilson recalls. 'All the maintenance people came out, realising this was history. The Wallabies deserved that lap of honour and the fans lapped it up. There were 33,000 there that afternoon and it told Australian rugby there were enough Wallabies fans to support them. I was just worried about the players collapsing — it's a heavy bloody cup. And it's even heavier when you pour in a dozen bottles of champagne. Not that we ever drunk champagne. We'd just pour a case of beer into it.'

Over the years, that victory, that lap of honour, those jubilant scenes, have become the stuff of Australian rugby legend, with each player who took part offering unique perspectives about what it meant.

Chris Handy: 'We took away their space and we took their ball and I felt, as a Test pack, we had totally matured. The Kiwis had downplayed our win in Auckland the previous year with the line, "But it won't happen in Sydney." So it was extra sweet. Credit to Brock. He was crazy, but rugby crazy.'

Mark Loane: 'We won because we played like a New Zealand team. They played a territorial game that was regularly converted into points. It's something we learned from New Zealand: that the uncontested three statistically beats a contested five all day long. I cannot comprehend that Australian teams still don't have a go at taking the three points whenever they are on offer.'

Dave Brockhoff: 'We were midgets in the lineout and outweighed, yet we took on the All Blacks technically up front and climbed home. Like two bull terriers with teeth on the jugular for 80 minutes … release your grip and you're dead.'

The footage of Brockhoff running along, in blazer and slacks, has been re-run many times in the decades since. What many on the field that afternoon recall, though, is the coach wiping tears from his eyes, and uttering these heartfelt words: 'The most significant thing as far Australian rugby is concerned is that we took them on at their own game — and won.'

Later that night, both teams attended the traditional Test dinner at the University of NSW in nearby Kensington. The celebrations went long into the night, but Brockhoff rose early the next morning to visit his father. He dished out two big bowls of corn flakes. Instead of pouring milk over the top, he poured whisky, a crunchy salute to his final match as Wallabies coach, and the fact that the Bledisloe Cup was finally out of the cleaner's cupboard and on the shelf where he felt it belonged.

I know: what a legend.

STU WILSON IS SITTING in the Members Stand, in the seats in front of the away dressing-room, just another face of the 48,698 at the SCG as a 21-year-old Indigenous fly half mesmerises the mighty All Blacks in a manner few had ever seen.

'Wow, this kid's special,' Wilson said to his teammates sitting next to him. 'No wonder they rate him so much over here.'

Mark Ella *was* special, announcing his Wallabies arrival in spectacular fashion against the All Blacks in a three-Test series in 1980, with the first and third matches played in Sydney. He made his debut alongside dazzling fullback Roger Gould in the opening match of the series. The recent inclusion of young centres Michael Hawker and Michael O'Connor, and then the selection of Ella and Gould, had transformed the Wallabies backline into a formidable point-scoring machine.

Ella seemed to have a sixth sense — an ability to read the play and defence before anyone else. After the electronic scoreboard was installed on the Hill in 1983, he was shrewd enough to use it to his advantage. During a Test match against New Zealand at the SCG in 1984, he would watch the live feed to see if Australia won or lost the lineout, using that extra nanosecond to adjust his positioning so he was in the right place to take the pass from his halfback. He was a genius.

In the first Test of 1980, he set up the match-winning try for winger Mick Martin after slipping through a gap in the New Zealand defence as if he was a Tally Ho paper. It would be a scene repeated all over the country, all over the world, for the half-decade that followed as Ella defined himself as a true Wallaby great.

Coached by Queensland's Bob Templeton, the Wallabies triumphed 13–9 in the first Test in front of 36,068 spectators, only to lose the second Test at Ballymore 12–9, which set up a mouth-watering decider at the SCG. The heaving crowd didn't leave disappointed with Australia romping through the All Blacks' defence to win 26–10. It was their first series victory at home against New Zealand in 46 years. Because of Brockhoff, the Wallabies beat the All Blacks at their own game. Because of Ella, they beat them with a distinctive Australian game — the game of running rugby.

For the second consecutive year, the Wallabies completed a lap of honour and this time in front of a larger crowd. 'In 1979, we'd beaten the All Blacks in a war of attrition,' Tony Shaw, who had been reinstated as captain for the series, said. 'We'd gone from that to this open, free-flowing style in 1980. We'd won it fair and square and played fantastic rugby. We had to nail them in that last Test and we knew from the second Test that they were never dead. I remember being in the guys' faces, real finger-in-the-chest stuff, urging them on and telling them, "We've come this far, we've got to go on with it." It's the most intense I've ever been in a game.'

History records it as a famous win, but many remember it for the food poisoning that ripped through the All Blacks in the lead-up to the match — and the sensational claims of foul play four years later from Wilson and his fellow winger, Bernie Fraser, in their book, *Ebony and Ivory*.

'I believe it had something to do with a big betting plunge,' Fraser wrote. 'If he'd seen our boys agonising their way through the night, queuing up to use the two receptacles at once, he'd have gone and doubled his bet.'

The theory has been widely dismissed by former Wallabies and some All Blacks, many firm in the belief that Wilson and Fraser were simply trying to ramp up book sales. Similar food poisoning claims were made in the aftermath of the 1995 World Cup in South Africa, it being alleged that All Blacks players were poisoned by a mystery waitress called Suzie before the final against the Springboks.

Wilson didn't back down when I spoke to him, and he made some curious points about that day at the Travelodge in Camperdown, which hosted many travelling football teams during that period. He says he and Fraser were injured for the third Test, which meant they didn't eat with the team for much of that week. Instead, the two wingers ate with members of Fraser's family. Wilson and Fraser got sick — but they did not.

'Two All Blacks who never ate with the team, who ate in a different part of the restaurant, and from a different part of the menu, became ill while others didn't — I couldn't work that out,' Wilson says. 'We weren't playing, we were injured, so we never ate with the team. They ate early, so we went in a couple of hours later. We were in the same area as the public. Then the whole team that night came down with a bad run of food poisoning — and so did Bernie and me. But his family members didn't. Nor did anyone else. We were all eating off the same menu. I found that all quite strange.'

Wilson didn't play that afternoon, but Fraser was called up to start on the wing. Perhaps he was needed because there were fears the All Blacks may have struggled to field a starting side. Players were violently ill right up until kick-off, with No. 8 Murray Mexted and prop Gary Knight needing fluid injections just so they could take the field.

Does Wilson truly believe they were sabotaged, as his co-author Fraser claimed?

'I don't know — it just seemed a little bit suspicious,' he says. 'But we were probably going to lose that match, even if we were 100 per cent fit, because the Aussies were running hot. You had to go hunting to beat the Wallabies. You couldn't sit back because they'd come back at you like a dunny door.

'And they had Ella. He stood out. When a player stands out against the All Blacks, he must be good!'

WRITING THIS CHAPTER SERVED as a great reminder about the often-forgotten beauty of rugby union and the pride in the Wallabies jumper. In the early 2000s, years after rugby had gone professional, I'll never forget an Australian Test player remarking at a promotional golf day: 'God, I'm sick of rugby'. For him, the sport had become a grind, a means to an end, not the passion it had been for players of the past.

I trust Dave Brockhoff never heard an Australian player utter such words. I suspect it would have broken his heart. He was from a time of true amateurism, when players and coaches weren't paid whenever they took time off for internationals and tours, which in some cases was for months at a time. They did it for the love of the game — and the company of one another, no matter the colour of the jumper.

No country hurt Wilson more than Australia. He played 85 Tests and lost just six — four of them against the Wallabies. In the decades since retirement, though, he's maintained a close relationship with the men in gold.

'I've got closer mates who have worn the Wallabies jersey than the All Blacks one,' he says, surprisingly. 'We always had a beer with our rivals in those days. The highlight of the day was the third half — the half when you had a beer with Paul McLean or Mark Loane. We're still good mates. A few cold beers, a couple of durries along the way. The rugby was pushed aside, and we formed closer friendships.

'The games were so tight and rugged but, at the end of the day, you would line up with the guy who smacked you or stood on your head and he'd shout you a drink at the bar. We did that for three or four years. It was a great time. The Wallabies, on their day, could rip your heart out. They ripped my heart out four times. But those friendships are everlasting.'

That bond also existed between player and coach. McLean grew close to Brockhoff, who pursued business interests after 1979 and never coached the Wallabies again.

'He coached us to do simple things well,' McLean offers. 'People often didn't understand what he was trying to do, but I spent a lot of time with him and really appreciated what he had to say. He was a rare beast. He spoke in riddles but he understood the game as well as anyone I've ever known.'

Brockhoff died in 2011 at the age of 83 following a fall. It didn't take long after his passing for stories to emerge of his passion for rugby. How he attended Waratahs' training sessions late in life, even if it was raining. How he never failed to see off Wallabies teams before they flew out for tours, always there to greet them at the airport resplendent in blazer and tie, always there upon their return regardless of the result. How he would be a lone figure in the back of the grandstand watching club rugby or standing around a fire as the sun went down, beer in hand, telling captivated colts players stories of yesteryear, the youngsters hanging on every word.

'He just gave so much to the game,' Loane says. 'He gave so much emotion. He respected the players and always thought, "If you're playing in the Test match, you have to take responsibility for it." Everyone had this immense love for Brock. Before the match in '79, he told us about the Bledisloe Cup. We said, "Oh that's good, Brock … What is it again?"

'To see him jump the fence and grab hold of it made it all worthwhile.'

CHAPTER 6

Creating Origin History

Steve Mortimer

THE LOGICAL PLACE TO start this chapter is with the obvious: NSW rugby league captain Steve Mortimer collapsing to his knees and kissing the turf of the Sydney Cricket Ground.

If the black-and-white image of Norm Provan and Arthur Summons embracing in the mud after the 1963 grand final represents rugby league's spirit of mateship, the iconic vision of Mortimer on the night of game two of the 1985 State of Origin series represents relief. Sheer relief. The sort of relief that comes when you want something so bad, for so long, that you wonder if it will ever happen, and then suddenly it does and you find yourself making out with the sacred mud of the SCG in front of 40,000 people.

NSW five-eighth Brett Kenny had just scored a typical Brett Kenny try, bending his ankles as if they were made of rubber before selling the perfect dummy to no less than Queensland captain Wally Lewis, to then step back inside, reach out and score. Those four points and Michael O'Connor's conversion extended the Blues to an untouchable lead with seconds remaining.

The players came together, embracing and screaming and jumping about, then the enormity of what was happening suddenly struck Mortimer like a bolt of lightning. NSW had secured the match *and* their first series win since the Origin concept was introduced in 1980.

Mortimer shifted away from the jubilant pack, then broke down into tears, collapsed to his knees and buried his face in the dirt. Prop Steve Roach stood over the top of him, put one hand on his back and whispered in his ear.

'We've done it, mate,' he said. 'We've done it.'

So that's the logical place to start this chapter — but let's not. No, let's go back to the start of the series in Brisbane, where we find ourselves on the NSW team bus as it snakes its way towards Lang Park.

The bus is approaching notorious Caxton Street and the players can hear it before they see it. It's like that on most nights when there's a headline fixture further down the hill at Lang Park, but particularly so whenever Queensland is playing NSW. All along the strip, fans in maroon jumpers are soaking themselves in XXXX or Bundaberg Rum or both. They are spilling out onto the footpath from various bars and restaurants, despite the falling rain. The command centre for the militant Maroons faithful on this night is, of course, the Caxton Hotel.

Quietly sitting on the bus are a handful of players who are either making their NSW debut or have played just one match. One of the debutants is Benny Elias, the Balmain hooker. In two-and-a-bit seasons of first-grade football, Elias has established himself as one of the smartest, craftiest and most supremely confident hookers in the country.

But not now. Not here on Caxton Street, even in the safety of the bus. He's looked into the bloodshot eyes of the Queensland supporters on the street and they give him an insight to the hostility waiting for him and his Blues teammates down the road.

'Excuse me, driver, stop the bus,' Mortimer says.

'Why?' the driver asks.

'Just do it, please.'

The bus grinds to a halt. Almost instantly, the Queensland fans start banging on the sides. Then the windows. Then they start rocking it. Then they start hurling cans, some empty but most of them full. Yes: *full* cans. As any NSW supporter worth his weight in Tooheys New will tell you: 'Ever tasted XXXX? You'd throw away full cans of it, too.'

Mortimer waves a finger at the delirious mob pressed against the bus like sardines and looks at his players.

'Look at these blokes out there,' he says. 'They're smiling, having a great time. And they think they'll be smiling when they come back here after the game.'

The Queensland faithful have every right to feel confident. They have owned this Origin thing since the first match was played at Lang

Park in 1980. They won the one-off matches that year and in 1981. They have claimed the series every year since, too, and have no reason to believe things will change.

The primary reason for this optimism is a player who can seemingly change the course of any match he plays in. He's Wally Lewis. He's the best player in the world. He's an Immortal-in-waiting. He's the Emperor of Lang Park. The King.

Mortimer played his first game for NSW in 1977, the year after he made his premiership debut for Canterbury, but he's been in and out of the team ever since. He took over the captaincy for game three in 1984 and, along with new coach Terry Fearnley, was charged with the responsibility of drawing a line in the sand.

This is the night it starts. He's had enough of losing matches and the series and the brawls and then getting lashed in newspaper print about how winning means more to Queensland than to those who play for and support NSW. Mostly, he's sick of the people thumping on the bus coming back here to Caxton Street and toasting their state's dominance. Things have to change, and it starts right here on this bus.

'So, let's stick it up them,' Mortimer tells his players. 'And let's make sure they aren't smiling when they come back.'

THE FIRST MATCH BETWEEN NSW and Queensland was played on July 11, 1908 — in the year the game of rugby league was first played in Australia — although it wasn't held at the SCG. It was played at the nearby Sydney Showground, then known as the Agricultural Ground. NSW won 43–0 and the editorial in the *Sydney Morning Herald* the next day was scathing: 'There can be no doubt the NSW men are improving a good deal ... They cannot be blamed for the farce, for it was nothing else. If the Australian team depends on Queenslanders to strengthen it, one is afraid it will be found wanting. They are quite the weakest lot of footballers I have ever seen come down from Queensland. The play needs no detailed description as it was simply a practice match for NSW, and certainly did not advantageously advertise the new game.'

It wasn't until June 7, 1915, that the interstate rivalry made its way onto the SCG. Teams were allowed to change in the Sheridan Stand, not the dressing-rooms in the Members Pavilion, which was sacrosanct, reserved for cricket teams. NSW's flying winger Harold Horder scored 29 points — five tries and seven goals — as NSW triumphed 39–6.

Queensland dominated interstate rugby league for much of the 1920s, especially from 1922 to 1925 when they enjoyed 10 wins from 11 matches, but after that the series usually belonged to NSW. In part, and especially after World War II, this was because the NSW team included Queensland-born and bred footballers who had ventured to cashed-up Sydney clubs to play and earn a living. When the NSW government passed legislation in 1956 that allowed gaming machines in licensed premises, a flood of Queensland players soon followed. By the late 1970s, the interstate series was on its knees, with matches played at suburban grounds in front of tiny crowds.

Comedian Paul Hogan was the guest speaker at a rugby league function in Brisbane in 1977. 'Every time Queensland produces a good footballer,' he said, 'he finishes up being processed through a New South Wales poker machine.' The NSW Rugby League was so dismissive of the series that season that it told Queensland Rugby League it could host the two matches. In its mind, the Sydney premiership and Test matches were the game's future.

For the proud rugby league officials of the QRL, this was no laughing matter. What if teams were selected on the basis of where they played their first senior match, instead of where the player was presently contracted?

Former Australian and Queensland player Jack Reardon, who became an acclaimed rugby league writer for Brisbane's *Courier-Mail*, had been beating that drum since 1964. But it wasn't until 1979, when another *Courier-Mail* reporter, Hugh Lunn, was sitting next to Federal Labor senator and QRL president Ron McAuliffe on a flight from Canberra to Brisbane, that the notion of a 'State of Origin' series started to take hold.

'You can take the Queenslander out of Queensland, Ron,' Lunn said. 'But you can't take the Queensland out of the Queenslander.'

McAuliffe wasn't sure. He thought the risks might be too great.

'What if we recall our boys from Sydney to play, and we are beaten?' the senator asked. 'Where would we go from there?'

Thankfully, the QRL had some powerful people behind them and they keep pushing. Entrepreneur Barry Maranta and his business partner, Wayne Reid, were deep believers in the Origin concept. Reid called NSWRL president Kevin Humphreys, who tentatively agreed to the idea of a one-off match in 1980 at Lang Park.

Still fearing the consequences of a NSW victory, McAuliffe knew the Queenslanders needed an inspirational player to lead them. Three years earlier, Jack Gibson had coached the Queensland Country team and McAuliffe valued his judgment.

'I need fellows who you'd want in the trenches when the going gets tough,' McAuliffe told Gibson over the phone.

Gibson knew a player who would be perfect: an out-of-shape 35-year-old forward who was struggling to keep his place in Parramatta's first-grade side.

Arthur Beetson was perhaps the best example of why the Origin concept needed to happen. From 1966 to 1977, he played 18 matches for NSW and 17 of them were against Queensland. He captained the Blues to a series win in 1977. 'Big Artie' might've played for Balmain and captained Eastern Suburbs to premierships, but he was born in Roma and played his first senior game for Redcliffe.

'If he says yes, he will give you the game of his life,' Gibson told McAuliffe.

Of course, Beetson played for Queensland in that first match and, as promised, he turned in the game of his life. The Maroons won 20–10. Interstate rugby league would never be the same again.

That was Beetson's only Origin match as a player for Queensland, but he took over as coach and proved just as successful. The Maroons won the only Origin match played in 1981, and then won the first Origin series a year later, with a 10–5 win in the deciding third match at the SCG. The following year, Queensland prevailed again in the final match, this time winning 43–22 at Lang Park.

The powerful rugby league media in Sydney were initially dismissive of the Origin concept. By 1984, they were wondering when the NSWRL would get its act together and roll back the Maroon tide. Accordingly, the suits at the League's Phillip Street bunker decided that from '84

Blues players wouldn't have to play for their clubs on the weekend before a midweek Origin match.

Steve Mortimer was selected at halfback for the first match at Lang Park but was suspicious when his Parramatta rival Peter Sterling was picked on the bench. He withdrew with a hamstring injury, but years later admitted he faked the injury because he was worried about how much influence he could have on the side that was led by Sterling's club teammate Ray Price and included several Eels players.

This wasn't the only example of rugby league politics at play. The push was well and truly on for Price to be named ahead of Lewis as captain of the Australian side for the upcoming Ashes series against Great Britain, with Price declaring that the winner of the first Origin match should settle the argument. Queensland were already howling because Beetson had been overlooked as Australian coach, the job going to his NSW counterpart Frank Stanton. There had long been — and still is, in some ways — great mistrust between NSW and Queensland, and especially so around national team selection.

So the Maroons had a point to prove, apart from continuing their Origin dominance. Each time during the match the TV cameras flashed to Beetson sitting in the Lang Park stands, he was either dragging back on a cigarette or reaching into the top pocket of his camel-coloured blazer to get one. When NSW backrower Noel Cleal scored with 20 minutes to go, giving his side a 15–12 lead, Beetson nervously fumbled around for another Winfield Blue.

Lewis was playing injured after the Blues, each of them wearing comically inflated shoulder pads in comparison to the Queensland players, pounded him at every opportunity. He had outsmarted the defence to sneak down the blindside from dummy half and score in the 30th minute but, ultimately, the difference between the two sides was Maroons winger Kerry Boustead, who raced in for three tries to lead his state to a 29–12 victory.

At Queensland's post-match function at the Gazebo Hotel, Lewis chuckled when told that 23 fans had been arrested for 'alcohol-related offences'. Good to see them celebrating, he thought. Then it was announced that he had been named Kangaroos captain for the first Test against Great Britain at the SCG in 12 days' time. The room roared its approval.

In many respects, the politics around the selection of the Australian team in 1984 fuelled the fires of Origin that year and for many to come. Lewis led the Kangaroos to a 25–8 defeat of Great Britain, but he will always recall the Test as the afternoon when the Sydney faithful booed him when he ran onto the field.

'I remember it as the lowest moment of my life,' he told me in an interview in 2011. 'Every time I played in Sydney, that was the reaction I got, even when I got the ball. I always used to say that there were three national anthems in Sydney: *Advance Australia Fair*, *Wally Sucks* and *Wally's A Wanker*.'

There was also simmering tension in the Australian dressing-room. As detailed in Adrian McGregor's biography *King Wally*, the relationship between Price and the Queensland players was strained. Apart from Price's regular jibes in the Sydney press that Lewis would struggle with the grind of the Sydney competition, they believed the Parramatta forward faked injuries and cramp, whether it was on the field or whenever the press entered the Australian dressing-room. 'It was like a Monty Python movie,' Lewis told McGregor.

Such was the subtext bubbling beneath the surface for the second match of the 1984 Origin series, at the SCG on June 19.

Desperate for victory, NSW ushered in several changes. The most significant was Mortimer and his Canterbury teammate Terry Lamb in the halves, replacing Sterling and Manly's Alan Thompson. Another Bulldog, Andrew Farrar, replaced Parramatta's Steve Ella in the centres, while plucky Penrith hooker Royce Simmons came into the side to make his state debut. Queensland made no changes, save for a positional switch with Chris Close moving back in the centres and Mal Meninga shifting out to the wing. They were still huge — in both their forward pack and backline — and ready to seal the deal in Sydney.

'The only difference is Greg Conescu has one less tooth, having had it knocked out in the first Test against the Poms,' said Channel Nine's Mike Gibson as he went through the starting line-ups while the teams ran out of the Members Pavilion and onto the field.

As *Advance Australia Fair* played before kick-off, with rain bucketing down, the television cameras flashed on Beetson in the front row of the Ladies Stand, laughing as the crowd chanted, 'Wally's a wanker! Wally's a wanker!'

The hate had helped sell tickets. Like the local press, Blues fans had been sluggish in buying into the Origin concept, but if they were ever needed it was now. Despite sideways rain, 29,088 turned up to see if the Blues could send the series into a decider.

They were treated to a dreadful match, played in dreadful conditions.

The upshot, perhaps, was that they could tell their grandkids they were present for one of the most infamous all-in brawls in State of Origin history. It erupted on the second tackle of the match and went for more than two minutes.

The kick-off found Queensland fullback Colin Scott, who made his way to the 20-metre line. The ball was then fired back to centre Gene Miles, with Mortimer screaming up out of the line to tackle him. Simmons and front-rower Peter Tunks came in from the left, then came NSW's other prop Steve Roach from the right. He threw a wild punch at Miles' head and from that moment it was on. Close ran over the top of other players to get to Price, and when he did the pair started trading blows as they fell to the ground. Brett Kenny came in and held down Close. All over the ground, players grappled and threw punches at anyone who came into their field of vision and was wearing the other team's jumper.

'I ran from halfway to punch Colin Scott,' NSW fullback Garry Jack recalls. 'We started throwing punches at each other. Then Mal Meninga grabbed me and held me down. "Stay there," he said. Things were different then. In those days, you just knew punches would be thrown from the kick-off. You knew it was going to be on, so you had to steel yourself for that. We didn't really like each other, because we didn't really know each other. It was the most intense footy you could find.'

In the commentary box, Nine's Ian Maurice deferred straight to Jack Gibson sitting alongside him: 'Well, Jack, what an explosive start to this match!'

It's unclear if Maurice was making a subtle reference to the actual fireworks still being set off around the ground.

'Well, they advertised it all week,' Gibson said, referring to newspaper predictions that there would be a fight early in the match. 'It surprises nobody.'

A lengthy analysis of the fight shows Paul Vautin throwing uppercuts, Miles sneaking in a knee, and Close trying to fight just about everyone, pinging from scuffles with Price to winger Ross Conlon and then Tunks. Somewhere along the line, his shirt was torn off him.

'When Price grabbed my jersey, I thought the only way I could keep going was to rip it off,' Close has said. 'It was the first time they used the electronic scoreboard at the SCG and after the game my wife said, "How embarrassing, your guts took up the whole screen."'

Somewhere in among it all was referee Barry Gomersall, a Queenslander, better known as 'The Grasshopper' because of his thin legs and tight shorts. He had a reputation for letting on-field fights run their course before signalling a penalty, arms and hands waving about as if he was conducting an orchestra. NSW supporters considered him outrageously biased towards his home state, although Maroons fans had the same opinion of NSW whistleblowers such as Kevin Roberts and Mick Stone.

'How do you account for the fact that in your nine matches Queensland won seven and NSW won only two?' Gomersall, a charming man away from football, was asked years after he retired.

'Well, surely anyone's entitled to two bad games,' Gomersall quipped, or so legend has it.

He refereed his first Origin match in 1982 but this was his first at the SCG. When the brawl eventually simmered, he gathered in Lewis and Price, laid down the law, and then blew the penalty to

Queensland. The Blues howled but, in fairness, he was signalling the same penalty for offside he had awarded Queensland before the melee broke out.

NSW didn't let up. Minutes later, Tunks was penalised for a swinging arm. Then Simmons gave away one. When Roach wrestled with Conescu for a little too long, Gomersall raced in, blew his whistle, and awarded them another. With rain driving down harder, Meninga lined up a shot at goal from 40 metres out. Queensland were more than prepared to win it this way. They had decided before the match, given the conditions, to play it in NSW's half and take points whenever they could. On this occasion, facing the wind, Meninga's kick fell a few metres short of the black dot.

As the rain continued to flog down, and the middle of the field turned into brown slush, the Blues had no choice but to play it the same way, rucking it out from dummy half or with hard yards from their big men up the middle. On the last tackle of the set, Mortimer would boot it high and hope Scott would drop the ball.

'If it's a loose ball, you have to make a prisoner of it,' Gibson told Nine viewers.

When Roach copped a punch in the mouth from his opposite number, Greg Dowling, Gomersall awarded the penalty. 'Thank you!' Roach boomed at his Kangaroos teammate as he ran downfield.

From 30 metres out, right in front of the posts, Conlon had the chance to kick the first points. Unlike Meninga, he was a round-the-corner kicker, and his trademark shuffle before each kick was as notable as his accuracy. It's why he had been picked ahead of Meninga for the first Ashes Test, of course to the chagrin of Queensland. But, on this rain-soaked night, even the deadliest of kickers struggled; the attempt faded away to the right.

For the rest of the first half, that's how it was: few chances but many errors as the white leather ball became the proverbial cake of soap. Whenever Gomersall missed a Queensland error, the SCG crowd howled.

Terry Lamb sniffed a chance late in the half, chipping over the top of the defensive line, but Lewis was there to punch it over the dead-ball line. One of the linesmen came racing in to report that Queensland forward Wally Fullerton Smith had taken Lamb out after the kick, but Conlon missed the penalty attempt that resulted, the ball skewing off the upright.

When the muddied players left the field at halftime, there had been no score, but another statistic was telling: Queensland had dropped the ball 19 times while NSW coughed it up on just nine occasions. In the dressing-room, the players sat quietly as Stanton told his players that points would come sooner or later if they could hold onto the ball. Surely, at some point, Conlon would land some critical attempts at goal.

Instead, the first points of the second half came in comical style — and they belonged to the Maroons.

Lewis placed a perfect bomb just over the top of the left upright. Jack managed to latch onto the cake of soap despite the rain, the wind, the ball being obscured by the goal post and a wall of Queensland players — some of them offside — bearing down on him, but from the ensuing drop-out Noel Cleal only managed to kick it two metres in the mud and Gomersall rightfully gave a penalty in front of the posts because it hadn't travelled the required 10 metres. Replays showed Cleal barely touched it.

In the first half, Lewis had managed to boot the ball just 12 metres or so from a drop-out, such was the difficulty of kicking it in the slush. The next time he had to restart with a drop-out, he waited until the referee wasn't looking and reefed it downfield without letting it hit the ground. A suspicious Gomersall made sure he watched each Lewis drop-out closely for the rest of the game.

Meninga poked the ball between the posts to give the Maroons a 2–0 lead and suddenly, with the rain getting harder and the field getting wetter, the pressure was building on NSW to save the series. They tried to play expansively, despite the conditions, while Queensland shut the match down. 'All we're going to see from Queensland now are exciting two-yard runs,' Gibson said on Nine.

It wasn't a two-yard run that allowed Queensland to extend their lead; it was a freakish turn of luck, followed by a freakish piece of skill from Greg Dowling.

Conescu was tackled five metres out from the NSW line, just to the left of the posts. On the last tackle, the ball was fired back to Lewis, who was standing deep behind the ruck. He took off, as best he could in the conditions, arcing back towards the posts. Sensing that Jack was out of position, he attempted a chip kick over the fullback's head. Instead of landing in the in-goal area, the ball hit the black dot in the middle of the crossbar and bounced back into the field of the play.

Who was there? Dowling, the bearded menace of the Maroons pack, with distinctive red electrical tape pinning back his hair and ears. He bent down, caught the ball with the tips of his fingers just centimetres from the ground, and splashed over the tryline. He looked up and smiled, before being pulled up by his teammates.

Meninga's conversion gave the Maroons an 8–0 lead, which was considerable given the conditions.

'I grew up in Ingham, one of the wettest places in Australia,' Dowling said years later, when recalling his try. 'At best, we would play a couple of games a year when it wasn't pouring rain. But on reflection, I look at the replay and still find it hard to believe I actually bent down that far and picked up a slippery leather football so cleanly. Wally was so skilful that he probably was aiming for the black dot on the crossbar and expecting a rebound. But I just happened to be in the right place at the right time. I was actually racing through to smash Garry Jack and stop him from getting back into the field of play. But old Wally, in his wisdom, was one step ahead of me — as he usually was.'

Standing on the Hill that night was a fresh-faced 12-year-old with a flattop haircut from Penrith in western Sydney. He was there as a spectator, but in the years to come he'd wear the same sky-blue jumper of his heroes, win matches in it, win series as captain in it and then do the same as coach.

'That try, with Wally hitting the crossbar and Greg Dowling scoring, was my first memory of Origin,' Brad Fittler recalls.

Other patrons on the Hill that night were not so gracious. After the Dowling try, some pelted oranges and other garbage at the Queensland players as they took their positions for the restart. The grubby tactic worked, as the ball was fumbled after the kick-off and then trickled over the dead ball line. The Maroons were required to drop it out, and Lewis' restart only went a matter of metres, too, but just long enough to ensure there wasn't a repeat of the Cleal fiasco. Later in the set, however, the Queensland captain did concede a penalty, illegally stealing the ball off NSW second-rower Wayne Pearce in front of the uprights and right in front of Gomersall.

As Conlon was kicking the penalty goal, Brett Kenny limped from the field with a hamstring injury and was replaced by Steve Ella. 'They all seem to limp a little more when they're being replaced,' Gibson, who coached both men at Parramatta, said.

The NSW crowd could feel a shift in momentum. *Blues! Blues! Blues!* The chant soon changed when Gomersall penalised NSW for pushing the scrum off the mark, despite having the loose head and feed. *Bullshit! Bullshit! Bullshit!*

Some of Gomersall's decisions baffled both sides. 'I don't know about Gomersall,' Gibson said. 'I know they haven't picked him on looks. I don't know if they've picked him on ability or not.'

With 12 minutes to go, NSW were awarded a penalty when Gomersall ruled Conescu had pounced on a loose ball from an offside position after Meninga had spilt it backwards. The replay was clear: Conescu was behind him. So much for Queensland bias. Once again, though, Conlon missed the penalty kick from a simple angle, spraying it across the face of the posts.

Queensland buried the result — and therefore the series — soon after when Miles dashed out of dummy half on the last tackle and scored, carrying Blues replacement forward Pat Jarvis and Jack across the line with him. That sparked wild celebration from the exhausted Maroons players, as well as an all-in brawl up on the Hill to rival what they had seen on the field during the first half.

Lewis was named man of the match, although he remains adamant the honour should've gone to Dowling.

'Fans remember me for two things — that try from the crossbar and my sideline stoush with Kiwi Kevin Tamati the next year,' Dowling has said, referring to the headbutting duel that ensued after he and Tamati were sin-binned in a Test match at Lang Park. 'One was ugly, one was pretty good — a lot like our life experiences I suppose. But to me, it was all about having a go.'

After fulltime, Mortimer wiped the mud from his eyes and plodded from the SCG wondering how this would play out … with the public and with the selectors. Maybe they would sack him again. Maybe they would go back to Sterling. Maybe he had played his last game for his state.

In the end, he was retained and, most importantly, given the captaincy for the third match of the series, back at Lang Park.

It happened by chance, if anything. Price announced his retirement from representative football after the final Ashes Test. Wayne Pearce, who was captain of Balmain and seen by most to be Price's logical successor as NSW skipper, was ruled out because of injury. Mortimer wasn't even captain of his own team because of internal politics at Canterbury-Bankstown, where coach Warren Ryan had controversially given the role to Terry Lamb.

The Blues selectors decided to use the dead rubber to blood some new talent. In game one, a banner in the Lang Park crowd advised: 'Pricey and your pensioners — go home!' For this match, Parramatta's Peter Wynn, Mortimer's younger brother Chris, and the St George quartet of Jarvis, Steve Morris, Brian Johnston and Chris Walsh were brought into a starting side that performed as if they had nothing to lose.

NSW won 22–12 and Mortimer was named man of the match. Blues players recall him dancing on the massage table after fulltime. Maybe he knew of bigger things to come.

'We stuck it up them,' recalls Mortimer of that result. 'It put us in a good frame of mind for 1985.'

WHY DID HOLDING ALOFT the State of Origin shield mean so much to Steve Mortimer? In truth, playing for NSW had hurt him. Repeatedly. It hadn't always been pretty.

Mortimer's first match for his state was in 1977, the year after legendary Canterbury secretary Peter 'Bullfrog' Moore signed him up soon after the then teenage halfback from Turvey Park in Wagga Wagga — hence his nickname of 'Turvey' — led Riverina to a shock Amco Cup win over the team known as the 'Berries' (they would become the 'Bulldogs' in 1978).

'He'll never play against a Canterbury-Bankstown side again,' Moore famously declared. And Mortimer didn't.

With his clever kicking game, electric running of the ball from a standing start and signature cover defence, he was picked for NSW to play against Queensland — at the age of 20. Ominously, Western Suburbs' veteran Tommy Raudonikis was on the bench, and after Mortimer struggled in the opening half, he was taken off by coach Terry Fearnley in the 45th minute.

Raudonikis came on, immediately started a fight and NSW won 14–13 after trailing 13–4 with seven minutes to go.

From then on, Mortimer was in and out of the state team, duelling with Raudonikis and then Parramatta's blond genius Peter Sterling for the No. 7 jumper. He played for NSW in 1981, but then Sterling edged ahead of him — for both the Blues and the Kangaroos.

While the selectors showed indifference about their halfback, Mortimer had identified after his first match in 1977 the indifference his NSW teammates felt towards interstate matches. He had played in that NSW side alongside the likes of Beetson, Ray Higgs and Rod 'Rocket' Reddy, all Queensland born, and after fulltime they had walked straight into the Maroons' dressing-room to be with their own. It made a lasting impression on the young halfback.

'It showed me that once a Queenslander, always a Queenslander,' Mortimer said in Neil Cadigan's *Greats of Origin*. 'When Origin came about, you could see the Sydney-based Queenslanders felt they were home. For me, every time I've picked up a NSW jersey I felt privileged. But when I took the field, it was a case of, "Okay, we'll do the best we can." But I never felt a real bond there with all the players.'

That's why Mortimer stopped the bus on Caxton Street, waving a finger at the Queenslanders with their faces pressed up to the windows. Something had to change, he figured, and it was starting tonight.

Also sitting on the bus was Michael O'Connor, the former Wallabies centre who had switched to rugby league in 1983 to play for St George. There had been doubts about how O'Connor would perform on the grand stage that is Origin, especially when that stage was a wet and angry Lang Park.

Instead, he revelled in it, scoring all of NSW's points — two tries and five goals — in an 18–2 win.

While O'Connor contributed the points, it was the defence from Roach, Tunks, Wynn and Jarvis that set up the victory. The man responsible for this was coach Terry Fearnley, who had replaced Frank Stanton and was also set to take control of Australia for the upcoming Test series against New Zealand.

Fearnley was no rookie. He had played alongside Jack Gibson at Eastern Suburbs and then travelled with Gibson on a fact-finding mission to the US, spending time at the San Francisco 49ers. The pair returned with a new, professional approach to coaching, which Fearnley put to good use when he became first-grade coach at Parramatta in 1976, steering the Eels into the grand final in each of his first two seasons. In 1977, he also coached NSW and Australia, after which he concentrated on club football, building a reputation as one of the best coaches in the business. No one in Sydney criticised his appointment as NSW and Australian coach in 1985. Fearnley knew there was one way to beat Queensland, even if it was easier said than done: stop Lewis.

'He was very measured and methodical,' Garry Jack says of the coach. 'The game plan was clear: Queensland would shift the ball wide, from Lewis to Mark Murray. We were told to come up and put pressure on him, because Wally could pass 25 metres across the field. We didn't want to give him any time or space with the ball. Wally was in his prime then, so we had to shut him down.'

The growing tension between the states wasn't just fed by politics around Australian team selections; a robust Sydney press also didn't mind poking and prodding the Queenslanders via a platoon of aggressive, straight-shooting columnists. Peter Frilingos from the *Daily Mirror* wanted Lewis sacked from the Australian team after the Maroons' loss at Lang Park, as did Bob Fulton.

Having been booed as Australian captain at the SCG the year before, the anti-Wally sentiment was again running high for Origin II. Almost 40,000 fans crammed into the SCG. The prospect of finally winning the series meant Blues fans were now firmly invested. Funny that.

At halftime in the curtain-raiser, Lewis and Mortimer left the dressing-room and made their way over to the turf in front of the Brewongle Stand for the coin toss. Lewis looked up towards the gathering crowd and saw his own name.

'Wally who?' read one banner. 'Wally's a Wanker' said another. There was even a reference to his receding golden locks: 'Old Baldie'.

Then the chant started: 'Walllly suuuucks! Walllly suuuucks! Walllly suuuucks!'

As Lewis made his way back towards the Members Pavilion after the toss, he was greeted by long-time Queensland manager Dick 'Tosser' Turner.

'I'm sorry about that,' Turner said.

'Tosser, that was a set-up,' Lewis said. 'I'm never going through that shit again.'

There were more theatrics when it came time for the teams to take the field. As was the way back then, the players were introduced one by one. After Queensland's No. 5, winger Dale Shearer, was introduced, it was Lewis' turn. A NSW official held him back, so halfback Mark Murray copped the wrath of the SCG crowd who'd been waiting for The King.

Lewis eventually came out for this Origin after prop Greg Dowling. The captains were supposed to come out last. The crowd howled at him anyway.

Up in the commentary box, Mike Gibson went through the team lists as the players took their positions on the field.

'Queenslanders are known as Cane Toads, New South Welshman are Cockroaches and now we have the Grasshopper,' said Gibson. 'We've got the whole menagerie here tonight.'

Only two tackles in and the Grasshopper blew his whistle with the cheapest penalty in the book, ruling the Blues were inside the five metres.

When the Blues finally found the ball in their hands, they used it; whether it was forwards Roach and Cleal standing and off-loading in tackles, or halves Mortimer and Kenny spreading it out wide with long, cut-out passes to Canberra's John 'Chicka' Ferguson on one wing or Parramatta's Eric Grothe on the other. Eventually, something had to give. NSW's first try came from a Mortimer kick, perfectly placed to land just over the Queensland line and adjacent to the right upright. His brother, Chris, soared above the pack to score.

Their second try was also of Mortimer's making. Rugby league is the definitive game of momentum, with the damage of each run and the subsequent speed of the play-the-ball having a domino effect on the defensive line. After Queensland had booted the ball deep into NSW territory, Mortimer scurried out of dummy half and, on the next tackle, scooped up the ball again after a quick play-the-ball from Ferguson to send Wynn searching into Maroons territory.

Queensland were scattered. Benny Elias darted out of dummy half to the open side, getting away from Chris Close at first marker. With legs pumping, he slipped through a gap created by Paul Vautin and Greg Conescu and went over. With O'Connor landing both conversions, the Blues were up 12–0 after only 16 minutes.

Could this really be happening? Was it really going to be this easy? Are NSW really about to do a Queensland on Queensland?

Well, of course not. The Maroons were back in it within minutes, after Close bustled down the left edge, breaking out of one tackle and then sneaking a pass to Shearer, who passed the ball back inside to Murray as soon as he caught it. Murray found lock Bob Lindner, who raced away and scored between the posts.

Queensland was now warming into the Origin. The NSW defence stiffened, as did the stiff arms, and when Mortimer threw one in a tackle on Dowling a touch judge came trotting in and Gomersall blew the pea out of his whistle. Meninga landed the penalty kick: 12–8 to NSW.

Until this point, Lewis had been relatively quiet. As they had done in the series opener, the Blues were rushing up on him every time he got the ball, with the crowd rising and barking their approval whenever his head was squished into the ground. Lewis hurt his jaw early in the match when tackling Grothe and was brutalised for the rest of the half, whether he had the ball or not. But champion players can never be fully silenced. As halftime approached, the ball found him flat-footed on the last tackle on his own 30-metre line. But the NSW defensive line was out of shape, and that was enough; he took off, sprinting downfield and it seemed there was only fresh air separating him from the tryline and an unlikely Queensland lead. But then Garry Jack came spearing across the field, taking the Maroons captain in a signature tackle around the laces. Gomersall ordered Lewis to hand over the ball, and NSW went one-out as they counted down the clock.

As Mortimer made a short run out of dummy half, Murray swung his arm and clipped his forehead. Gomersall awarded the penalty and the NSW captain stayed down for a nanosecond, but then he got to his knees and started barking instructions to his teammates. He was still barking instructions as NSW trainer Alf Richards tried to stop the blood gushing out from a cut on his temple, and was still barking as the two sides left the field at halftime.

One man who didn't leave the field was Lindner. He had twisted his knee in a tackle and was writhing in pain. Lewis rushed over, immediately realised the seriousness of the injury, and called for a stretcher. Queensland fullback Colin Scott had left the field in the same way after suffering a similar injury, which meant Queensland had no more fresh reserves. If they were to retain their Origin crown, they would have to pull out their greatest performance of the past five years.

And they almost did …

The second half started like most first halves in State of Origin football — with a fight — and it surprised few that the combatants were Roach and Dowling. 'Looks like round one,' drawled Jack Gibson. Gomersall dispatched the two players to the sin bin for five minutes. In true rugby league style, they returned after three and a half.

Perhaps the timekeeper was caught up in the chaos with the rest of us as Queensland, led by an injured Lewis, whose jaw was given another unwanted jolt while he was trying to tackle Wayne Pearce, came surging back. Two of his kicks close to the NSW line might have yielded tries if not for Garry Jack snuffing out both chances. If Fearnley's strategy to shut down Lewis was to rush up on him, Queensland coach Des Morris' second-half tactic was to play it down the Blues' end, with Lewis kicking early in the tackle count. Sooner or later, their chance would come.

It eventually arrived via the boot of Dale Shearer, who found touch with a booming kick downfield. Queensland then pushed over the top of the Blues in the scrum and gained possession.

This was it. Who would break NSW hearts this time: Lewis? Close? Meninga?

No, it was Dowling again. And this time, there was no luck about it. He spotted that Cleal was slow getting back onside and motored towards him. Roach came across from the left to help with the tackle, but Dowling reached out with one hand and threw the perfect 'round the corner' pass to replacement forward Ian French, who was supporting on the inside. French poked his head through the line, despite the attempts of Mortimer and Elias to reel him back, to score the try.

The crowd fell silent. Mortimer gathered his team near the posts as Meninga lined up the conversion. Big Mal's toe-poke could be wildly inaccurate at times but not now: his kick snuck inside the right upright and the Queenslanders were — somehow — up 14–12 with 25 minutes left on the clock.

Much like the corresponding match at the SCG the year before, going behind on the scoreboard sparked the Blues into using the ball. Jack broke through on one play; Chicka Ferguson bounced off several tackles like one pinball off another. Roach worked his way down the short side on both edges of the field. Lewis' side refused to yield but NSW soon had the chance to level the scores when Gomersall penalised Chris Close for taking out Mortimer late after a kick. Replays showed there was nothing in it. 'He went down soft but he made it look hard,' Gibson said in the commentary box. 'But he got what he was after.'

O'Connor landed the penalty: 14–all.

The night before the match, Fearnley had asked every player to gather in his room. 'Here we are,' he told them. 'Here it is. You're 80 minutes away from doing what we set out to do.'

Now it was 12 minutes.

'This was the moment when we were going to know if all the hard work, all that mateship we'd talked about, meant anything,' Wynn recalls. 'If we really were a special bunch of blokes.'

Queensland kicked off but Jack gobbled it up on the full and kicked straight back down the field, wanting to keep the ball down the opposition's end as much as possible. When the Blues got possession, they shifted the ball to the right, first through Ferguson, then Wynn, then Mortimer linked with Pearce, who found Grothe lurking outside him. He pushed Maroons replacement Tony Currie out of the way before second-rower Paul Vautin came scrambling across in cover. Grothe could see Pat Jarvis hunting up on the inside, though. His desperate one-handed pass found him. Jarvis scored! The SCG erupted! So did the players!

But standing back on the sideline where Grothe had gone out was the touch judge with his flag in the air. Grothe, he said, had put a foot on the sideline. As the players trudged back onside, a replay flashed on the SCG's big screen and it clearly showed Grothe getting the ball away before he had gone out. The crowd voiced their thoughts …

BULLSHIT! BULLSHIT! BULLSHIT!

All that passion and pride that Mortimer had been trying to evoke in his team had specifically been for moments like these. Such a critical call could rock a team's self-belief, especially one that been crushed in this arena by this same opponent like this before. But NSW didn't panic. When they next had possession, they worked the ball towards the centre of the field. Come the last tackle, they were 10 metres from the Queensland line. Lewis spotted Michael O'Connor behind the line and knew what was on. He barked at his markers to get away quickly, but they were fractionally slow, Elias' crisp pass from dummy half smacked into O'Connor's hands and he kicked the field goal that gave the Blues a 15–14 lead.

What followed in the concluding minutes was mayhem — which would, in decades to follow, become the hallmark of most Origin matches — as exhausted bodies tried to squeeze out one last effort, one last point, one last victory.

Cleal gave the Queenslanders a sniff when he knocked on, but Elias and his pack regained possession in the scrum. When the Maroons regained the ball they spun it wide, but Shearer kicked the ball out on the full. As the fulltime siren neared, Lewis found himself in a similar position to O'Connor, albeit a few metres further back. Conescu fired the ball back to Lewis for the field goal attempt, but Elias had sprinted up and charged down the kick.

'Very quick off the mark, aren't they?' Lewis recalled in *King Wally* as Adrian McGregor showed him a replay of the missed field goal. 'I hate watching that game. It was a bastard of a match.'

Then Kenny scored his ankle-bending try, close to the line, and all hell broke loose.

'And look at Steve Mortimer!' Ian Maurice beamed in commentary as Mortimer collapsed to the ground. 'Ecstasy! Pure heaven!'

The siren sounded before play could resume. One of the first to congratulate the NSW skipper was 'Fatty' Vautin.

'Turvey, you just did a Queensland on Queensland,' Vautin said.

'Piss off, Fatty,' Mortimer said. 'We did a NSW on Queensland.'

In the dressing-room afterwards, Mortimer announced his retirement from representative football. Job done.

MORE THAN 30 YEARS later, Steve Mortimer is getting emotional again. He sits across the table at a café in Pyrmont, and he is talking about that moment.

I haven't shown him the vision of him collapsing to the ground. Instead, it's an image taken by *Sydney Morning Herald* photographer Peter Morris. Mortimer is perched on the shoulders of Cleal and Pearce, with Wynn, Jarvis and Jack also in shot. The scoreboard on the Hill and lights from the SCG's giant towers illuminate the scene. The captain has both clenched fists in the air, his head thrown back and he's looking up at the heavens.

I push the image under Mortimer's nose. What was he thinking in that moment?

'Without sounding corny, I was saying my prayer to God, on behalf of myself and the boys,' he says, voice cracking. 'I had the privilege of representing our team in receiving the trophy, but I also had my faith. In that moment, in that photo, I am saying thanks on behalf of all the boys. I thanked the bloke above.'

Terry Fearnley's presence as Australia's coach in 1985 caused an enormous rift. Although Australia won the first two Tests against New Zealand, he sacked four Queenslanders — Close, Dowling, Murray and Conescu — for the third Test and shared a frosty relationship with Lewis. But Mortimer, like many people in the game, adored Fearnley and respected his football intelligence.

'He was the most humble man you could ever meet,' Mortimer says. 'He was a caring person, too. He didn't say too much, but what he had to say you listened to.'

Fearnley, 81, died of cancer in 2015 but like each of those players he will forever be linked to the moment when NSW turned back the tide. He also knew the benefit of an influential captain. Mortimer asked him before the second game if he could speak to the players individually.

'We have a great opportunity here to create history,' Mortimer told each player in the SCG dressing-room before they went out on the field that night. 'By creating this history, 30 years on we'll shake hands and hug each other, and know exactly what we've achieved.'

'And is that how it turned out?' I ask. 'Do you all realise how important that win was?'

'We all do.'

CHAPTER 7

Plugger's Points

Tony Lockett and the Sydney Swans

THERE HE IS! PLUGGER! The No. 4 for St Kilda, dominating the scene at full forward at the Randwick end of the Sydney Cricket Ground.

'They won't catch him,' declares Channel Seven caller Sandy Roberts, sitting high in the stands in the commentary box.

Won't *catch* him? Tony Lockett has never been noted for his speed and agility. More brute strength and force and an angry mullet because, let's face it, all mullets are angry.

'He's drifting into the right forward pocket now,' Roberts continues. 'Now, half forward. This is incredible!'

The Swans' defenders don't know what to do, clutching at thin air as Plugger evades them with deft, fleet-footed aplomb.

Darren Holmes has had enough of this malarkey. Here he comes, zeroing in from behind, smothering Plugger in a ball-and-all tackle.

'Ohhhh!' booms Roberts. 'What a magnificent tackle from Holmes!'

On the surface, it seems as if we're talking about St Kilda legend Tony Lockett wreaking havoc in typical Tony Lockett style.

Instead, these were the comical scenes of August 1, 1993, at the SCG when someone decided to buy a piglet, paint 'Plugger' on one side and then No. 4 on the other, and let it run onto the field in the middle of a match between the Swans and St Kilda.

The real Plugger wasn't even there. Lockett was injured but watching from his lounge in Cranbourne. When he saw the pig on his television screen, he didn't laugh, couldn't see the funny side of it.

'I was livid when I saw it,' Lockett said in his autobiography *My Life*. 'I didn't think it was funny at the time and I certainly failed to see the joke. I doubt anyone who was being made fun of on national television would see the humour … I vowed to make the Swans pay every time I came up against them.'

When the two sides met at the SCG a season later, in round 7, Sydney paid. Unfortunately, so did Swans defender Peter Caven — with his nose. Ken Williams almost paid, too — with his head.

Williams is the Swans' most fanatical supporter and probably their oldest. Most certainly their loudest. He was part of the 75,754-strong crowd that watched South Melbourne beat Richmond in the 1933 VFL grand final. He was at Princes Park in Melbourne in 1945, cheering on the Bloods in their infamous 'bloodbath' grand final loss to Carlton, when the police were needed to help the umpires restore order.

Four years later, he brought some racehorses to Sydney, was supposed to stay for a fortnight, and decided to stay for the rest of his days. He's now in his 90s. 'It was such a good place,' he says, 'I ended up getting married and bringing up a family here.'

When South Melbourne was transplanted in Sydney in 1982, Williams became an instant member of the Swans' family, too. Sitting in the front row in the old Noble Stand, he quickly became identifiable as their No. 1 supporter.

On a sunny autumn afternoon in Sydney in May 1994, Williams was sitting in his signature position when Tony Lockett — the man, not the pig — placed a sizeable target on his forehead. It had been that kind of afternoon, you see. In the first quarter, Lockett and Caven were running from different directions to mark the ball. It was like watching a slow-moving car crash and not being able to do anything about it. Lockett's right arm collected Caven's face, and as Caven crashed into the turf it was obvious to the 9295 people at the ground, and all those watching on TV, who had fared better from the ugly collision.

Caven clutched at his nose. Actually, the bone protruding from his nose as blood gushed out. After a lengthy delay, he was stretchered from the field and taken to hospital.

'I couldn't see how badly he was hurt,' Lockett said in *My Life*. 'But I knew I'd find out later.'

Caven was taken away for emergency surgery but the incident didn't rattle Sydney. Instead, they rallied, and led by 18 points at quarter-time. Then 25 at halftime. At one stage, in the third term, the home side kicked out to a 51-point lead before the Saints booted two to cut the lead to 38. By anyone's measure, it was a deficit too large to reel in, even with Lockett stalking the goal square like a cranky, caged lion. When the Swans kicked another two goals seven minutes into the final quarter, they led by a staggering eight goals. This match was over.

Saints coach Stan Alves thought differently. He'd told his side at the end of the third term that they only had to swing the momentum their way and Sydney would faceplant. They just needed someone to trigger the resurgence.

Sitting in the stands, the Swans faithful started to chirp — and their target was Lockett. In his book, he says he heard something uttered 'about my family' from a mob of Swans fans. That was enough for the adrenaline to kick into his weary bones. From a set shot right in front, he homed in on the head of one particular Swans fan. 'I got the chance to drill one straight at my "mates" in the stand,' Lockett said. 'I missed but I'm sure they realised I'd been listening to them all afternoon.'

Years later, it was revealed that one of those 'mates' was poor old Kenny Williams.

'Plugger used to kick low torps at him when he was playing for St Kilda and try and kill him,' former Swan Jude Bolton once mused as if it was an everyday occurrence.

In the final quarter, the Saints booted 8.4 (52) to the Swans' 2.1 (13) to win by a point. Lockett finished with 11 goals, kicking three in the final quarter. He raised his arms in the air in triumph. Barely anybody at the SCG cheered.

'If you could write the script, the one person you want with the ball in their hands in that situation is the No. 4,' Alves said.

When Lockett arrived back in Melbourne, the heaving media pack at the airport gate gave an indication of the storm about to the engulf him and the club. Lockett was no stranger to controversy — nor the AFL tribunal. He'd been reported six times and suspended on five occasions. But the longest penalty had been for four matches. The Caven incident was on another level. There was talk of Caven taking legal action, something Swans coach Ron Barassi dismissed instantly.

'That's one of the worst sides of American life and we don't want to see it in this country,' the legendary coach told Channel Ten's Eddie McGuire. 'The personnel of both clubs would do well to keep cool for the next 48 hours.'

Lockett's manager, Rob Hession, thought nothing of the incident. 'Fair bump,' he said. 'It's a contact sport — not netball.'

Hession also said the umpires had told Lockett during and after the match that he had no reason to fear being charged. But the tribunal saw it differently. Lockett was suspended for eight matches. Caven was sidelined for 12 weeks on the advice of a plastic surgeon.

'I honestly believe what happened with Peter Caven in 1994 was just one of those things that occurs in a game of football,' Lockett said. 'A reflex action where somebody, unfortunately, got injured.'

The way Plugger saw it, the thrilling Saints win was payback for the embarrassment he had felt the previous season when Plugger the pig was set free and allowed to run wild at the same venue.

'It could not have been better payback if a script had been written,' he said. 'I didn't care if the Sydney fans hated me or not. As a matter of fact,

I probably enjoyed the fact they were so passionate in their displeasure. I got my own back. I thought, "They've had fun at my expense, now it's my turn," and I hoped they were all feeling nice and sick.'

Who could ever have imagined, after the heady events of those two matches, from little piglet to signature Plugger brilliance and brutality, that Tony Lockett would become one of the Swans' favourite sons? A revered figure who gave the code true gravitas in a city and state besotted with rugby league and rugby union? And that, after avoiding decapitation that sunny afternoon at the SCG, Ken Williams would become mates with Lockett?

That Anthony Howard Lockett would be responsible for two of the most memorable moments at the SCG, with thousands of fans streaming into the middle of a ground the man himself called 'The Fortress'?

Former Swans chairman Richard Colless remembers the precise moment when the Sydney faithful forgot the past of Tony Lockett, St Kilda full forward, and oozed excitement about the imminent arrival of an Australian football superstar.

'He was reviled,' Colless says. 'Then he put the red-and-white on and he was loved — forever.'

JIMMY BRESLIN, THE BRASH New York columnist famous for writing stories like his landmark piece about the gravedigger who buried John F. Kennedy, cut his teeth on sport. The best stories, he argued, were to be found in the losing team's dressing-room. Damon Runyon, no less, offered the same dictum to aspiring sportswriters.

There's losing and then there's the horror run of the Sydney Swans in the early 1990s. Over two seasons, 1992 and 1993, against all the other 15 teams then in the AFL competition, in every capital of the mainland states, including 12 matches at their beloved SCG, involving three coaches and 51 players, the Swans lost 26 matches straight.

Twenty-six! It started in round nine, May 17, 1992, with a 32-point loss to Richmond at the MCG. For the next 413 days, the Swans couldn't buy a win. They were rooted to the bottom of the ladder for three straight seasons.

Sitting in the old press box in the Bradman Stand, looking straight down the ground, reporters struggled to muster their inner Breslin. Michael Cowley, the *Sydney Morning Herald*'s AFL reporter, was struggling to find inventive ways to describe what the rest of Sydney already knew: the Swans sucked.

In 1993, prominent broadcaster Mike Willesee gave Cowley an easy column to offer his editors in a city more interested in the rugby codes. Back in December 1988, Willesee stood alongside businessmen Basil Sellers, John Gerahty, Peter Weinert and Craig Kimberley in the Noble Stand to announce they were buying the Swans. In reality, they were rescuing them. The halcyon days of the mid-1980s, when the Swans' owner, the flamboyant entrepreneur Geoffrey Edelsten, outshone the players via the cut of his suit and the pinkish hue of his private helicopter, were long gone. Willesee and his partners soon discovered the hole the club was in was bigger than they'd imagined. By May '93, as the losing streak continued, Willesee told Cowley they were floating the idea of making the Swans a public membership-based club.

Give the Swans to the people.

Then Sydney suffered another humiliating defeat. 'No doubt the public will be happy to return this generous gift,' Cowley wrote.

Early into the 1993 season, Cowley was chatting with Swans coach Gary Buckenara, a Hawthorn great who was finding his first coaching job rather challenging. He'd watched his side lose 18 matches in a row.

'I wouldn't be surprised if I was sacked at some stage,' he told Cowley.

Two days later, he was.

'They really stank,' Cowley recalls. 'During the losing streak, it looked like there were more people on the field than in the stands.'

Buckenara's sacking forced the Swans into making some serious changes. The AFL had taken over the licence again, even if it was still owned by Willesee and his partners, but what the team needed was a winning culture. Who better to turn the beat around than one of the most respected individuals in the code's history?

Initially, Ron Barassi didn't have the immediate influence on the broken Swans side that many had hoped. Ahead of Barassi's second match in charge, Cowley sensed the streak was coming to an end. The Swans were due to fly to Brisbane to play the slightly less bad Brisbane Bears at the Gabba. The sports editor took some convincing to send his reporter north, but in the end Cowley got his way.

Sydney were down by 20 goals at halftime and lost by 162 points. It was the club's second biggest loss in their history.

Having won six premierships as a player for Melbourne, then two each as coach at Carlton and North Melbourne, Barassi was accustomed to winning. He knew the Swans' ship would eventually turn. And it did. At 4.45pm on the Sunday afternoon of June 27, 1993, the streak ended with a 40-point win over Melbourne at the SCG. Fans were crying in the stands. So were the players. After a brief moment of reflection in the middle of the ground, they retired to the rooms.

Barassi, considered one of the hardest men in football in his day, admitted to reporters he shed a few tears.

'I feel extra good,' he told them. 'I haven't been here as long as those other guys. They're *really* crying.'

That was the Swans' only win that season. In 1994, they notched four. But on Barassi's watch there was at least hope. It was clear they needed a marquee signing, ideally a true ball-magnet anchored to the goal square. Such a player would give the Swans credibility off the field, and strike power on it.

Barassi knew of such a man: the brute who had rearranged the face of Peter Caven.

Lockett was grumpy in Melbourne, hating how the press shadowed his every move. He once tried to spear Eddie McGuire with a crutch after the Channel Ten reporter and his cameraman followed him into a Melbourne hospital to get the latest report on Lockett's injured ankle. Now he wanted a change of clubs, although Sydney was a long way down his list. He spoke to Collingwood, Richmond and Brisbane but in the end decided on the 'Pies', only for some nervous directors to pull the contract at the 11th hour. He then focused on Richmond, but they couldn't negotiate a satisfactory trade agreement with St Kilda.

After finishing last for the past three years, the Swans had some bargaining power in terms of draft selections. But Lockett was wary. 'I had mixed feelings about the deal,' he'd say. 'It was hard to see them winning a premiership before I anticipated retirement.'

Then Lockett met with Barassi and Swans chief executive Ron Joseph, who told Lockett that if he committed, so would Paul Roos, who might have been in his early 30s and with his best days at Fitzroy behind him, but who was still one of the most respected players in the AFL. Lockett started to warm to the idea. He understood the lingering stench of what happened to Caven — 'I'm sure the Sydney supporters would've hanged me if they could' — but changing states as much as clubs appealed.

'Moving to Sydney was going to be a whole lifestyle change,' he said. 'And, at the time, that held a special sort of appeal for me. I was stale in Melbourne and getting away was the best option.'

Then, at the last minute, Lockett got cold feet. He told his wife Vicki that he was staying put. But Joseph had spent weeks hounding Lockett, lobbing on his front porch in Cranborne or phoning at least three times a day. Eventually, he convinced Lockett to sign.

When the big man walked through the doors and into the old ambulance rooms at the RAS Showground where the Swans did their weights, and took a whiff of the old smelly carpet, he wondered if he'd made the right decision. New facilities were being built at the SCG, but Lockett knew straight away that he'd dispatched himself to an AFL outpost. Life was going to be different.

At this first training session, the Swans took the heat out of any potential storylines surrounding what Lockett's arrival would mean for Peter Caven, organising a photoshoot in the middle of the SCG with the two men and Barassi. 'I think Cavo understood what happened last year was in the past,' Lockett said.

The other fundamental change to the club that occurred at the same time as the Lockett coup was the appointment of Richard Colless as club chairman. Willesee had been butting heads with AFL head office, which was pushing for Colless to take over. Colless was the inaugural chairman of the West Coast Eagles, but had moved to Sydney in 1988 to pursue business interests.

As it turned out, securing Colless was a masterstroke, Willesee recalled in his autobiography, *Memoirs*, in 2017, because it helped the fledgling club navigate delicate relationships with the AFL at a time when the Swans were fighting for survival.

'Richard was far more important for the club than any single coach or player,' Willesee wrote.

In 1995, the revolution started to bear fruit. Led by tireless captain Paul Kelly, who chased the ball like a sheep dog that year all the way to the Brownlow Medal as the AFL's best and fairest player, there was marked improvement. The Swans finished the season 12th with eight wins and a for-and-against percentage of 100.7. By comparison, Brisbane, who finished eighth, won 10 games and had a percentage of 95.3. The Swans had lost their away match to the Bears earlier in the year because of a contentious free kick. If they'd won that game, Colless argues, the Swans would've made the finals.

'With the value of hindsight, we hadn't realised how far we'd come,' Colless says. 'Bad sides don't have percentages of a hundred or more.'

The person who saw the most potential was Barassi, who was coming out of contract and unsure what to do. 'Should I stay for one more year?' he asked himself. Or should he hand the reins to his more than capable assistant coach, Rodney Eade?

'You're Ron Barassi,' Colless told him. 'You can do whatever you want.'

Barassi opted to retire, knowing the club was in safe hands with what he'd built over his nearly three seasons in charge.

'There was certainly internally and externally a sense we were a long way off being a force,' Colless offers. 'But no longer the basket case and object of ridicule we'd been the previous three years [before Barassi became coach].'

And this revival was in no small part due to Lockett, even though he was — in his own way — still coming to terms with the city as much as it was coming to terms with him. Geelong maestro Gary Ablett (the father of 21st-century champion Gary Ablett junior) claimed the Coleman Medal for most goals kicked in a season with 122 from 22 matches, but Lockett wasn't far behind, kicking 110 goals from the 19 games he played.

'Lockett was the embodiment of the marquee player,' Colless says. 'As good as Paul Kelly was — and universally loved and admired and crazy brave — and we had Roos playing as a 32-year-old, Lockett just added that element of seniority to calm people down. His impact on the club and game was extraordinary.

'I'm not for one minute saying Tony wouldn't be a star in today's era, but the game was changing. Full forwards had to be more mobile. They couldn't be anchored to the square. But he was something else.'

In one *Herald* story, Colless theorised that Lockett looked like a front-row forward who played like a halfback. An angry Lockett phoned Colless when he read the remarks.

'What do you mean I play like a halfback?' he grumbled down the line.

'Tony, do you know anything about rugby league?' Colless asked calmly.

'No.'

'In rugby league, the halfback is the playmaker, the architect, usually the best player on the field.

'Oh. I thought you meant a halfback flanker.'

In Australian football in 1995, halfback flanker wasn't a particularly glamorous position.

'That's OK, then,' Lockett said before hanging up the phone.

KEVIN SHEEDY IS SITTING in the away team's coaches' box at the SCG, wondering how it had come to this. The Essendon coach had watched his team lead by as many as four goals, then two goals deep in the final quarter, but now Tony Lockett is standing at the top of the 50-metre arc at the Randwick end. Any score will put the Swans into their first grand final since 1945; their first since relocating from South Melbourne to Sydney.

A mouthful of expletives pours from Sheedy's mouth as the siren sounds in the preliminary final. What was that, Sheeds?

'I'm a Catholic, I don't want to repeat it,' the retired coach laughs now.

In the home team's coaches' box, Rodney Eade isn't swearing. He's praying. In normal circumstances, the man you need in this sort of situation is Lockett. Actually, his booming right foot. But Eade and his assistants are palpably aware that Lockett's injured groin might prevent him achieving what his head and foot want to achieve.

Down on the ground, Paul Roos is standing in the back line and thinking the same thing. Lockett had badly torn his groin in the second last round against the Bombers at the MCG. This grand-final qualifier was his first match back, having missed the qualifying final against Hawthorn.

'Bloody hell, I wonder how his groin is?' Roos says to himself. 'Is going to have to go a torpedo? A drop punt?'

Recalls Roos: 'Normally, this would be like shelling peas for Plugger. He'd kick this over the fence. But that groin was the issue.'

When Lockett took the field that evening, he hadn't kicked a ball any further than 30 metres in the past month. Now, he was straight in front but requiring a kick of 50 metres plus interest to get the Swans into the grand final against North Melbourne at the MCG in a week's time.

He moves back, goes through his signature ritual from a set shot. Pulls up his socks. Takes in a deep breath. 'Well, this is it,' he says to himself. 'Just hit it right and give it everything you've got ...'

Not even Lockett could've imagined in March that he'd be lining up such a history-defining kick. Adelaide had mugged the Swans in the first round, beating them by 90 points at Football Park in Adelaide. Welcome to coaching, Rodney Eade. A week later, at the SCG, Fremantle won by 29 points.

'Rodney's credibility was on the line,' Lockett recalled of that dark start to the 1996 season.

But Eade stayed calm. He believed in himself and so did the Swans board, who had backed him to replace the great Barassi. The players believed in him, too. And he believed in the players, knowing the quality at his disposal: a premier on-baller in Paul Kelly, years of experience in Roos, a hard-as-nails midfielder in Daryn Creswell. And, of course, Plugger.

Memories of the Fremantle loss at home were quickly erased with three wins in a row, including a gritty result against Richmond at Waverley Park in Melbourne. 'They were bullies,' Colless says. 'That was an important win.'

So, too, a thrilling draw against Essendon at the SCG in round 6. The Swans went on to win 13 of their next 16 matches, and the good people of Sydney loved them for it. As that season went on, the hottest ticket in town suddenly became a cold, plastic seat at the SCG.

'During that period, the SCG became known as "The Fortress",' Lockett said in *My Life*. 'We became unbeatable at home. Whenever a Swans game was in progress, the ground rocked like nothing I had ever experienced.'

Colless could feel the groundswell, too. 'Suddenly people started coming to the game in droves,' he says. 'Almost half the people who came that 1996 season had never seen a loss because that was their first season.'

For Roos, the feeling was surreal. He played his very first senior match in the VFL when Fitzroy met the Swans at the SCG in 1982. 'We had our arses kicked', he recalls of a 56-point loss. Now he was part of something altogether different.

'It's strange when you think that match was my first connection to that club and that ground,' says Roos, who went on to coach the Swans to the premiership in 2005. 'If you played for a Victorian club in the 1980s, you never travelled much, so playing on the SCG was different. It was an unusually shaped ground, but I loved coming there because of the history of the ground. You knew you were going to the very heart of sport.'

The Swans' emergence that 1996 season couldn't have been better for the AFL, which always had one eye on swinging fans away from the rugby codes. Indeed, that year, the Super League War was gathering momentum, ripping rugby league down the middle as media giant News Limited wrestled with the establishment of the Australian Rugby League for control of the game's best players.

'It was the perfect storm in many ways,' Roos says. 'The Swans, Lockett and the SCG itself, all coming together.'

Yes, Sydney was learning to love the Swans but the figure they truly adored was Lockett. 'Lockett was *the* story,' Colless says. 'Even rugby league people were fascinated by him.'

Lockett was a marketing department's dream. He wasn't the 'fool forward', as the flamboyant Warwick Capper called himself in his 2005 autobiography. Rather, he was a colossus standing strong and proud in the goal square, kicking bags of goals with impudence. He kicked 11 against Brisbane, 10 against North Melbourne, then a dozen against Richmond as the finals drew near.

In July, the Swans hosted Geelong. This one sold itself: Lockett at one end, Gary Ablett at the other. The crowd swelled to beyond 44,000. For safety reasons, officials opened up the adjacent Sydney Football Stadium and thousands watched on the big screen.

Lockett barely spoke to the growing throng of journalists at Swans training because he didn't have to. 'He was icy,' Michael Cowley laughs. 'He never had a great relationship with the media. It was because of the character he was, and the way he played. He'd had his fair share of negative stories over the years. But it was a fun time to cover the Swans because they were something different. Lockett had been so hated by the Sydney public. Then suddenly he became the legend, the hero, the icon.'

Eade wasn't overly concerned about the bigger picture. His focus was on the next game. But the coach could see how Plugger was infecting the city with Swans fever. 'The Sydney public, because of its roots in rugby league, liked a player with a big, physical presence like Plugger,' he says.

Eade was conscious about ensuring that the Swans weren't a one-man team, no matter how dominant Lockett had become. The full forward himself helped make this happen. 'His presence, which you can't measure, gave his teammates this incredible confidence,' Eade explains. 'He just had a magic effect on the rest of his team.'

In round 21, disaster struck against Essendon at the MCG. Lockett was chasing the Bombers' Gavin Wanganeen as he ran towards the wing in front of the Members Stand when a crash between defenders and a rather large Sydney Swans full forward ended with bodies sprawled on the ground. During the collision, Lockett turned to one side and felt his groin go 'pop'. He'd had a history of groin issues, but hadn't strained either one in years. At halftime, he required painkilling injections to finish the match but, as the week went on, he learned of the seriousness of the injury. Scans revealed he needed surgery on both groins. He also had two hernias that needed attention.

Lockett watched the final-round match against West Coast on a Saturday night at the SCG unsure if he would play again — not that season but ever. Sydney needed to win to claim the minor premiership, but the conditions were atrocious. Lightning struck one of the light towers before play, meaning the left forward pocket near the Members Stand was mostly shrouded in darkness. Still, the Swans triumphed by 35 points, setting up a qualifying final against eighth-placed Hawthorn at the SCG. Without Lockett, the Swans struggled to put the Hawks away but did so eventually via a late Creswell goal.

The victory sent them straight through to the preliminary final against Essendon, meaning Lockett and the medical staff had two weeks to do whatever they could to allow him to take the field. In the later years of his career, Lockett prided himself on ditching the hamburgers with the lot and the packets of cigarettes he'd inhaled when he was younger. But when he trotted out onto the SCG, he knew he was underdone. The plan was to make himself the target, draw in the Bombers' defenders and let his teammates do the heavy lifting.

It was a brutal match from the first bounce. Bombers' sharpshooter Matthew Lloyd was rushed to hospital with broken ribs. Wanganeen played on despite a bad shoulder injury. Nevertheless, Sheedy's men hung tough after taking an early lead. The Swans fought their way back to be a point clear at three-quarter time, but let the Bombers out to a two-goal advantage as the fulltime siren loomed.

Colless had been watching from a private suite on the lower level of the Brewongle Stand, hosting VIPs and sponsors. He wouldn't show it externally but he was pessimistic. 'For many, the Bombers were the premiership favourites,' he says. 'We hadn't played in a grand final for 51 years. I don't think we were pre-ordained to lose, but we weren't used to going that deep into the finals, so when they came at us it was hard to see us reeling them in.'

With four minutes to go, and Essendon clinging to a two-goal lead, Colless made his way down to the race. As he did so, he could hear the crowd screaming. Dale Lewis had kicked a goal. Sydney trailed by six points.

When the umpire restarted play from the centre-bounce, 2 minutes 9 seconds remained on the clock. The Sherrin found Kelly, who kicked it to left half-forward, where Simon Garlick handballed to Stuart Maxfield, whose left-foot kick found Lockett running strongly onto the ball in the pocket. Instead of lining up the shot himself from a narrow angle, Lockett had the presence of mind to place a centring kick towards Daryn Creswell, who marked in front. 'Creswell, 48 metres from home,' Seven's Sandy Roberts said in commentary. 'He kicks! It's there! He's got it! Scores are level! Listen to that roar!'

In the mad scramble of that final minute or so, the ball slipped out of the players' grasps as if it was a cake of soap. With 21 seconds to go, with the Swans pressing their backline, Essendon tried to clear but the ball found Wade Chapman, who marked. In an instant, he knew what to do. He kicked towards the top of the 50-metre arc.

'Look out!' shouted Roberts' fellow commentator Gerard Healy, a glamour player for the Swans from 1986 to 1990.

Look out? For whom? Lockett, of course. He gobbled the ball into his stomach, prompting the crowd into meltdown. For Kevin Sheedy to swear like a wharfie. There were 12 seconds left.

Suddenly, the entire SCG's focus became The Groin. Plugger's Groin. It pervaded everyone's thoughts as Lockett lined up his kick, but the big man himself wasn't concerned. He knew he'd get the distance, no matter what it did to his groin.

'Any score will do,' Roberts told the viewers. 'Otherwise we have extra time. Lockett ... the most important kick of his career. Any score will do ...'

Lockett moved in. Not the torp, as Roos had wondered. A drop punt ...

The explosion from the crowd told the story. The Swans were into the grand final. Before the great full forward could see the goal umpire's signal — point or goal — he was smothered by his jubilant teammates. 'Get off me!' he bellowed joyously. 'I can't breathe.' Then reality sank in. He was off to his first grand final. Only Derek Kickett among his teammates had previously played in a premiership decider. It wasn't until long after the match that Lockett, Eade, Roos and most of the players realised that Lockett had kicked a behind, not a goal. The crowd's reaction suggested he'd kicked a major. It didn't matter.

Sheedy was rocked by those last few minutes. He still is. 'One of the toughest moments I've had in footy,' he says. 'We had the game sewn up until the last three minutes. We should never have let it past our forward line.'

As a player, Sheedy represented Victoria against South Australia in an interstate match watched by a crowd of 20,752 at the SCG in 1974. 'That was the game when the game said, "We're coming,"' says Sheedy, who would become Greater Western Sydney's inaugural coach, forever the ultimate salesman for his sport.

But the venue had been an unhappy hunting ground for him. As a coach, his Bombers often met the wrath of Tom Hafey, Sheedy's hero and mentor at Richmond before Hafey went on to coach the Swans. 'Some of Hafey's greatest coaching was with Sydney in the 1980s,'

Sheedy says. 'His teams kicked over 30 goals three weeks in a row, and I was on the end of one of those terrible losses. In those days, the ground announcer played the team song every time they kicked a goal. I had to listen to it 31 times one day.'

But the loss in 1996 stung much more. Afterwards, a reporter approached him for comment: 'Sheeds, how do you feel?' Recalls Sheedy today: 'It's still the dumbest question I've ever been asked.'

Fans stormed the field on fulltime to congratulate the players. Soon after, they were trying to make their way into the Carroll-Kippax Room in the Noble Stand for the official post-match function. 'I'm not sure how many it was licensed to hold but I was just opening doors, letting people come in,' Colless says. 'The power brokers at the AFL were beside themselves.'

When the players eventually found their way into the dressing-room, Lockett plonked down next to teammate Craig O'Brien, who he'd also played alongside during some lean years at St Kilda.

'OB,' Lockett said, 'we're in the grand final.'

The Swans, of course, lost the following week to North Melbourne by 43 points.

'I don't think anyone was devastated that we lost,' Colless reflects. 'Two years before that, we'd been bottom for the third year in a row. We were an object of ridicule. People in Melbourne said it wouldn't work. People in Sydney were asking, 'What are you doing here?' You didn't feel threatened, but nobody took you seriously, nobody respected you.'

Now the Swans had the respect of the entire AFL. As time has passed, Eade has come to understand just how important Plugger's Point was.

'It was the point when the Swans were accepted in the city,' Eade says. 'That was the tipping point. Sydney, from that point, thought, "The Swans are ours." The way we won only added to the legend. You teach younger players the importance of persistence. That group had a tough mental edge to them. They hung in and got the result.'

Lockett himself felt immense pride in what he'd achieved but was typically deflective of the praise. 'I felt honoured to be the one who kicked that point,' he said in his book. 'However, as far as I was concerned, everyone who was there contributed to the win. The crowd played a massive role. The way the crowd lifted the team and the way the team lifted for the crowd was incredible.'

A few weeks after the grand final, Lockett underwent five surgeries: two groins, two hernias and an arthroscopy on one knee. As he limped around with the aid of a walking frame, he wondered out loud to more than a few people in his inner sanctum if he'd played his last game of football.

'As you get older, you have to be honest about whether you can keep up with the expectations,' he said. 'At the end of 1996, I just didn't know if I could.'

SITTING IN THE BACK row of the plane, Mark Doran looks out the window and over the Emerald City. He's flown from Melbourne on this day to record history. Now he's wondering what to say. How to capture it. The Channel Seven broadcaster is searching for the right words to say in the middle of the SCG later this day after Tony Lockett breaks Gordon Coventry's record of 1299 goals.

Commentators have different approaches to the moments that will be replayed forever. Bruce McAvaney, who would be one of the play-by-play callers for this match for Seven, rarely comes armed with pre-meditated lines. When he called Cathy Freeman's gold medal in the 400 metres at the Sydney Olympics, he made a point of *not* preparing what he'd say if Cathy won. Dennis Cometti, however, was the master of the one-liner, having an armoury of phrases to call on but delivering them as if they'd just come off the top of his head.

As the plane makes its descent towards Sydney, Doran decides to go with the McAvaney approach.

'No, I won't plan a glib line here,' he says to himself. 'I just want to say what happens.'

Doran was a St Kilda fan who adored Lockett. The great Robert DiPierdomenico was initially scheduled to work the boundary, but Doran pleaded with Seven's executive producer of football, Gordon Bennett, to send him instead.

'When he kicks it, I'll be the first one to him with the microphone,' Doran promised.

He laughs when he says this now. 'That was complete rubbish because you can't promise it,' Doran says. 'I just wanted to go — and I think Gordon knew it.'

Lockett first learned of Gordon Coventry — a Collingwood legend in the 1920s and '30s — after seeing large posters of him around VFL Park in Melbourne. Coventry retired in 1937 with 1299 goals, a highwater mark which Lockett never dreamed he would reach. Even in 1998, when he kicked 100 goals in a season for the sixth time in his career, he didn't think he'd break the record. Hawthorn's Jason

Dunstall was considered a better chance, until he broke down with a series of injuries.

By the end of that '98 season, Lockett was 24 short of the record. The following season, after he kicked three against West Coast in round 9, he was left with two to kick against Collingwood the next week at the SCG to equal Coventry's record.

Typically, Lockett hoped the media interest would've petered out after the West Coast match. 'What else was there to write?' he asked. Colless knew better.

'Regardless of what sport you followed, you knew this was a once-in-a-lifetime experience,' he says. 'He downplayed his records, but I suspect they're more important to him than he lets on. All players, deep down and no matter how grounded they are, talk about their record.'

Before the match, Lockett had a decision to make: wear his normal Puma King football boots or a souvenir pair of '1300' boots. Plugger was a superstitious footballer, wearing the one pair of jocks on match day for a whole season. He wore the same blue socks to each game before pulling on the red and white.

This time, however, Lockett broke with tradition. He wore the '1300s', and came out and quickly kicked two goals. With seconds remaining in the first quarter, Paul Kelly was awarded a free kick right on the boundary, in front of the Members Stand. Lockett sprinted away from Mal Michael, who was marking him that afternoon. Kelly eyed his close mate, kicked it over the fingertips of leaping Collingwood players, and Lockett marked. He was 35 metres out on a 45-degree angle.

'It wasn't just a matter of converting,' Lockett recalled. 'I've always considered the pocket in front of the Members Stand as the worst on the ground, so it wasn't going to be a pushover.'

He was about to take the kick when the quarter-time siren sounded, forcing him to stop and set himself again. In the commentary box, Bruce McAvaney was thinking about the right words to use — and then delivered them in a typically McAvaney manner.

Perfection.

'For 90 years, the Collingwood Football Club has held the record,' McAvaney said as Lockett steadied himself. 'For 62 years, it's stood at 1299. Will he write his name in the record book forever? With this kick?"

Sitting next to McAvaney was Jason Dunstall, who many had thought would haul in this mark ahead of Lockett.

'Come on Plugger,' Dunstall said under his breath but loud enough to be heard on the broadcast.

Lockett moved in, kicked … and threaded a wobbly kick between the posts.

'GOT IT!' Dunstall boomed.

That's when things got hectic. Fans jumped the fence as the ball left Lockett's foot. Several were standing next to the goal umpire when he signalled the major score.

It had long been the custom for Australian football crowds to run onto the field whenever a player kicked over 100 goals in a season, or reached a significant milestone, although the practice was being increasingly banned by the late 1990s. The Swans players formed a ring around Lockett after he kicked the 1300th goal as supporters in their hundreds, maybe thousands, streamed onto the ground.

'Aren't we privileged, to be a little part of it?' McAvaney continued. 'A remarkable player. However long we play the game, he will be remembered forever. Who knows who the greatest of them all is? But we can tell you now that nobody in the great game has kicked as many as this man. He deserves to stand on the highest peak.'

Somewhere in the mass of bodies was Doran, right behind Paul Kelly but not close enough to Lockett to interview him, as he'd promised.

'Mark Doran, can you hear me?' McAvaney asked.

'Yes, I can!' Doran screeched. 'I'm right in the middle of this huddle! This is unbelievable! I had no idea what I'd be feeling here, but I can tell you this is the most amazing thing I've ever done.'

The Swans players slowly edged towards the race, and then took Plugger off the field, down into the sanctuary of the dressing-room so the ground could be cleared, which took some time.

Reaching the milestone proved to be a distraction for Lockett and the Swans. After leading by 37 points at quarter-time, they allowed Collingwood to kick three of the next four goals to cut the lead to 17 at halftime. Lockett didn't kick a goal in the second term.

'What about you?' Eade said during the halftime break, pointing at Lockett. 'You've broken the record and now you've just put the cue back in the rack.'

'I remember it vividly,' Eade recalls now. 'I never usually said anything to Tony — but I did on this occasion. His eyes rolled back into his head and steam came out of his ears.'

The Swans went on to win the match by 51 points with Lockett booting nine goals.

Above: Wally Lewis (No. 6) dances with delight and Queensland halfback Mark Murray (right) looks on as referee Barry Gomersall confirms prop Greg Dowling has just scored a miracle try in the deciding State of Origin match of 1984.

Below: A year later, NSW captain Steve Mortimer is chaired from the SCG after NSW's first Origin series win. The other triumphant Blues are (from left) Peter Wynn, Noel Cleal, Wayne Pearce, Pat Jarvis and Garry Jack.

The moment on June 6, 1999, when Tony Lockett kicked his 1300th goal, breaking Gordon Coventry's longstanding VFL/AFL record.

Above: Another famous Lockett
kick ... the behind in 1996 that gave
the Sydney Swans a one-point win
over Essendon and put them into
their first grand final in 51 years.

Right: Steve Waugh strides onto the
SCG on January 3, 2003, day two
of the fifth Ashes Test of 2002–03,
knowing he needs a big score to
prolong his career.

The square cut for four that took Steve Waugh past 10,000 Test runs.

The view from the Hill after Waugh hit the last ball of the day for four, to complete one of the SCG's most memorable hundreds.

The SCG shines brightly as Silverchair take to the stage at the Wave Aid Tsunami Relief Concert on 29 January 2005.

Two weeks later, Missy Higgins, Donna Simpson (The Waifs), Peter Garrett (Midnight Oil), Phil Jamieson (Grinspoon) and Ben Gillies (Silverchair) were among the artists who returned to the Members Pavilion for the handing over of funds raised from the event.

Daniel Johns (left) and Nick Cave (above) were just two of Wave Aid's headline acts.

Peter Garrett takes an excellent catch during a celebrity Twenty20 game staged at the SCG in 2009 to support the Victorian Bushfire Appeal. Garrett was fielding on the same hallowed turf on which his great-grandfather, Tom Garrett, performed with distinction from the 1870s to the 1890s.

Above left: Phillip Hughes celebrates his century for NSW in the 2008 Shield final. Above right: Hughes batting for South Australia at the SCG on November 25, 2014.

The 63 bats placed on the field, one for each run Hughes scored in his final innings.

Mourners gather near the centre wicket, prior to Hughes' funeral being shown on the SCG's video screens.

Above: NSW and Australian off-spinner Nathan Lyon stops outside the home dressing-room to read and re-read the plaque placed there to honour his much-loved late teammate.

Left: David Warner reaches an emotional Test hundred against India at the SCG six weeks after Phillip Hughes' death. It was Warner's first innings at the ground since the accident.

The scenes that took place at fulltime aren't easily forgotten: Lockett in the back of a convertible car, holding the game ball aloft, with the SCG heaving with jubilant fans.

In the rooms, Kelly wore a knowing smile for the assembled media. 'I always liked to think that I'd be the one who would give it to him,' he said.

Lockett laughed about the quality of the history-defining kick.

'It was a shocking kick,' he said. 'It just floated through. But if you are going to duff it, you might as well duff it straight.'

Hours later, the players made their way into a special function at the Sydney Aussie Rules Social Club in Kings Cross. Jimmy Barnes performed, but before he did Kelly wanted to make a special presentation.

'For a guy who has everything, here's the cue you put in the rack at halftime,' Kelly said, handing over a pool cue.

In the end, Mark Doran did cement his place in history with a famous line. After Lockett marked Kelly's kick, Doran found himself directly behind him. He couldn't have been better placed to be the first person to rush the ground and shove a microphone under Lockett's nose.

But when the goal sailed through, he didn't. 'I paused just for a second,' Doran recalls. 'I didn't want to be first there. I didn't want to spoil it. It wasn't about me. So by the time I got there I wasn't close enough to talk to him at all. That was my doing. I should've been there and what a moment I would've had. But a part of me thinks it's wonderful that I didn't.'

He knew Lockett well enough to understand how he would've been feeling with so many people around him. 'Tony would've hated it,' Doran says. 'It's not why he played the game.'

As Lockett left the field, McAvaney crossed to Doran again and gave the boundary rider an opportunity to deliver the line he'd been contemplating on the plane earlier that day.

'If anybody ever says to you there's no passion about AFL in Sydney,' Doran said, his voice breaking with emotion, 'tell them to have a look at this.'

LOCKETT WAS APPROACHED REPEATEDLY for this chapter. He agreed to speak through a third party — former Swans chairman Andrew Pridham — but didn't return calls or texts.

When I told Roos I hadn't heard from Lockett, he chuckled. 'Nobody has,' he said. 'That's him.'

Which is OK. It adds to the mystique of the big man. While you could assume it was Lockett fobbing off yet another member of the media, it was explained to me by more than a few people who know him that Lockett is simply shy.

He retired at the end of the 1999 season with 1357 goals. He made a brief return in 2002, playing three more games and adding three more goals to his tally. Then he retired for good, having topped the AFL's season goal-kicking list on four occasions. In 2006, he was inducted into the AFL's Hall of Fame. In 2015, he was elevated to legend status.

But the numbers explain only part of what the man achieved and the legacy he left behind. Paul Roos is as qualified as anyone to talk about what Lockett did for the Swans and their relationship with the SCG.

Roos took over as coach from Rodney Eade in 2002, and coached the Swans to the premiership in 2005. That season, in the semi-final against Geelong on a wet, windy night at the SCG, Nick Davis kicked four goals in the final quarter to keep the grand final dream alive.

'I've continually said that's the best quarter of finals footy I've ever seen someone play,' Roos said. 'But Tony put the Swans on the map. Getting Tony was massive at a time when the club was down and out. His contribution to the game, to the Swans, to where it is now, is immeasurable. If he doesn't come to the Swans, and they don't make the grand final in 1996, and he doesn't kick that point, there's no way the AFL competition would've been advanced as it is now. That's how significant his role was.'

Perhaps the most astonishing achievement was the manner in which he won over the Swans faithful. One season, a piglet was released onto the field, mocking him. The next, he was drilling torpedoes directly at the Swans' greatest supporter, Kenny Williams. In the years that followed, though, they became great mates.

'When I look back, it was silly kicking the ball at Kenny because if it happened to hit him ... you know what I mean,' Lockett said. 'I am a spur-of-the-moment type of individual. You're out there and it's competitive and, yeah, you get worked up. I got to know Kenny pretty well. A more passionate supporter you couldn't find.'

As for Plugger, the piglet, he also refused to speak to me for this book. There are two stories about how he came to be on the sacred turf of the SCG that afternoon in 1993. Swans defender Scott Watters has said a bunch of players met a random pig farmer in a bar and they jokingly urged him to let a pig onto the field when they next played St Kilda. Years later, a mystery caller to SEN Radio in Melbourne insisted he was the one behind the plot, claiming several Swans players, clubs and even some senior football administrators were in on the prank.

Lockett did make a rare public appearance at the Swans' end-of-season presentation in 2014. He was there to present another imported lethal spearhead, Lance Franklin, with the Coleman Medal.

Master of ceremonies Adam Spencer rattled off Lockett's achievements with the Swans, including Plugger's Point and breaking the Coventry Record.

He looked at Lockett for a response. Silence. Lockett looked at him, smiling, before saying a very Tony Lockett thing, as you'd expect from a man who was only ever worried about what he did on the field.

'What do you want me to say?'

As always with Plugger, no words were required.

CHAPTER 8

Don't Be Home Before Six

Steve Waugh

PERHAPS NO SPORTING MOMENT elicits the question, 'Where were you?' more than Steve Waugh's last-ball-of-the-day, career-saving, heart-in-throat century in the fading light of the SCG on Friday, January 3, 2003, on the second day of the fifth Ashes Test against England. The official crowd figure that day was 41,931 — the biggest day-two crowd at the venue since 1975 — but there must have been three times that number if those who claim to have been there actually were.

Where were you? I was sitting at the back of the Noble Stand, slowly getting sunburnt from the glare off the green shine of the outfield. Another friend was sitting on a beach in Noosa with a growing crowd of strangers huddled around the radio on his beach towel as the final over was bowled, a roar coming from the nearby surf club with each run. Another was going bonkers in his car at a set of traffic lights, overcome with excitement and ignoring the green light as impatient people in the cars behind him kept honking.

Yet nothing quite tops the story, told by Waugh himself, of the man who was so excited, so overcome with emotion, that he literally popped an eyeball in celebration.

'One guy who was in hospital, hooked up to all this equipment, was about to have an operation,' Waugh recalls. 'He got so excited when I got the hundred that he jumped up in the air, ripped the connections out … and detached a retina. He was in there for an operation and wasn't supposed to move around but he forget about it and got caught up in the moment. He had to have a second operation. There are hundreds of those stories. I get them almost every day from different people telling me what they were doing when I got the century. It's quite amazing.'

Any others stand out?

'There was a race meeting in country Victoria,' Waugh continues. 'They were about to go into the starting gates. They stopped the race, pulled the horses out and played the commentary of the last over through the loudspeaker. I hit four off the last ball, the crowd erupted, the horses went back into the stalls and the race got underway.

'I've heard that many stories you could almost write a book on what people were doing at that time. It's one of those moments that people can relate to. It means it's special to them, which is nice for me.'

Surely he gets tired of talking about it.

'Not at all,' he says. 'It seems like a lifetime ago. But if people want to talk about it, I'm always happy to engage and hear their story. The fans were part of my journey that year. I was doing it tough, and the support of the people got me through those times. That hundred is theirs as much as mine.'

When Waugh flayed England off-spinner Richard Dawson through extra cover, the red cherry bouncing over the rope and into the fence in front of the Ladies Stand, and the crowd erupted, it was the release of a year's worth of tension surrounding the Australian captain. He'd copped it from the selectors, the media, past players and even himself, because no matter which way anyone dissects it, Waugh's lack of runs along with his age — 37 at the time — meant something had to give sooner or later. The Australian Test team had become so dominant on Waugh's watch that it was almost becoming harder to get dropped from the side than to get into it. But success could only hide poor scores for so long.

FOR MOST OF 2002, the Test positions of Steve and his twin brother Mark had been the subject of great debate. That Australia's Test team and, to a lesser degree, our one-day side were steamrolling all before them could only silence the critics — and hide scratchy individual innings with the bat — for so long. When Steve was dropped as one-day captain in February 2002 to make way for Ricky Ponting, it only heightened the belief held by some observers that the end was near.

A three-Test series against Pakistan, starting at the beginning of October, would be an ideal way for the Waugh twins to keep the critics at bay. The series was being played in Sri Lanka and the United Arab Emirates because of ongoing political unrest in Pakistan and neighbouring Afghanistan. On the eve of the opening match in Colombo, Waugh was asked about his future.

'I want to keep playing as long as I'm enjoying it and improving as a cricketer,' he said, as recalled in his book *Never Say Die*. 'I don't want to put an end date on it ... If you put an end date on it, you play accordingly ... I never thought about when I was going to start playing for Australia and I'm not going to think about when I'm going to finish.'

Australia swept the series — the sixth time they'd done so under Waugh's captaincy. He scored 103 in the Third Test, but Mark's numbers were again skinny. When the team returned to Sydney, a healthy media pack was waiting for them.

'The English will probably hope that we have a couple of changes in our side, but it really depends on what the selectors want and what they see as the future,' Steve told them. 'I think when you are running a business and being successful you shouldn't just throw a couple of guys out and replace them for the sake of it.'

Steve survived the chop. Mark didn't; he was dropped for the first Ashes Test at the Gabba with the selectors opting instead for Darren Lehmann. He announced his immediate retirement from international cricket.

If the continuing debate about the captain's future was a distraction, it wasn't reflected in the way Australia went about their business. They required no more than a total of 11 days of play in Brisbane, Adelaide and Perth to retain the urn. It was the eighth straight Ashes series victory that Steve Waugh had been involved in. The victory that sealed the series was his 32nd Test win as captain, equalling the Australian record of Allan Border.

But he'd merely 'teased' the scorers with the bat, scoring 7 and 12 at the Gabba, 34 from 40 balls at Adelaide Oval, and 53 at the WACA. Suddenly, the narrative around the skipper took on a life of its own, with the Sydney Test suddenly earmarked as the likely venue for his farewell. Sure, it had a nice symmetry about it — finishing up in his home city, a perfect coronation for the Ashes-winning team and his own career — but Waugh had no plans for calling it a day.

The Ashes were retained on December 1, the earliest this had ever occurred in a series in Australia. A day later, the selection panel, headed by chairman Trevor Hohns, turned the knife just a little more: it omitted Waugh from its provisional 30-man squad for the 2003 World Cup. 'I was very disappointed not to be considered in the top 30 players,' Waugh grizzled to reporters. 'I was hurt by it, and I want to prove them wrong.'

On December 6, in a one-day game at the SCG, Waugh belted 24 runs from 12 balls, including three sixes in five balls, to steer NSW to victory over England. During the match, people in the crowd who had bought pies noticed stickers on the plastic wrappers. 'Pick Steve Waugh now!' they declared. The stickers had been placed there by catering staff. As NSW surged to victory, the fans chanted his name.

Waugh wasn't in a hurry to leave the building and it was hard to find someone who wanted him to leave the building. Indeed, the selectors would need a crowbar to get him out of the building: he wanted to force his way onto the plane to South Africa for the World Cup and, beyond that, to lead Australia on upcoming Test tours of the Caribbean and India.

'Waugh can only keep winning, trying to score runs and wait,' Peter Roebuck wrote in the *Sydney Morning Herald*. 'Like all players, he does not trust the selectors. It is not their job to be popular or close with any Australian cricketer, no matter how distinguished. Over the years, Australian selectors have acted early rather than late, and it has been a strength. Waugh must fear that they will tell him before Sydney that the game is up. Observers believe he has already been told this Sydney Test will be his last. His fighting talk suggests otherwise.'

Hohns, a former Test spinner, spun the narrative in favour of his besieged panel in the lead-up to the Boxing Day Test in Melbourne. 'At the moment Stephen has our support until the Sydney Test,' Hohns told reporters. 'The decision is then up to him whether he wants to continue or not. If he does, he will be judged on form, like any other player. He has our support for the time being. There has been no push. The decision is entirely Stephen's at this stage.'

At this stage?

At the moment?

These were throwaway phrases but loaded with ambiguity. If Hohns thought this statement would ease the pressure, he was mistaken. It put all the heat back on Waugh. Talkback crackled about the issue of his future and if Sydney would be a suitable place to finish up. Sydney's broadsheet newspapers took various stances but leaned towards moving Waugh on, while the Murdoch-owned tabloid *Daily Telegraph* smelled the breeze among its working-class readers and fell in firmly behind Waugh. The 'Save Our Steve' campaign was underway.

An old pro at the crease, Waugh was also equally adept at turning public sentiment his way. He played a straight bat to Hohns' remarks, taking the higher ground. 'I've never asked for a guarantee, nor did I want a guarantee,' he said. 'I've always played my cricket under the belief that you pick your best 11 players and that's never changed. I think it's wrong to give players guarantees. If I'm one of the XI then that's fair enough. I know I'm one of the best 11 players.' It was, to that point, his finest stroke of the summer.

Much of the debate wasn't so much stirred by the media as by a long line of former players prepared to offer their take on whether Waugh should stay or go.

Former Test spinner Gavin Robertson: 'Stephen Waugh has a bigger public following than any player in memory. He's the people's hero, not the Australian Cricket Board's hero, and I don't believe his mass of admirers will be satisfied with having a selectors' decision dumped on them.'

Former Test fast bowler Geoff Lawson: 'A Sydney finish would be perfect, but cricket does not always provide perfect finishes. David Boon, Ian Healy and Mark Waugh were all given a message, because it is difficult to make the decision yourself, and I would be surprised if Steve Waugh was any different.'

Former Test captain Mark Taylor: 'I don't think the selectors will take too much notice about what Steve Waugh's said about going to India. They won't worry about what Steve Waugh wants to do. They'll be worried about what's best for the Australian cricket team.'

At the media conference two days before the Boxing Day Test, there was only one topic the reporters wanted to focus on. They bombarded Waugh with questions about his future.

'Any questions about the Test, guys?' ACB media manager Brian Murgatroyd asked. No, not really. There was only one story in town.

In Australia's first innings, Waugh rattled up 77, taking on England fast bowler Steve Harmison as if they were playing a one-dayer, stepping back and punching him over point for four runs. But in the second innings, he was all at sea against Harmison and his fellow quick, Andy Caddick, being caught off a no-ball and then lucky to survive a late appeal for a caught behind. He was dismissed for 14, caught in the slips, his Test career apparently in tatters.

'We all agreed he was gone,' Kerry O'Keeffe, who was calling the match for ABC Radio, remembers. 'He looked late on the ball, he was 37, it looked like the twilight had arrived. It later emerged that he'd been suffering from a migraine.'

Former Test captain Ian Chappell understood the impasse Waugh and the selectors had reached. Here was an immovable captain not known for conceding an inch when at the crease or in the field at loggerheads with a selection panel with one eye on the future, as the guardians of Australian cricket, trying to ignore a growing tide of public sentiment washing up against them.

'Waugh is a man who has made a glittering career out of being stubborn,' Chappell wrote in his column for London's *Daily Telegraph*. 'If he was pounded with short-pitched deliveries he dug in deeper to defy the fast men and wear them down; if his team were in trouble his concentration sharpened, his defence tightened, and his resolve increased and a big score usually followed; if critics said he was struggling with the bat, it would motivate him once again and a substantial knock was virtually guaranteed. Now the selectors are hinting it's time to go. Is his attitude likely to change? They say a leopard never changes its spots.'

The media conference staged underneath the Bradman Stand the day before the Sydney Test was packed with reporters, not all of them your typical cricket roundsmen. Waugh was the story of the day, the summer. There was also a sense of finality: this could be the last time this Australian captain would be fronting the media before an international match.

It was to be Waugh's 156th Test, equalling the world record of Allan Border. He needed one more century to equal Sir Donald Bradman's total of 29, the most by an Australian player. The gravity of the moment was too tantalising to ignore.

'What's been the most defining moment in your career?' a reporter asked, a question usually reserved for retiring players.

'Well, perhaps it will happen in this game,' Waugh famously replied.

As the Sydney Test grew closer, rival publications seemed to pick sides. You were either with Waugh or against him. The man himself could see right through it, as he later observed in *Never Say Die*: 'The "Save Our Steve" campaign mounted by the News Limited tabloids in the days leading up to the Test was, on face value, nice to have, but, in reality, I was just the meat in the sandwich. The rival paper's slant seemed just as persuasive the other way. Each day produced another headline and many more opinions. It was like watching a novel unfold, with twists and turns everywhere.'

The *Australian*'s Malcolm Conn was a fearless columnist who'd blown apart the biggest stories in Australian cricket. He wrote: 'Steve Waugh will try to enter what should be his retirement Test in a bubble, determined to avoid all outside pressure and emotions as Australia aim for a 5–0 clean sweep of England in Sydney.'

Waugh had first come to the SCG 30 years earlier, when he and his teammates crammed into the old ute belonging to one of his first cricket coaches for the drive from Panania in Sydney's south-west to watch a Sheffield Shield match between NSW and South Australia. 'The SCG was just this magical place,' he recalls. 'Sitting on the Hill, seeing how big the crowd was, you'd look across at the Members, the Ladies Stand, the Bob Stand. You could hear the willow on the bat. It was like going to another place, another world, and we loved it.'

Sitting alongside him was his under-10s teammate Brad McNamara, who developed into a capable medium-pace bowler and stubborn batsmen who claimed Sheffield Shield titles with NSW as Steve and Mark made their way into the Australian side. Waugh once described him as 'one of my favourite teammates I've ever played with' but they were more than that. When Waugh married his childhood sweetheart Lynette, McNamara was best man.

When McNamara's 16 years as a cricket professional came to an end, he transferred his knowledge to television, becoming a producer with Nine's Wide World of Sports and then, in 2008, executive producer of its all-important cricket coverage. He didn't like what he saw at the MCG, regardless of the migraine that had made it near impossible for Waugh to concentrate. McNamara was his greatest supporter. His closest ally. But even McNamara could see the end was nearing, no matter how much he didn't want to admit it.

'It looked like the dismissal of a player in his twilight,' McNamara recalls. 'When the short stuff worries them, it's a tell-tale sign that they're near the end of their career. Steve always played short stuff awkwardly, but he wasn't getting knocked over by it. Now he was and it was starting to look like this was the end.'

On New Year's Day, on the eve of the final Test of the Ashes series, the lifelong friends crossed paths at the SCG. Just as McNamara was making sure everything was in place for his work over the next few days, so too was Waugh with a last-minute net session ahead of the game that would determine the course of his career.

'How you feeling?' McNamara asked.

'I'm hitting the ball well,' Waugh replied with usual casualness. 'I just can't score any runs. I'm going to take them on in this Test, mate. Anything's possible.'

MATTHEW HAYDEN STORMS UP the steps, past his teammates sitting on the balcony and then inside the dressing-room. *BANG!* Some poor inanimate object has felt the opener's wrath for falling lbw to Andy Caddick, the first Australian wicket of the innings.

Shane Warne, who isn't playing in this match because of a shoulder injury, walks out the door onto the balcony and chuckles. 'Matthew's kicked a chair so hard his foot's stuck in it!' he reports.

Earlier in the day, Australia had dismissed England for 362. They were cruising along nicely at 0–36 before Hayden's dismissal, but his departure creates a stir in the dressing-room. As Ricky Ponting makes his way out into the middle, Steve Waugh begins his pre-innings ritual.

First, he puts on his thigh pad. Then his protector. He distracts himself from what's happening in the middle, reading a newspaper or watching the coverage on television. But this day is different. He knows it. He can feel it in the sea of faces all around the ground, each of them here to see if he can save his career.

Ponting is coming back sooner than anybody expected, caught behind by England gloveman Alec Stewart, again off the bowling of Caddick, who is having plenty of fun on a deteriorating SCG pitch, a worrying sign on the afternoon on the second day of play. Waugh puts on all his equipment, bar his gloves and helmet. Other essentials for a trip to the middle are added: lucky red rag — check; wad of chewing gum to work like a piston with jaw — check; steely Iceman-like demeanour, ready to prove the critics wrong — check, check, check.

Waugh sits on the balcony in front of the home dressing-room, no longer trying to distract himself from the match he's playing in. Instead, he's sitting in silence, scanning the play, getting a read on the opposition. But his mind wanders and conjures sinister mental images of a career-ending duck, the shoulders of 40,000 fans in the SCG dropping in unison in disappointment.

Waugh has a meeting with himself. 'Wake up to yourself,' he thinks. 'You've done it a hundred times before. Just trust yourself.'

Justin Langer top-edges Caddick to deep fine leg and Waugh's focus suddenly sharpens. The ball hangs in the air for an eternity before dropping into Matthew Hoggard's hands. As soon as the dismissal is confirmed, Waugh is up and out of his seat, the adrenaline carrying him down the steps of the Members Pavilion and sling-shotting him onto the ground well before Langer reaches the fence.

Sitting in ABC Radio's commentary box, Kerry O'Keeffe is channelling his inner Eminem. No, seriously, he is. Before play, he imparted to fellow commentators Jim Maxwell, Jonathan Agnew and Peter Roebuck the words from the American rapper's chart-topping song *Lose Yourself* … 'The moment, you own it, you better never let it go.'

'You only get one shot,' is Eminem's message. 'Steve Waugh has one shot, one opportunity to save himself and that's today,' O'Keeffe tells listeners as Waugh trots to the middle. 'This is his "lose yourself" moment.'

The crowd knows it, too. They are giving Waugh a standing ovation, as a tide of unfettered support for their embattled captain sweeps over the entire ground. It is 3.26pm on a warm Friday. Australia have suffered a mini collapse, teetering at 3–56. It's a moment Waugh relishes — a dogfight, a challenge. The dual challenges of reviving the innings and his own career are now at hand.

Getting to the middle early is an old Waugh trick. His aim is to get there before the field is set and to show the opposition he's going to be batting on his terms, not theirs. But he also wants to shut out the din of the crowd. Emotion and adrenaline won't play the shots for him. He takes guard on centre stump, walks down the wicket for some signature gardening, patting down raised parts of the pitch, real and imaginary, before making his way back for the first ball.

England captain Nasser Hussain does exactly as Waugh predicts, bringing on fast bowler Steve Harmison to terrorise the Australian skipper, just as he's done all series. Hussain knows that the game situation is at a stage where Waugh is at his most dangerous: 'three-fa-stuff-all' instead of 'three-fa-plenty'.

Harmison bangs in a couple of bouncers, which Waugh ducks under with relative comfort. Hoggard is brought into the attack and Waugh clips the medium pacer off his pads. No running required, an easy four.

Deep within the confines of the dressing-room, Adam Gilchrist is rummaging through his kit bag, getting ready as the No. 7 batsman. He can't see his captain's confident start but certainly hears it as the crowd oohs and ahhs every Waugh stroke. His teammates on the balcony report the good news: the skipper looks good. So far.

The umpires call for the tea break and, while he's only been in the middle for 15 minutes, Waugh's bursting with confidence. He and Damien Martyn have moved the score to 3–67. Waugh's on 9, and hungry for more in the final session.

He doesn't jog out to the middle after the tea break. Instead, he looks around the ground, drinking it all in. His name is daubed on multiple banners, too many to read. He doesn't want to be distracted by their words of encouragement, but he's savvy enough to know when to ride their energy. To make them a part of the innings. This is going to be one such afternoon.

Harmison and Caddick work in tandem, peppering him with short-pitched deliveries, but Waugh handles them with ease. His defence is sound, he's leaving the balls that need to be left. There's a half-appeal for lbw. Another delivery thuds into his body but it doesn't hurt. Rather, it enlivens him, a wake-up call to the job at hand. He picks off Caddick for two runs before spanking three fours.

His colleagues and fans alike joke that Steve Waugh is made of ice. On this afternoon, he's bullet-proof. His weaknesses become his strengths. All series, Hussain has used Harmison as his attack dog, but this time Waugh uses the pace of the fast bowler to his advantage, whipping a delivery to backward square for four. Waugh pokes his head into the 40s.

Andrew Denton is sitting on the balcony outside the Australian dressing-room, wedged between the intense Justin Langer and the slightly more relaxed 12th man Brad Hogg. The TV and radio personality is there after buying a 'Test day experience' at a charity auction some months earlier. He was originally allocated a day later in the match, but politely asked if it could be moved forward because he was flying to Canada in a few days' time. Little did he know when making his winning bid that he'd be given premium inside access to one of the landmark days in the history of Australian sport.

Despite the pressure, Waugh was determined to give Denton the complete experience of being part of the Australian cricket team's inner sanctum. On the morning of the first day of play, Denton attended the team's net session and was chatting to coach John Buchanan when batsman Martin Love smoked a straight drive so close to Denton's head it moved the hairs on one of his ears. Waugh insisted Denton join the slips cordon for catching practice. To Denton, it showed that the skipper was focused on the routines of the game. There were no signs he was under additional pressure; he appeared as shrewd and discerning as ever.

But as the shadows begin to lengthen across the SCG, and the mood around the ground fizzes with anticipation, the mood in the dressing-room changes with it.

Drinks are called and one of the coaching staff nudges Denton.

'Why don't you take the drinks out again?' Duncan Kerr asks him.

A chance to be part of a moment in history? Denton doesn't hesitate, walking out into the middle of a sporting venue he's admired his entire life. He takes it all in … the crowd, including the Barmy Army on the seats where once had been the Hill, the English players gathered near one part of the wicket, and the sight of Stephen Rodger Waugh, Australian icon.

'How you going?' Denton asks Waugh.

'I'm enjoying myself,' Waugh replies, using his fraying red rag to wipe away the sweat pouring from his brow.

Earlier in the day, during the drinks break in the morning session, Waugh had purposely spilt some water on Denton's foot.

'You're now initiated as 12th man,' Waugh smiles.

Denton chuckles at that memory. But here in the late afternoon, for the first time in his life, he is lost for words. He doesn't want to say anything out of line but feels as if he should say *something*. But what? The moment is passing, the time to return to the dressing-room fast approaching. Denton says the first thing that pops into his head.

'Don't be home before six,' he quips, and then turns and walks away.

'That was the perfect thing to say,' Kerr tells him.

Waugh reaches his half-century with a piercing cover drive from a Caddick half-volley, through the gap and smoking along the super-fast outfield into the boundary rope. While it's his third fifty in as many Tests, he understands better than anyone that the job is far from done. He and Martyn need to keep the scoreboard ticking over, and also occupy the crease. But when Martyn is out for 26, caught at wide mid-on, and then Martin Love falls for a duck, the match changes complexion once more.

On his day, Adam Gilchrist is the most devastating batsman in the world. No player hits the ball with such purity and assuredness. But this is the captain's afternoon and Gilchrist knows it. Waugh dances down the pitch and effortlessly pushes Richard Dawson through midwicket for another four runs.

So far, Waugh's innings has been chanceless. Now, on 64, he stands alongside Gilchrist awaiting a potential run out decision from third umpire Simon Taufel. Waugh tells Gilchrist not to worry — he's certain his bat has slid beyond the crease in time — and when the green light is signalled high in the Bradman Stand it isn't just a signal that he's not out but that history beckons.

Waugh went into the game needing 69 runs to become just the third batsman, after Allan Border and Indian great Sunil Gavaskar, to reach 10,000 Test runs. He hasn't allowed himself to think about it too much, but when the landmark gets within a boundary, he wants to knock it over and move on. He shuffles to the legside and cuts a ball from Dawson that is neither short nor wide for four. The crowd roars, Waugh raises his bat briefly to acknowledge them, and briefly thinks to himself: 'Maybe this is my day.'

In the dressing-room, Waugh's teammates are already thinking as much. With every signature backfoot cover drive, every effortless turn of the wrists for a run, they sense something special is brewing. 'He's gonna to do it,' Langer oozes. 'He's gonna do it, he's gonna get a hundred today.'

With the captain's score now on 76, Harmison thunders in, bowling around the wicket, once again reverting to the short stuff to unsettle the batsman as he had done in Melbourne. Waugh leans back, winds back the clock, and punches him through the covers. The crowd roars again.

Up in the Channel Nine commentary box, Brad McNamara's mind is racing with competing thoughts. After a relatively quiet first half of the day, the match has sprung to life. McNamara is torn between the fact his besieged best friend is on his way to a career-defining century and the looming 6pm news. He understands that nothing is more imperative to a free-to-air network than its nightly news bulletin, and it requires something special to push it back, especially for the best part of an hour, which seems likely. The problem is England's meandering over-rate: they are a long way off achieving their required overs for the day. McNamara does the sums in his head. Six o'clock is fast approaching, the light remains clear and Waugh is scoring at nearly a run a minute.

Discussions start bouncing between Nine's news director Paul Fenn and chief executive David Gyngell, who is also talking to Kerry Packer, who is watching the cricket at his property at Ellerston in the Hunter Valley.

'This is going to be close,' McNamara declares to the commentary team of Richie Benaud, Billy Lawry, Tony Greig, Ian Chappell, Ian Healy and Mark Taylor. The thick glass of the commentary box shuts out the roar of the crowd, but the coterie of cricketing greats can fully sense the occasion through their earpieces, feeding off the cheers and the sound from the stump microphones of the players in the middle.

McNamara takes a moment to step outside and onto the balcony, standing near the cameras trained straight down the wicket over the bowler's arm. That's when the outpouring of support for the captain, willing him to triple figures, truly hits him.

The word comes back from Gyngell: stay with the cricket. *Nine News* and *A Current Affair* can wait.

STEVE WAUGH IS NOW 80 not out, and for one of the few times in his career, Adam Gilchrist is playing second fiddle. He's on 8. That's about to change. For some reason, England's bowlers start bowling short to him. 'Don't play the hook shot,' Gilchrist tells himself. 'Don't chase the short ball.' But he ignores his own advice, slashes away, hooks gleefully, and before anyone seems to notice he's raced to 42, the tempo of his innings suddenly at limited-over pace.

By the second-last over of the day, Waugh has reached 88. He starts to make some calculations in his head as Hoggard prepares to bowl. Does he dig in, to make sure he doesn't throw his wicket away ... or score 12 runs from the next 12 balls.

Death or glory? He barely wastes a second considering it.

Let's go for it.

Waugh slashes at the first delivery, gets some bat on it, and it flies just out of the reach of the slips but fine enough to beat the third-man fieldsman for four. Now he's in the 90s. His mind drifts to the 10 times he's been dismissed just short of a hundred, but only briefly.

Three balls later, he glances the delivery down the legside to backward square, scampering through for two runs. But it was tight, as he turned 'blind' on Harmison's throw and had to dive to make sure he got home in time.

Two balls left in the over. Waugh hatches another plan: hit a four then a single to retain the strike for the final six deliveries. Instead, he pushes a single to mid-on, leaving Gilchrist on strike for the last ball of the over. Hoggard bowls short, Gilchrist ducks, and tucks his bat under his wing, ready to walk from the field unbeaten with his skipper.

That's when it hits Gilchrist: 'Oh, it's not the last over.' That's when he realises that he's miscalculated. There's one over left for the captain, on strike, to score the five runs he needs to reach three figures.

As the fieldsmen and umpires move to their positions, Waugh makes his way to the striker's end, passing wicketkeeper Alec Stewart.

'Do you write your own script these days?' Stewart says with a grin. It eases Waugh's mind — for about a second.

Hussain keeps Dawson on for the last over, perhaps a curious decision given the off-spinner's lack of experience. But Waugh respects the bowler, and the situation, carefully defending the first three deliveries.

Around the ground, the tension is palpable. In the ABC Radio commentary box, respected BBC caller Jonathan Agnew has been joined by Kerry O'Keeffe, who's replaced Peter Roebuck, who's frantically rewriting his copy for the next day's *Sydney Morning Herald*. It's a similar scene in the nearby press box, where those who had been etching the words onto Waugh's tombstone are now under tightening deadline pressure as they write about his glorious resurrection. Most first editions of the newspaper are 'off the stone' before 7.30pm. Now Waugh is making *them* sweat.

'You know, I've been incredibly privileged to have seen a number of theatrical occasions, events, dramas, whatever, doing this job,' Agnew tells O'Keeffe. 'But this is the most gripping of all.'

Dawson bowls his fourth delivery of the final over. It's short and Waugh gobbles it up, punching it towards deep point, forcing Caddick's long limbs to chase after it. The batsmen run three, which takes Waugh off strike.

'Now, there are two balls remaining,' Agnew tells the listeners all around the ground and the nation, including the jockeys behind the barriers at a race meeting in country Victoria and the bloke about to have surgery, who's supposed to be staying completely still but cannot.

'Steve Waugh is at the non-striker's end on 98. Can Gilchrist nudge a one or three or manufacture a five and get Steve Waugh on strike for the last ball? How does Gilchrist feel?'

How does he feel? What Gilchrist is thinking is that he should have just kept that last effort to two runs not three and kept his captain on strike. But Waugh's directive was to squeeze out every run possible and he obeyed.

Hussain sizes up the situation. How best to take advantage of Waugh willing himself to his century? He approaches vice-captain Marcus Trescothick.

'What shall we do?' he asks. 'Keep Gilchrist on strike so Waugh can't get back on strike?'

'Oh yeah,' Trescothick says. 'Let's do that. Let's keep him sweating over his 100 overnight.'

Hussain decides on an alternative strategy. He wants Waugh on strike for the final delivery. He wants him to have a rush of blood, to flay wildly. He's hoping that in such a bid for glory Waugh will fall to his death.

The delirious mob reminds Gilchrist what he must do. *Single! Single! Single!* Like he needed any advice. He nonchalantly flicks Dawson to the fieldsman at deep midwicket.

'It's hard to believe there's still three days left in this match,' Agnew says. 'But everyone wants and expects Steve Waugh to score two from this last ball of the day, to ram home, in the most emphatic possible way, his message: he's not finished. One ball remains. And Hussain's dragging out the agony here, he's strolling up to have a word with Dawson ...'

Hussain takes his time, clearly drawing out the moment to put pressure on the opposition captain.

'I've got nothing to say to you, actually,' Hussain says, zinc covering his bottom lip, pretend-laughing as if he and Dawson are old mates catching up for the first time in years. 'We're just trying to stall a bit here … Bowl it full and straight and quick.'

Waugh meets briefly with Gilchrist in the middle of the pitch. The instruction is brief: 'Run hard because, wherever it goes, we're going for two.'

'Will Waugh dare come down the pitch and try to hit Dawson over the top?' Agnew asks. 'He could come back tomorrow. Wait for Harmison, a loosener on leg stump, pick it off for two.'

O'Keeffe explodes.

'Stuff the silver, we've come for the gold!' he says. 'Poms would come back tomorrow! Aussies want it now! We're instant people! *COME ON STEPHEN*!'

In the Nine box, McNamara has one eye on the time, one eye on the TV screen in front of him. Hussain's field placing suggests he's enticing Waugh into a slog-sweep over midwicket. McNamara thinks Hussain is opening the gate for his best mate to play his 'bread and butter' shot.

'What's he doing?' McNamara thinks. 'He's brought a man in closer and left point open. This bloke doesn't spin the ball, unless it hits a rock, so a wide half-volley without a point is probably not the best tactic.'

A century off the last delivery of the day will mean many things to Steve Waugh: it will save his career, cement his place in history, add to the legend of Australia's most successful captain, and equal Bradman's record of 29 Test hundreds.

'He's the greatest player of all time,' Waugh had said before the match. 'But if a hundred comes along I'm not going to turn it down.'

Now he can do it with one shot. Maybe Eminem was onto something.

'Death or glory off the last ball of the second day,' O'Keeffe says.

Here we go. It's been a long day. The clock atop the Members Pavilion reports that it's 6.46pm. Few expected to be here when play started at 11am, let alone this far into the evening. They should be shoulder to shoulder at nearby pubs or piling onto the trains at Central.

Dawson moves in. It's a quicker-than-normal delivery, on a good length, but fractionally wide. Waugh opens his shoulder blades and drives through the offside …

A roar you could probably hear on the other side of the harbour tells the story. A sea of hands reaches for the sky in unison, in jubilation, the same wild scenes happening all over the country.

'That is extraordinary!' Agnew beams before putting down the microphone and allowing the sound of the crowd to tell the story. He eventually starts again: 'And Steve Waugh, a man of little emotion, can barely restrain himself now … his helmet is off … he's waving his bat. You could not have scripted anything more remarkable than what we have seen here this afternoon.'

Gilchrist is halfway down the pitch as the ball crashes into the fence. He attempts a high-five with his captain but then pulls out. He is also aware the skipper is more a handshaker than a hugger. 'It was great to be a part of it,' he tells Waugh, shaking his hand. 'Well done.'

Hussain also shakes Waugh's hand and offers his congratulations before instructing his players to stand back. This moment belongs to Waugh, who looks almost embarrassed as he raises the bat to applause that simply does not stop. SCG members slap his back red raw as he heads up the steps, into the dressing-room and plops down into his seat, always first on the left, right next to Matthew Hayden, who's worked out how to remove his foot from the chair he kicked hours earlier.

A semi-circle forms around Waugh, with few players or officials saying a word. Earlier, they had stood on the balcony, silenced by nervousness. Now they are mute in admiration. Outside the balcony, a growing crowd is gathering. They chant as one: 'We want Steve!' They stay there for the next hour as people come in and out of the dressing-room.

First, Waugh's father, Rodger, makes his way in. There's no bigger Steve Waugh fan. Waugh's wife, Lynette, and daughter Rosie are next, tears in their eyes. Prime Minister John Howard, a genuine cricket tragic, makes an appearance and shakes the captain's hand.

Waugh eventually makes his way from the dressing-room to the media conference.

'I don't think it gets any better than that,' he says. 'To get a hundred off the last ball in front of your home crowd and playing as well as I did today. I think it was one of those occasions that, as a sportsperson, they talk about being "in the zone". I think it only happens a couple of times in your career. To me, it felt very much like my first Test century in England, just the way I saw the ball and everything hit the gap. I wish I had more of those days than the bad days. It was almost a perfect day.'

As he makes his way back to the dressing-room, he bumps into McNamara. It's been a long day — for both of them. Waugh looks at his best man, his former under-10s teammate, and shakes his head.

'Told you I was hitting them well,' Waugh says, grinning out of the corner of his mouth. 'What was everyone worrying about?'

ONE PERSON WHO WASN'T at the SCG at 6.46pm was his twin Mark, who left early because he wanted to get across town for the harness racing at Harold Park. Contrary to popular belief, he didn't have a runner. It was merely his Friday night ritual. The first race was at 7pm. Mark watched the heroics from the SCG on a TV in the office of Harness Racing NSW chief executive Peter V'landys.

Like his brother, Mark has a bank of SCG memories from watching sport on the Hill, including the afternoon 'the tall bloke with the black moustache' karate chopped Ray Baartz. As one of the best batsman of his era, he added a few himself, including three Test centuries, against Pakistan, England and South Africa.

'Stephen was poking around and I wasn't sure if he was going to get his hundred that night,' Mark says. 'I just left and went to the trots. I think that's fair enough. I don't regret it. I saw him score plenty of hundreds! It was a great moment, scoring the boundary off the last ball of the day. He played up to the crowd there, waiting until the last ball.'

Mark had been honoured in the lunch break hours before his brother's heroics, completing a lap of honour in an open-topped 1967 Mustang alongside three other NSW Test representatives: Doug Walters, Len Pascoe and Geoff Lawson. At the completion of that ceremony, he was asked about his twin brother's future.

'Not sure what he's up to,' Mark said, typically laconic. 'Hopefully, he makes some runs and makes a decision from there.'

If the press had been split on Waugh's future leading into the Sydney Test, they were united in their praise the following day.

Peter Roebuck (*Sydney Morning Herald*): 'Steve Waugh has done it. In an amazing, nerveless display typical of the game's foremost fighter, he waited till the last ball of a rollercoaster day to strike the boundary that brought the century a sporting nation and history itself had demanded. Don Bradman and Doug Walters also hit boundaries off final deliveries to reach three figures, not bad company for an unpretentious young man from western Sydney.'

Robert Craddock (*Daily Telegraph*): 'Steve Waugh rescued his future yesterday by going back to his deep past. The Waugh we saw yesterday was much like the devil-may-care buccaneer who exploded on to the interstate scene 19 years ago. From the moment he surged from the dressing-room, crossing with Justin Langer about 15 metres inside the boundary, rolling his shoulders like a boxer, it was apparent every sense in his body was on red alert and humming. When Waugh plays one-day cricket he has a philosophy "Never hesitate — it's the worst crime you can commit." Yesterday he took that attitude into the Test arena.'

Malcolm Conn (*Australian*): 'Steve Waugh arrived in the perfect situation and played almost the perfect innings on what became a perfect day.'

The decision to stay with Waugh, and not switch to the 6pm news, was a ratings masterstroke for Nine. Almost one in nine Australians watched the final over: 2.1 million viewers. Nearly 665,000 watched in Sydney and more than 760,000 did so in Melbourne.

David Gyngell says he didn't hesitate to stay with the match because of two people: Brian Henderson and Kerry Packer. Henderson, the much-loved doyen of newsreaders, had retired in November after 45 years as the face of Nine News.

'The news ran the network, but I told them to stay with it,' Gyngell recalls. 'This was the day before multi-channels, but the cricket in those days would rate so heavily. But the newsroom was cutting up rough the whole time. When it got to 6.30pm I was thinking, "God, I hope he gets his century because the newsroom will be that angry if he gets out on 98." I was lucky "Hendo" wasn't there. If it was Hendo, I might have had less courage. It wasn't too hard to keep it on because Kerry wanted to watch it. He had an interest in the captain of Australia getting a century in possibly his last Test.'

The roar of the crowd that afternoon is still ringing in O'Keeffe's ears. 'It was the loudest sound I'd ever heard at a sporting event,' he says. 'Maybe Cathy Freeman winning the 400 metres at the Olympics. When that ball left his bat and went through the covers, it was like 40,000 rifles going off. Everybody in the ground had their hands extended above their head. A moment of triumph. I had not seen that before.

'We all got caught up in the emotion of that day. "Aggers" said he couldn't sleep that night. He was tired the next day because he got caught up, as did I. We all love an underdog, not that Steve Waugh is an underdog, but people could see the chairman of selectors was bullying him into going. He had to state his case — and he did.'

There's a framed and now faded photo in Denton's office of him and Waugh hugging each other in the dressing-room soon after the century had been scored. It is autographed: 'To the supercoach.' Waugh had given nothing away about the pressure he was under that day. 'But we spoke years later, and I got a better sense of what he was going through,' Denton says. 'At the time, I got no feeling he was carrying any extra pressure. He's a very ornery guy, that's why I always loved him as a player. When a punch-on happened, he was going to say, "Sure, hit me again." To walk onto the SCG, which I'd looked at my whole life, in the last session of an Ashes Test, into a moment of history like that, was surreal. It was like having a dream as a lifelong sports fan and then waking up and realising I was in the middle of it.'

We should probably add that Waugh was dismissed in the first over the next day without adding to his score and England won the Test by 225 runs. Minor details.

A year later, after a successful tour of the West Indies, winter Tests against Bangladesh in Darwin and Cairns, two home Tests against Zimbabwe and then four against India, after horse races had been run and won and retinas reattached to their rightful eyeballs, and after he had scored a further three Test centuries, Waugh retired. He finished by scoring 40 and 80 against India at the SCG in a drawn Test that meant India retained the Border-Gavaskar Trophy.

When I spoke to Waugh for this chapter, he was deflective of his efforts that afternoon against England, with everything on the line. The moment was less about him than about people who carried him to it: the fans.

'It was like this force was with me, protecting me, giving me energy and strength that whole Test match,' he says. 'I felt the vibe and connection with the crowd during that innings. It almost felt safe and secure, like a security blanket when I went out to bat. That's what I'll never forget.'

None of us will, no matter where we were that day.

CHAPTER 9

Power and the Passion

Wave Aid

IT'S JUST AFTER 10PM on a steamy Saturday in late January and the SCG is cloaked in darkness. You can't see the 47,000-or-so souls squeezed into the stands and on the field itself. But you can hear them. The tribes are rowdy.

Fireworks explode above, briefly revealing a seething mass of humanity below, pulling this way and that, like an elastic band too thick to break. Light beams begin shooting around the ground and the mob stirs even more.

It's been a long day. The previous act, Powderfinger, ran late so there's a rush to change equipment so the final act can play its set before the 10.30pm noise curfew. Only the meanest of bureaucrats would fine a rock concert raising money for a worthy cause, but organisers don't want to give them a reason to think about it.

White light illuminates the back of the stage, revealing band members holding their instruments as they find their marks. Eventually, the silhouette of the 193cm lead singer and his signature bald head comes to the fore. The crowd wails its approval.

Oooooils … Oooooils … Oooooils … Oooooils …

The lights get stronger and the darkness is replaced with brightness. Sweat fills the air. The beer-soaked throng surges again. Their call has been answered: Midnight Oil is here.

The baby boomers know the faces even if their kids do not. Rob Hirst on drums, Bones Hillman on bass, Jim Moginie and Martin Rotsey on guitar. As Moginie plays the distinctive opening chords of *Read About It*, the silhouette comes to life, too. It has a face and body. Arms and legs begin to flail, jerk and thrash in a manner that generations have mimicked in pubs and clubs all around the country, although none of these impersonations ever quite matched the man who pioneered it.

He seizes the microphone with his left hand. The right hand, with fingers spread wide, starts shaking in unison with his right leg, another signature move instantly recognisable to many in the crowd.

The melody builds, edging closer to the opening words, and when they come, they hit you right between the eyes just like every Oils lyric ever written: to the point, devoid of bullshit, appealing to your senses as much as your sense of what's right and wrong.

The rich get richer,
The poor get the picture,
The bombs never hit you when you're down so low ...

WHEN PETER GARRETT LEFT Midnight Oil in 2002 to pursue a career in social activism that eventually led him to federal politics, he figured he'd never sing these words in front of an audience again, let alone play with the band he'd joined in 1973 after answering an advertisement in a newspaper. 'No, not all,' he says. 'I thought we might do something for fun. But I didn't expect, as a newly elected member of parliament, to be out there tearing up the stage, across the road from the electorate of the people I was representing.'

Things can change quickly. In June 2004, Garrett was elected as the Member for Kingsford Smith, representing Sydney's south-east. Six months later, the world was gripped by a natural disaster, the magnitude of which it has rarely seen. The Boxing Day tsunami, triggered by an underwater earthquake off the coast of the Indonesian island of Sumatra, killed more than 250,000 people, displaced 1.7 million and caused devastation to cities, villages and entire regions in Indonesia, Thailand, India and Sri Lanka.

The water subsided but the pain and shock did not. Australians wanted to help. The music industry parked self-interest and record-label allegiance to one side, leading to a major fund-raising concert at the SCG on January 29, 2005. Featuring hugely popular bands such as Silverchair, Powderfinger and the John Butler Trio, solo legends Nick Cave and Tim and Neil Finn, and emerging talents including Missy Higgins and Pete Murray, Wave Aid wasn't just going to raise a lot of important money — it was going to rock the dust off the roof trusses of the Members Pavilion.

'The cricketers play cricket, the TV people do a TV show and the musicians play a gig,' Silverchair frontman Daniel Johns said on the eve of the concert. 'It should be a really memorable occasion.'

Particularly so with Garrett and the Oils coming together once more. The band's last gig together had been at the Twin Towns Services Club in Tweed Heads on November 20, 2002. The band cut its teeth on the pub and club scene throughout the 1970s, but the farewell didn't fit the legend.

Like an old boxer preparing to come out of retirement, they endured a tough sparring session at Manly Leagues Club two nights before the main bout at the SCG. They played in front of a crowd but were easily distracted.

'Because we hadn't seen each other for a while, we spent a lot of the time just swapping yarns,' Garrett laughs.

Surely, though, for bands like Midnight Oil, playing gigs is like riding a bike?

'No,' he laughs again. 'We spent many nights banging up and down the coast, playing all the great clubs, the pubs, the surf clubs. You do develop a condition for it. But the business of making the songs work, getting them where you want them to be, all of you hearing it the same way, there's a little bit more to it. I'm not a great rehearser by nature, but you do like to be mentally, emotionally and physically ready to give whatever you've got.

'In this case, I wasn't physically ready, but it didn't matter because the energy in the Cricket Ground that night was quite present. The feeling in the crowd was palpable. You could feel the electric current coming off the audience and onto the stage. When you're doing something that's bigger than what's going on in your own life, you play out of your skin and the audience goes with that.'

As the crowd stomped its feet in the middle of the SCG that evening, I wonder how many realised this wasn't the first Garrett to be enthralling the masses on the ground they were now trampling. Garrett's great-grandfather, Tom, was a bowling all-rounder who had played in the very first Test match ever played, between Australia and England at the Melbourne Cricket Ground in 1877.

Of the 19 Tests Tom Garrett played from 1877 to 1888, eight were at the Association Ground, as the SCG was known until 1894. He played 58 first-class matches for NSW from 1877 to 1898, 33 of them at the venue. As a medium-fast bowler, he generated plenty of bounce from his lanky frame. Later in his career, he was better known for his powerful batting and agility in the field. He stunned Sydney crowds with some spectacular catching, according to newspaper reports of the day. Tom Garrett died in Sydney in 1943, aged 85.

'It's a ground very familiar to most of us and certainly familiar to someone like me who's grown up in Sydney and with my family links,' Peter Garrett says. 'Whenever you bring people together in common cause, when the tribes come together on the hallowed turf of the SCG, it's always something special.'

The perspiration was just starting to form on Garrett's white long-sleeved shirt by the time the last strains of *Read About It* echoed through the SCG.

'Greetings everybody,' he said to the crowd. 'Thank you for hangin' around. Thank you for being part of the gathering. When people give a little bit of themselves, it always makes the world a better place. That's one of the things this band felt strongly about, still does in all its manifestations, and always will ...'

And, with those words, it was on. The 10.30pm curfew was looming. The crowd was begging for more. The Oils were just getting started.

The Member for Kingsford Smith had the floor.

THAT WAS THE FIRST and only time Midnight Oil played at the SCG. In fact, no Australian band had ever headlined a concert at the ground and only a handful of international acts had graced the hallowed turf before that night. Sport was given preference, which meant many large, outdoor concerts were held at the adjacent Sydney Showground and, from 1988, at the Sydney Football Stadium.

Legendary concert promoter Michael Chugg recalls bringing ABBA to the Showground in 1977. 'It was great, except for the fact that it rained,' he says. 'We built the stage in the rain, set up in the rain, the band rehearsed in the rain, and then performed in the rain. The seats were sinking into the ground. The problem with the SCG was availability. There was usually a game of cricket on, and they had first shot at it.'

American popstar Prince was the first to hold a concert at the SCG, in May 1992, despite the best efforts of South Sydney Council, who took the matter to the Land and Environment Court in an effort to block the performance. Approval was given to promoter Paul Dainty only four days before the concert was announced.

Given the green light, His Purpleness didn't disappointment, enthralling a crowd of more than 40,000 people. However, the mass of people left the playing surface in quite a state. Curator Peter Leroy was left scrambling to get it ready for sport again with the NSW Australian Rules State of Origin side scheduled to train on the SCG just 19 hours after the event.

A year later, an arguably even bigger act graced the turf: Madonna's 'The Girlie Tour', featuring songs from her controversial *Erotica* album. Tickets, at $65 apiece, were snapped up in record time.

Chugg was the promoter for that concert, too. The day before the first concert, security, ushers and food and beverage staff buzzed around the ground as Madonna and her band completed a sound check. Halfway through, she suddenly stopped, turned around and unloaded at a member of her band, an acclaimed artist who had performed with some of the greatest names in music history.

'You either get your act together and start playing with enthusiasm and passion, or you can get on the next plane back to Los Angeles,' the Queen of Pop bellowed, according to Chugg.

'The whole joint came to a grinding halt,' he recalls with a laugh. 'There were media waiting outside. I don't know how the story didn't get out.'

On the night of the concert, rain again poured down on Sydney, which was a problem for those not undercover because umbrellas had been banned. So wrote the *Herald* of the soggy night: 'The anticipation for 45,000 Sydneysiders was excruciating. The carnival music ended and the searchlights stopped their restless sweep across the crowd at the SCG. The red velvet curtain rose to reveal a harlequin, a white-masked Pierrot figure, who enigmatically retreated, leaving us with a dancer, bare-breasted atop a pole in the centre of the stage, slinkily making her way to the floor. Then suddenly, there was Madonna, rising out of the stage, clad only in spangly black hot-pants and the smallest of jackets above a matching bra.'

The Rolling Stones and the Eagles followed in April and December 1995 respectively, and then in November 1996, Michael Jackson's *HIStory* extravaganza rolled through the gates for two nights, complete with a 10-metre statue of the singer in military uniform that had been assembled at the Man O'War Steps at Farm Cove. Elton John and Billy Joel played four shows together at the SCG through March 1998, forcing the NSW Sheffield Shield team to reschedule a match against South Australia. Front-row seats cost $205 with a 33-metre yellow brick road — a nod to Elton's famous studio album of the same name — leading VIPs into the Members Pavilion for a post-concert cocktail party.

The next concert at the SCG wasn't held until March 22, 2003, when Bruce Springsteen and the E Street Band played for more than three hours in trying circumstances. Power cuts kept silencing the American rock legend, much to the dismay of the 30,000-strong audience, although he humoured them through to the end. 'Nobody use their cell phones!' he declared at one point. 'People are going around making sure no one is using an electric shaver around here and all hair dryers must be turned off in the suburbs of Sydney.' Those in the expensive seats that night who were close enough to clearly hear Springsteen and the band report 'The Boss' remained on point throughout a show that featured 27 songs.

THE FIRST SEEDS OF Wave Aid were planted just days after the tsunami struck. Phil Stevens, who managed folk band The Waifs and roots band John Butler Trio, phoned another leading agent, John Watson, who represented Pete Murray and Missy Higgins.

'We're thinking about doing a benefit gig at the Hordern Pavilion,' Stevens told Watson. 'Would Missy and Pete want to be involved?'

Watson's mind started turning over. This could be big, he thought. He also managed Silverchair, the Newcastle band that had been inactive for a couple of years with mystery surrounding their future. Their last gig had been a sold-out show at Newcastle's Civic Theatre in April 2003, and there had been a sense of finality about that gig for lead singer Daniel Johns, bassist Chris Joannou and drummer Ben Gillies. They'd pumped out four best-selling albums, including *Frogstomp*, *Freak Show* and *Neon Ballroom*, and many felt the ride was coming to an end. They did too.

'By 2005, Daniel wasn't even sure if he wanted to continue with Silverchair,' Watson says. 'This was an undeniable cause for them to play again, but it could've been their last gig.'

Watson then suggested to Stevens that they call Paul Piticco, who managed Brisbane band Powderfinger. They were in, too. Homebake festival promoter Joe Segreto was approached. Then Mark Pope, another leading promoter who had put together the ARIA Awards.

'You interested in doing something at the Hordern?' all three asked on a memorable conference call.

'Yeah, I would,' Pope replied. 'But this could be much bigger than the Hordern. You should have it at the SCG. If we do, we're better off getting Chuggy involved because of his connections with the SCG.'

Pope chuckles while recalling the story, revealing, 'One of the three — I won't say who — said, "No, we can't get Chuggy involved because he'll take all the credit." I crossed my fingers and said he'd never do that. All three replied, "Well, OK then. Let's do it."'

For Chugg, the Boxing Day tsunami hit close to home. He was building a villa on Bang Toa Beach on the Thai island of Phuket and was supposed to be there that day with his son. 'But we didn't go because there was no surf and he didn't want to go,' Chugg says. Phukct was swallowed up by the huge waves.

Instead, he was on a boat somewhere between Hamilton and Daydream islands when his mobile buzzed. It was Pope calling about the Wave Aid project. Chugg had a busy month ahead, preparing for the arrival of Bette Midler in April, but didn't hesitate to take it on.

'We were very aware that we had to make this something special,' Chugg recalls. 'But we only had four weeks. These were the days when the internet was just coming in. There was no real social media to spread the word. The adrenaline rush of pulling off a major stadium concert in four weeks is something none of us will forget. We were working 24 hours a day to get it done.'

More names were added to the line-up: Nick Cave, the Dark God of Australian Rock; Neil and Tim Finn of Split Enz and Crowded House fame; Kasey Chambers, the hugely popular country singer-songwriter whose name was all over the charts at the time.

John Watson had one last call to make. He knew Peter Garrett from his days working for Sony Music and felt the band deserved a better ride off into the sunset than the Twin Towns Services Club.

'The band didn't get to say goodbye properly,' he told Garrett. 'You guys deserve a proper farewell.'

'My pitch was the Oils deserved better than that,' Watson recalls. 'So did their fans. They were an inspiration to a whole generation of musicians. The spirit of the event was a new generation of artists trying to push a rock up a hill for a good cause. The Oils had done hundreds of benefit gigs over the years. This would be a great way to pass on the torch.'

Tickets were snapped up within days, including some by scalpers, many of whom tried to sell them on eBay for more than double their price. As the end of January neared, a Wave Aid ticket was the hottest ticket in town.

A sense of expectation hung in the air when reporters and artists attended the soundcheck and media conference the day before the event. So did an enormous banner from the stage proclaiming the Universal Declaration of Human Rights: 'All human beings are born free and equal in dignity and rights. They are endowed with reason and conscience and should act towards one another in a spirit of brotherhood.'

Many of the artists admitted to feeling nervous, given the magnitude of the event and the fact that some of them hadn't played together for some time. For the sports fans among them, there was the added anticipation of playing at the venue. Powderfinger's Bernard Fanning and Silverchair's Chris Joannou made their way through the home team's dressing-room, picturing the likes of Dennis Lillee, Rod Marsh and the Chappell brothers in the recently installed spa or having a well-earned post-match beer.

'Then we made our way out into the middle,' Watson recalls. 'It was hard to believe a rock concert was going to be played there the next night.'

PHIL JAMIESON STEPS INTO a lift, headed for the green room at the top of the old Bradman Stand. The lead singer of Grinspoon has just performed on stage with The Wrights, a supergroup formed by some of Australia's leading musicians in a nod to Easybeats legend Stevie Wright.

'Jamo!' says a voice from the back of the lift.

'Oh hey, Heath,' Jamieson replies.

Heath is Heath Ledger, the actor. He's there with his partner Michelle Williams, who is nursing their newborn Matilda. Also in the lift are Neil and Tim Finn. That's a lot of celebrity in a small space.

'I'll never forget that day for a number of reasons,' Jamieson tells me. 'But standing in a lift with the Finn brothers and Heath Ledger is one of them. I was also wearing questionable sunglasses from memory. It was the mid-2000s.'

Wave Aid took form as celebrities and the common people alike streamed into the SCG that warm afternoon in late January. The concert began with The Waifs, who had left Toowoomba at 4am and cancelled a gig in Brisbane that night to make sure they could open the concert with *London Still* right on 2pm.

The crowd kept flowing in as Missy Higgins, Pete Murray and Kasey Chambers took their turns to light up the SCG. All three were accustomed to smaller, more intimate venues, but sounded at home on the vast stage. Nick Cave eased his lean frame behind a piano for his set and provided the most incongruous scene. As he played a darker-than-usual version of his gothic folk hit *Red Right Hand*, a group of young men started playing a game of cricket on a patch of grass at the Paddington End.

By the time the Finn brothers took the stage, the SCG was truly heaving. After playing Crowded House classics such as *Weather With You* and *Don't Dream It's Over*, they covered Hunters and Collectors' *Throw Your Arms Around Me*, much to the delight of the fans sprawled out in front of them, many of whom were wearing boardshorts and bikini tops because of the heat.

'Who was it who said people are not kind?' asked Kamahl, who didn't perform but was one of the MCs for the day. 'You have been more than generous — some of my relatives who live in Sri Lanka have been affected.'

Just after 6.15pm, The Wrights stepped up to perform *Evie*, the trilogy Stevie Wright had released in 1974. The group was a collection of some of the country's leading musicians that had formed the year before to perform at the ARIA Awards in tribute to Wright. Jet lead singer Nic Cester sang *Evie Part 1*, Bernard Fanning performed *Part 2* and Jamieson sang *Part 3*. The rest of the group was Kram from Spiderbait, Chris Cheney from The Living End, Davey Lane from You Am I and Pat Bourke from Dallas Crane.

'But I wasn't even pencilled to be in it at all,' Jamieson says. 'I had to convince Nic Cester to let me in. I knew that song like the back of my hand, even though *Evie Part 3* is challenging. It's not the easiest track to sing. Stevie Wright made it very difficult. But back then I had enough nous and swagger to say, "This'll be right."'

Jamieson, who had performed with Grinspoon at the Big Day Out festival at the Sydney Showground on Australia Day, three days before Wave Aid, had turned up late to the media conference the day before. There were stern looks from organisers, but Garrett was more understanding. Upon learning Jamieson and his partner were about to welcome the couple's first child, he simply offered, 'It goes really quick.'

As Jamieson looked over the ground, the scale of the occasion struck him. 'We're walking onto the SCG to do a gig,' he says. 'There is something so mind-blowing about that ground. You take deep breaths when you're walking on there because so much history has played out there. You are walking on hallowed turf.'

After Cester and Fanning performed the first two parts of *Evie*, Jamieson — wearing a large red tie, black shirt and indeed dubious sunglasses — took the stage.

'I was reasonably hungover, as was the case in those days,' he says. '[And] playing alongside those guys, who were my contemporaries, peers who I'd long admired. People like Bernard Fanning and Nic Cester.'

Two days earlier, The Wrights had recorded the song in a studio with proceeds from sales going to Wave Aid and the Salvation Army, and to Stevie Wright, who had been battling ill-health for some time. 'I felt humbled to be a part of it — it was a great privilege,' Jamieson says. 'But I was there for a hot minute and had to leave, off to re-join the rest of the Big Day Out tour.'

Next up, Chugg took the stage to thank the artists and all those who had helped put the day together in such a short period of time, including SCG Trust staff who had worked as tirelessly as anyone. He then prepared to call for a minute's silence for those who had been killed by the tsunami. At this moment, a group of young men at the back of the huge crowd were misbehaving, making a racket, and Chugg delivered a spray not too dissimilar to Madonna's a decade earlier. The louts quickly fell quiet.

'And now,' Chugg said, 'a minute's silence.'

The moment was talked about for days with *Herald* cartoonist Cathy Wilcox capturing it with a drawing of Chugg saying, 'F...............k.'

Silverchair came on just before 8pm, with dusk falling on the SCG. A shirtless Johns strode to the middle in the manner of future Test cricketer David Warner, guitar in hand, buzzing with nervous energy. The band hadn't played in two years and now, here they were, after just a week of rehearsal, performing before a huge crowd.

'We haven't played for a while,' Johns told them. 'Here's to those who said we've been *beaten*.'

What followed has become the stuff of Australian rock legend. Silverchair were back in their natural environment, enthralling the masses as they sang along to hits such as *The Greatest View*, *The Door* and *Ana's Song*. This didn't sound like a band on the way out. It didn't sound like a farewell gig. They were just getting started, as Australia's leading music author Jeff Apter wrote in *The Book of Daniel*, his 2018 biography of Johns: 'Anyone who had witnessed the awesome sight of Daniel Johns strutting across the Wave Aid stage like a man who had just rediscovered the simple pleasure of plugging in and making a hellacious noise, could see that Wave Aid marked Silverchair's new tomorrow. They were back ...'

For all three band members, it was a reawakening.

Daniel Johns: 'The gig wasn't close to the best we've ever played; it felt a bit like an infomercial. We hadn't played for years ... we only had about five rehearsals, so we decided to just try and sound like a great rock band. And the cause was the big thing, so it wasn't about showboating or making a big artistic statement; just try and enjoy it.'

Chris Joannou: 'We had those few days of rehearsal beforehand, but it wasn't until we played — in fact, after the gig — that we went, "Holy shit, how much fun was that?" It probably wasn't the greatest show we've ever played, but the energy after that show was amazing.'

Ben Gillies: 'I was less nervous at Rock in Rio [in 2001] than Wave Aid. I was nervous. But it was incredible, the whole day. It would have to be in the top five moments of my life. It was just incredible.'

AS SILVERCHAIR WERE CHURNING through a memorable set, Watson was off stage biting his fingernails.

'The thing for me was we were running out of time,' he says. 'The show was running late enough. Then Powderfinger went over and, in the back of my mind, all I could think about was the local member of parliament, who was a noted environmentalist, [and us] breaking the EPA (Environmental Protection Authority) guidelines. It was a mad scramble.'

If the pioneering town planners of Sydney had their time again, there's every chance they might've laid things out a little differently. Perhaps they would have put some extra distance between the sliver of residences near the SCG that are most impacted when big, loud events held are in the Moore Park precinct. Indeed, the SCG Trust operated under a noise-prevention notice, which meant the volume generated by events at the ground couldn't exceed 70 decibels.

There were no such issues during the Wave Aid concert. In fact, media articles from the day note that the songs were quieter than expected, although Midnight Oil sounded louder than the other acts. The SCG Trust denied the volume had been turned up for the last performance.

'Any gig in that part of town, in that area between Fox Studios and Centennial Park, there's a pocket of people who hate noise,' Watson says. 'They are notorious complainers. It's always been an issue for promoters with concerts at the Sydney Football Stadium and the SCG. Dealing with sound restrictions has been difficult over the years.'

The 10.30pm curfew is strictly adhered to because the fines from the relevant authorities for going overtime are substantial. With this in mind, Midnight Oil was forced to drop two songs from their set. After Powderfinger left the stage, they found themselves in the lift with the Oils' long-time manager Gary Morris, who was furious that the headline act was now in a race against time.

'It got tense in that lift,' Chugg remembers with a chuckle. 'Peter mightn't have known about it, but we were all there and it happened. It was quite funny.'

If Garrett and the Oils were cranky about having their time cut down by Powderfinger, they didn't show it when they eventually took the stage. Standing there provided a unique viewpoint for Garrett.

'For many people who grew up in the era I did, particularly those of us who follow cricket, when you get to see a game the first time it's quite incredible,' he says. 'As a kid, the ground is so big because TV makes it look quite small. Then, when you get in, it reverses itself.'

On this evening, as Garrett looked out at the surging sea of faces and bodies, illuminated in red and then blue as the lights from the stage changed, it seemed enormous. The band's set list of all-time classics was punctuated by Garrett's captivating oratory, so seamlessly delivered you'd have thought he was reading. He wasn't. It was from the heart.

'A big thanks to the bands that made it happen. Their managers that made it happen. The staff around this place that are doing it for nothing that made it happen. And finally to you for making it happen. You've gotta have some power, and you need some passion, especially if you live in Sydney like we do.'

The band launched into its 1982 song *Power and the Passion*. A fan near the front of the stage thrust a banner, written on cardboard with black texta, into the air. 'PETER GARRETT FOR PM' it proclaimed. When the trumpets and horns that end the song eventually died, Garrett said: 'Even though one of us has headed off on a slightly different road, the principles remain the same. The locations are different. I'm probably the only Labor MP who's singing in a rock band tonight, but I reckon I'm the luckiest bloke on earth. If you come from Kingsford Smith, just remember in two and a half years, all right?'

There was no identifiable ring rust on display as the band rattled off songs that are very much part of the nation's DNA. *King of the Mountain, Beds Are Burning, The Dead Heart, Forgotten Years ...* each of them delivered as if the Oils had stepped back in time, three decades in fact, to the sweaty confines of the Royal Antler Hotel at Narrabeen or Selina's at the Coogee Bay Hotel. At one point, Garrett climbed down to the front fence and into the arms of the faithful, who clutched and grabbed at him. He wrenched himself free, clambered back up to the stage, and put the night into perfect context:

'You might have noticed when you came into the SCG this afternoon, there were two hallowed principles operating in the arena. The first hallowed principle was that patch of green over there, which everybody takes very seriously, and I do, too. I love it. The other hallowed principle is above us, the universal declaration of human rights. The 21st century is about making this stuff come a little closer to the truth, however hard the job is. It can be done.'

It was some night. It was some performance. Midnight Oil closed with *Best of Both Worlds*, a poignant final reminder for the people at the SCG that night to have a sense of gratitude and perspective. As the final strains of the song echoed around the ground, Garrett lit a red flare and held it high in the middle of the stage, the smoke billowing over his fellow band members. Then he raised his arms in triumph, like Steve Waugh hitting a four off the last ball to save his career, acknowledging a job well done by all.

John Watson looked at his watch and breathed a sigh of relief. They'd made the curfew … by a minute.

WAVE AID CHANGED MANY lives, and not just those for whom it was intended. The net proceeds of the event topped $2.3 million. Those funds were distributed to charities including the Australian Red Cross, Oxfam, UNICEF and Care Australia. The organisers were steadfast in their view that the money had to be put to work immediately — and that's what happened, says Chugg today. 'A lot of greatness came out of that gig,' he says. 'Phil Stevens built schools in Indonesia. Along with some English ex-pats in Phuket, we built schools that taught poor kids how to speak English. Some of those kids have graduated from university.'

Wave Aid also provided a blueprint for future benefit concerts. Four years later, a natural disaster hit closer to home with devastating consequence. Bushfires ripped through rural Victoria on February 7, 2009, claiming 173 lives — Australia's most severe cost in human life from bushfire — and devastating communities. The day became known as Black Saturday.

As it had been with Wave Aid, the response from the music industry was swift and large. Within two days, the wheels were in motion to hold Sound Relief, which would see concerts held simultaneously at the MCG and the SCG on March 14. It was also decided that half the money raised in Sydney would go to victims of the Queensland floods that had devastated large parts of the south-east of that state in November 2008.

Chugg, Pope and Segreto joined Melbourne music giant Michael Gudinski to pull the event together. Again, the deadline was just four weeks. 'Come on guys,' Gudinski said via phone hook-up. 'I'm new to this charity game.' Gudinski was handed the MCG, which he adored, for the Melbourne concert, while Chugg was given familiar territory at the SCG.

This time, Midnight Oil headlined the MCG concert, supported by performances from Kylie Minogue, Split Enz, Paul Kelly and a reunited Hunters and Collectors. The SCG concert was headlined by Bee Gees icon Barry Gibb and Olivia Newton-John, and supported by a powerhouse line-up that included British group Coldplay, Australian bands Hoodoo

Gurus, Icehouse and You Am I, as well as Marcia Hines. The two hottest Australian rock bands of the day — Jet and Wolfmother — did an extraordinary job playing in both Melbourne and Sydney.

The Sydney gig had one more addition. Nineteen-year-old Taylor Swift was a highly popular country singer-songwriter with two best-selling studio albums and she happened to be on tour in Australia at the time. 'EMI Records pitched her to us,' Pope recalls. 'And we gladly took her on board.'

The two concerts started in different cities under contrasting skies. In Melbourne, fans shivered as rain fell during Jet's set. The cruel irony wasn't lost on anyone: not only was this the state's first sight of decent rain in weeks, it was falling on a bushfire relief concert.

In Sydney, a blazing sun greeted those in attendance as Coldplay opened. At one point, lead singer Chris Martin ran into the crowd while singing *Fix You*, but didn't get back in time for the end of the song. The crowd finished it for him. He eventually emerged.

'When you come to Australia and you've only really got two hit singles, which we've already played before, you think to yourself, "How am I going to impress everyone from row one to row 5000?"' Martin said. 'Ladies and gentlemen, please welcome … to sing the Australian national anthem …'

For days, the rumour had been running strong that a well-known Australian artist would join the band on stage at some point. The smart money had been on John Farnham to sing the country's unofficial anthem, *You're The Voice*.

Long-time music journalist Kathy McCabe recalled the moment in the *Daily Telegraph*: 'And then that secret that wasn't a secret happened.

It was everything you wanted a moment to be. There was no doubt Farnham was having a ball up there, singing with the world's biggest rock act as his backing band. But it was the crowd who made the moment. Their voices swelled as one for the *You're The Voice* chorus, Farnham revving them to sing louder and louder with an emphatic, "Come on!"

'Those front rows weren't the mums and grandmothers he would be used to hanging on his every note. They were the kids and grandkids who had grown up hearing their elders flog Farnham's signature song. It is ingrained in their DNA and cool or not cool, they love it. They love it so much that 120,000 people sang it even louder when it was replayed later in each of the concerts. It has some powerful magic.'

The day was punctuated with a score of memorable moments: Kylie Minogue singing Peter Allen's *I Still Call Australia Home* at the MCG, with her performance on the big screen at the SCG; actress Toni Collette introducing Prince William and Prince Harry, who both offered their well wishes and support; then, just on dusk, the music and light stopped in the name of the bushfire and flooding victims and both venues were asked to observe a minute's silence to remember those who had lost their lives.

After rain doused the MCG, it became Sydney's turn, as day turned to night. One thunderstorm swept through, clearing the ground. When a second thunderstorm dumped on the SCG, electro duo The Presets were just finding their voice with their track *Talk Like That*.

This time, nobody clambered out of the rain. They welcomed it. In fact, many in the stands surveyed the scene below — with the confluence of the thumping beats of The Presets, an impressive light show and sideways rain — and decided to run into the middle of the

SCG, forming one huge, bouncing mass of people as the band ended with *My People*, their biggest hit.

I'm here with all of my people,
Party time all of my people,
So let me hear you scream if you're with me

'With the thunder and lightning, it was like Armageddon,' Pope recalls. 'The audience and band were as one. It was magical.'

McCabe was one of those who ran out into the rain, wanting to be part of the mob. 'It had been this stinking hot day and this classic Sydney thunderstorm came through,' she recalls. 'There was lightning everywhere. Sheets of rain. It bucketed down. People just ran down from the stands into the rain and danced to The Presets.'

Afterwards, McCabe took refuge in the Ladies Stand, which was one of the designated VIP areas for the event. 'Everyone was squeezing out their clothes in the female bathroom,' she says. 'Outside, I saw one girl say to her dad, "That was a spiritual experience." That's a father-daughter moment they won't forget in a hurry.'

Then it was time for Barry Gibb to take the stage with Newton-John, who had turned up 10 hours earlier to watch Coldplay simply because she is a fan. They rattled through a playlist of classics from the '60s and '70s: *To Love Somebody*, *Jive Talkin'* and *You Should Be Dancing*. Newton-John's *I Honestly Love You* brought real tears to glass eyes. They closed the show with the Bee Gees' *Spicks and Specks*.

Nobody who left that night would've seen the distraught look on Gibb's face before the show. 'Barry Gibb was shit scared beforehand,'

Pope says. 'So was John Farnham. Both just so nervous. They're superstars, but they have this human frailty about them like all of us. They think, "Maybe it's past me." But it wasn't past them. They nailed it.'

More than 40,000 people attended the SCG concert, while upwards of 80,000 packed the MCG. Together, the concerts raised more than $5 million, with a further $1.5 million in DVD sales in the days that followed.

Silverchair fans are still thankful for Wave Aid, because it led the band to Midnight Oil. 'After it, we thought, "We didn't even try and people really responded,"' Daniel Johns told Jeff Apter. 'We realised how easy it felt, it was so natural, the songs kept coming out. And then watching Midnight Oil, who were just absolutely killing it. We figured we only had one opportunity to be a great, great band. The great ones are the bands who have been together since they were kids, sorted out their shit, and kept going and 20 years later they were still killing it.'

They recorded a new album, *Young Modern*, which included the pulsating chart-topping hit *Straight Lines*, and toured the country. At the 2006 ARIA Awards, Silverchair were asked to perform before Midnight Oil's induction into the Hall of Fame. During a performance of the Oils' 1981 single *Don't Wanna Be The One*, Johns spray-painted 'Peter Garrett for Prime Minister' on the stage wall.

Garrett never reached either of the highest offices in the country — prime minister or captain of the Australian cricket team — but he did become minister for the Environment, Heritage and Arts when Kevin Rudd was elected prime minister in 2007. Two years later, Garrett found himself at the SCG once more, playing in a charity cricket match to raise funds for the victims of the Victorian bushfires, as part of a side captained by Steve Waugh.

'He'd watched me bowl and bat and stuck me in the outfield, which was the smartest thing to do,' Garrett laughs.

Garrett's friend, the former Test fast bowler Mike Whitney, was the square-leg umpire as former footballer Anthony Mundine bowled to former Test captain Mark Taylor, who skied his shot towards Garrett.

'Run, Pete! Run!' Whitney screamed. 'You might catch it.'

Garrett ran, long arms outstretched, and took a spectacular outfield catch — just as his great-grandfather had more than a century earlier on the same patch of turf.

Garrett left politics in 2013 after deciding not to seek re-election after three terms in parliament. Soon after, he and his family moved out of the Kingsford Smith electorate to a house in Paddington, close enough to the SCG to hear the roar of the crowd. Occasionally, he'd walk over to watch the Swans or the cricket. Inevitably, he'd be dragged around to the Members Reserve to look at the framed picture of his great-grandfather on one of the walls.

'The SCG is about culture as much as sport,' Garrett says. 'Steve Waugh scoring his ton is fantastic. But to me it's what the ground represents ... it brings the tribes together. When we played at Wave Aid, we brought the tribes together again. This time, there was a tribe that doesn't usually follow sport in the middle of the SCG in an inspiring arena.'

Three years after he left politics, inspired by what happened at Wave Aid and then Sound Relief, Midnight Oil reformed. In 2017, they toured 16 countries, performing 77 concerts. They recorded live albums and, more importantly, remain an important voice for the Australian conscience. And Garrett continues to attend events from time to time at the SCG.

'As summer's approaching, you smell frangipani, the evenings are getting longer,' he says. 'You know the SCG is about to loom in your memory.'

CHAPTER 10

63 Bats

Phillip Hughes

DAVE WARNER WAS SITTING in the second tier of the Bill O'Reilly Stand when Tony Lockett kicked the 1300th goal of his career to break Gordon Coventry's 62-year record for most premiership goals.

'I sprinted down, over the fence and out onto the ground — and then froze,' Warner says. 'I didn't know what to do!'

Warner's first cricket coach, Laurie Heal, was an SCG member and would often take the spritely young batsman to Swans matches, although never cricket. What Warner reveals next will surprise you.

'I'd never seen a game of cricket at the SCG until I played there,' says one of the game's most dominant batsmen of the modern era. 'I've never watched a cricket match at the SCG. I've only played there. My mum and dad didn't like crowds. As a kid, we'd be praying for matches to be sold out in Sydney because the [television] coverage would stop at 3pm if it wasn't. My first game of cricket at the SCG was a country championship final. Let's just say the pitch wasn't as well prepared as it was for a Test match.'

Why would Warner need to watch cricket at the SCG when he was destined to make history in the middle of it? After plundering runs in Twenty20 internationals and then the one-day format, Warner has feasted at the SCG in Test matches like few others in recent times. Heading into the 2021–22 season, he'd scored four centuries in nine Tests at the ground at an average of 57.69.

Arguably his most impressive numbers came in the first session of the Test match against Pakistan on January 3, 2017. That morning, Warner lit up the ground as few have, dispatching the second, fourth and fifth balls he faced to the boundary and then racing to a hundred in 78 balls. He became the fifth batsman — and first since Pakistan's Majid Khan dismantled New Zealand in Karachi in October 1976 — to score a century in the opening session of a Test, and the first to ever score a ton before lunch on any day of a Test in Australia.

'Whatever I saw in front of me, I just played,' Warner reflects. 'Everything was moving in sync. The SCG is a ground where it won't traditionally always bounce over the stumps, so you can go big on day one or two. Someone of my height can climb into those deliveries. You're allowed to play straighter and square of the wicket. If you can capitalise on some early half volleys, the bowlers start bowling back of a length and someone of my height can get on the back foot and punch it through.'

Michael Clarke also hadn't seen a game of cricket at the SCG until he played in one. His first game was a 'kanga cricket' match during the change of innings in a one-day international during the late 1980s. He was seven years old. Could anyone sitting in the stands that afternoon know they were watching a future Australian captain as he faced up to Test fast bowler Merv Hughes, who presumably eased back on his pace for the young'uns that day?

A child of solid working-class stock from Sydney's western suburbs, Clarke's family couldn't afford tickets to the headline matches at the SCG. But he rapidly climbed the ranks of Australian cricket, making his first Test appearance at the ground in the summer of 2004–05 against Pakistan. Suddenly, Clarke was seeking as many tickets as possible from officials so his family and friends could watch him play. In the years that followed, they would sit in the same seats in the Ladies Stand, with Clarke scanning the sea of faces to find them before each day's play.

He rarely disappointed his personal fan club. In an emotionally charged Test against India in January 2008, a fresh-faced Clarke niggled at captain Ricky Ponting all day to allow him to bowl his slow, left-arm orthodox. Australia were desperately trying to dismiss a daunting Indian batting line-up that included the likes of Rahul David, VVS Laxman, Sourav Ganguly and, ominously, Sachin Tendulkar.

'Ricky, give me a go,' Clarke, who was fielding in the slips, chirped at the start of India's innings.

He didn't let up. Ponting eventually grew tired of it, and moved him.

'Go and field at cover,' the skipper said. 'Get away from me.'

As the day dragged on and Australia struggled to dismiss the tailenders, Clarke kept nagging.

'Give me a bowl! I'll get you a wicket.'

Ponting eventually relented.

'Righto,' Ponting said. 'Go get me one then.'

Clarke didn't get one wicket but three. He dismissed Harbhajan Singh, RP Singh and Ishant Sharma with the first, second and fifth deliveries of his second over, spinning Australia to victory.

'That over was a fluke,' Clarke grins. 'I was a terrible bowler but in the right conditions, on day five of a Test, if you put it in the right spot, and you're a part-timer, you can break the batsman's concentration. I was young and confident then. Ricky chucked me the ball, it landed on a bit of dust, and it spun.'

Unfortunately, Clarke's feats, along with Andrew Symonds' unbeaten 162, are often forgotten when people remember that Test, otherwise known for Symonds' claims that Harbhajan Singh called him a 'monkey'. The Australian team didn't leave the SCG until 2am; not because they were celebrating. They were locked in interviews with the match referee.

Four years later, Australia played India again and Clarke, who had taken over from Ponting as captain the year before, once again shone, although this time with his bat, scoring an unbeaten 329 in Australia's first-innings total of 4–659. Clarke declared when he was just five runs short of Sir Donald Bradman's Australian record highest Test score of 334, a mark The Don shares with Mark Taylor, who famously declared in Peshawar in 1998 to avoid going past Bradman's landmark.

The way Clarke was batting that day, he could've knocked off every record in the history books. Matthew Hayden's 380 and Brian Lara's world record 400 almost certainly would have been reached. But Clarke had a different target in his head. He closed the innings during the drinks break in the middle session of day 3, challenging the Indian batsmen to bat for two and a half days in their second innings to save the Test. They'd be all out for 400 late on the fourth afternoon, giving Australia victory by an innings and 68 runs.

And what does Clarke think of his decision now?

'I wish I hadn't declared!' he booms with a good-natured laugh. 'We'd still be batting now. I'd never get to 300 again. What was I doing? That innings is a good example of where my head was at when I took over the captaincy of Australia. I wanted to win and I wanted us to be the best in the world. Nothing was going to stand in my way. There was so much time left in the game, I could've kept batting to beat the record of 400. I actually didn't care about 400. People said I didn't want to beat Sir Donald's score. It didn't even come into my mind.'

In the dressing-room after the Test had been won, Clarke and his teammates shared beers with the cellarmen and groundstaff. He says the players shared a connection with the people at the SCG more than any other ground at which he played.

'Some of the Test-match cricket played at the SCG will stick with me forever,' he says. 'I wanted to perform there even more because that was my home turf. You can feel the tradition and history in that dressing-room. Cricket is a sport that's built on those who have come before you. The SCG echoes that more than any other ground in Australia.'

THE SCG HAS MANY meanings for many people but, for elite young cricketers, it's the 'Dream Factory': the place where childhood ambitions transform into real-life moments.

The most hurt they're supposed to feel in this place is to their pride and ego. Players are dropped, careers ended by form or injury, and that kind of pain hurts more than a bad ball dispatched to the boundary or the occasional misjudgment of a delivery that sneaks through an armoury of padding and thuds into the body.

It's not meant to be a place where their best friend loses his life playing the sport they all love.

The SCG was Phillip Hughes' Dream Factory. It's where he made his first-class debut for NSW against Tasmania during that same 2007–08 season in which Michael Clarke took three Indian wickets in five deliveries. He played his first Test in Australia against Pakistan there in January 2010. He played more first-class and Test matches at the SCG than any other venue.

On Tuesday, November 25, 2014, Hughes was playing for South Australia against NSW in a Sheffield Shield match, looking to spark the next chapter in his 26-Test career. He was less than a week away from his 26th birthday. The man he was likely to replace in a reshuffled batting line-up for the looming first Test against India in Brisbane was Clarke, who was struggling with a hamstring injury. A big score against his former state, which featured current Test players Warner,

Shane Watson, Brad Haddin and Nathan Lyon, would help convince the selectors he deserved another opportunity.

As Hughes took the crease, Clarke was doing some rehab training in Moore Park under the watchful eye of the Australian team's trainer, Duncan Kerr. He was ticking every box possible to get the injury right, yet he remained in serious doubt for the start of the Test series. When Clarke finished his session, he looked through the gap between the stands and could see the scoreboard. Hughes was 20 not out.

'I thought I'd get home, quickly shower, then come back and watch him bat,' Clarke recalls. 'If I didn't pull up fit for the first Test, a hundred would get him in. If I wasn't playing, I'd love nothing more than my good mate to be there instead.'

Inside the ground, Mark Waugh was taking a keen interest in what was unfolding. He was the Australian selector on duty that day and was to report back to chairman Rod Marsh about how Hughes played. Sitting in the Ladies Stand was Hughes' mother Virginia, who had come down from the family farm in Macksville with Hughes' sister Megan. His brother Jason, a talented cricketer in his own right who played club cricket in Sydney, sat alongside them. Now that their son and brother was no longer based in Sydney and was playing for South Australia, chances to see him play were rare. His father, Greg, had stayed in Macksville to attend to the farm: 220 acres of land where they had 70 head of prime Angus cattle.

Hughes had come into the match suffering from a virus, but he was determined to score the big innings that would deliver him a Test recall. He was on 63, batting at the Randwick end, when NSW fast-medium bowler Sean Abbott delivered the third ball of the 49th over. Hughes tried to pull but mistimed his shot ever so slightly, the ball striking him on the back of his neck. After a moment, he fell forward onto the pitch.

Malcolm Conn wasn't at the SCG, but he was just around the corner in his office at Cricket NSW headquarters, which were located near the Sydney Football Stadium. Conn was now working as a media manager for Cricket Australia, after leaving the newspaper business. After decades of examining cricketers, he was now advising them. Conn was watching the live stream of the Shield match on his computer when Hughes fell. The sight of frantic players gesturing towards the dressing-room, screaming for help, was worrying.

'He's in serious trouble,' Conn thought. He raced out of the office and down to the front of the Members Pavilion.

When he arrived, the scene before him was confronting. Hughes was on a Medicab, being taken from the middle to the edge of the field. At the same time, SCG Trust staff were ushering Hughes' family away to a private room, as players pulled a white sheet up around their fallen mate. Frantic calls were placed to Triple Zero, but to the people on the ground it felt like nobody outside the confines of the SCG understood the seriousness of the situation.

NSW team doctor John Orchard knew straight away. He saw the panicked reaction of the players and rushed onto the field, where he performed mouth-to-mouth and CPR on Hughes in the middle of the ground and on the Medicab. Orchard also intubated Hughes, desperately trying to keep the flame flickering inside the stricken batsman.

That's when Conn heard the words that gave everyone who had ever been touched by the diminutive kid from the NSW north coast a sense of hope, however fleeting.

'I've got a pulse!' Orchard said. 'I've got a pulse!'

'PHILLIP HUGHES IS A tough, pesky 20-year-old lefty from the sticks who bats and lives by his own lights. Australia's new opening batsman scores an awful lot of runs in any company, but in every other respect he is an ordinary lad, with a short haircut, a slight earring, a fondness for clothes, plenty of mates, no tickets on himself and a love for rugby league so strong that he spent his youth crash-tackling boys twice his size. Armed with a willow, though, he enters another world, becomes astute, bold, confident, tenacious and resilient.'

So Peter Roebuck described Hughes for the *Sydney Morning Herald* in March 2009 after Hughes had scored centuries in both innings of a Test against South Africa in Durban. Born in the sleepy north-coast town of Macksville on November 30, 1988, Hughes often seemed in a hurry, just as he was during that match.

It was just Hughes' second Test appearance. When he was handed his baggy green for the series opener, as the replacement for the retired Matthew Hayden, he became Australian Test player No. 408.

He'd played rugby league alongside Macksville's other great sporting export, Melbourne Storm and South Sydney star Greg Inglis, but cricket was his calling. He played A-grade cricket at the age of 12 and moved to Sydney when he was 17, to play with the Western Suburbs Cricket Club, for whom he scored an unbeaten 141 on debut. A year later, he was given a rookie contract with NSW. When he made his first-class debut at the age of 18, he was the youngest player to do so in Australia since Michael Clarke.

Hughes became the youngest player to score a century in a Sheffield Shield final when he scored 116 for NSW in the 2007–08 decider against Victoria. He'd make three more first-class centuries at the SCG, earning adulation from his teammates and generating much pride for his family, who regularly made the long drive down from Macksville to see him play.

The same scene was repeated around the world after he made his Test debut. It was impossible not to like Hughes, who put a premium on making runs, having a good time, being a good mate and identifying quality cattle for his farm.

Alas, Test-match cricket is difficult. Popularity doesn't guarantee runs and he found himself in and out of the side, earning a recall when players were injured or retired. He moved from NSW to play for South Australia for the 2012–13 season, gained another chance at the top level, but was dropped after the first two Ashes Tests in England in 2013.

By 2014, however, his form was turning again. An unbeaten 243 for Australia A against South Africa A during a game in Townsville in August had the selection panel interested again. All he could do was keeping making runs. Clarke's injury was keeping the selectors up at night. A big score from Hughes in the Shield match against NSW would make him an enticing option for the first Test at the Gabba.

A few weeks earlier, Clarke had predicted publicly that Hughes would soon earn a recall and become a hundred-Test veteran. But in the days before the match, Hughes was suffering from a virus, something confirmed by Greg Hughes in his son's official biography, written by leading cricket writers Malcolm Knox and Peter Lalor.

'He wasn't well,' Greg Hughes told Knox and Lalor. 'But he was so determined to score runs. He'd thought he'd batted himself out of the Test team when he didn't make runs in the previous match, but now it was clear that Clarkey was struggling with his hamstring. Phillip knew how important this match was, and he saw that bigger picture.'

South Australia won the toss that Tuesday morning and, unsurprisingly, elected to bat first on a dry wicket. Hughes and his fellow opener, Mark Cosgrove, weathered the first hour, getting through to the drinks break without losing their wicket. Hughes looked particularly determined and his former NSW and Australian teammates knew what that could mean for them. They set out to unsettle him with short-pitched bowling and a healthy spell of banter, something he'd become accustomed to in domestic and international cricket.

'He would never say a word, he'd just flick up his collar and look you in the eye and never lose your gaze,' NSW spinner Stephen O'Keefe said in Hughes' biography. 'Then he would bully you around. He slog-swept me for four, and then whipped one violently from off-stump out through midwicket, and then hit the single. When he got down my end, he said, "You spin the ball in, eh?"'

'I looked at him as if to say, "At least give me an over to settle."'

South Australian coach Darren Berry noticed that Hughes looked tired when he sat down in the dressing-room during the lunch break.

'You're on today,' he told him. 'Make sure you go big.'

'Tough work out there, coach,' Hughes replied. 'But I like it that way. They're not getting me out today.'

Hughes was determined not to fall to the hook shot, no matter how many bouncers were sent his way. He reached 40, taking his tally of first-class runs to 9000. He'd scored 26 centuries. Very few Australian batsmen — only legends such as Bradman, Harvey, Greg Chappell, Hayden and Ponting — had achieved these figures at such a young age.

As he reached his half century, the sledging from the NSW players gathered momentum. The hour leading into lunch had been 'torrid', according to Berry, and the Blues continued these tactics in a bid to unsettle their obstinate little mate. Hughes refused to bite, repeating to friend Nic Maddinson at bat-pad the same message he'd uttered to Berry in the lunch break. 'You're not getting me out,' he said.

Hughes reached 63, and a career-changing century looked likely. Abbott moved in, pitched the delivery short, Hughes tried to hook but was late on the shot. When the ball struck him in the neck, and he collapsed on the pitch, the players and umpires immediately sensed the seriousness of the situation. The NSW players who had been taunting him now raced to his aid. Abbott cradled Hughes' head as Warner sprinted for the change room to request an emergency phone call before sprinting back to the middle. Shane Watson and Brad Haddin placed their friend in the brace position.

Warner refused to leave Hughes' side, holding his hand as the Medicab made its way towards the boundary.

'I was standing at gully when it happened — and it all happened so *fast*,' Warner recalls. 'I'd been talking to him the over before, pointing to my little girl Ivy on the boundary. At lunch, he'd walked over and said hello. Twenty minutes later, he was struck in the head. It was heartbreaking.'

Mark Waugh was watching Hughes closely from the stands.

'He was batting really well,' he recalls. 'He'd copped a lot of short-pitched bowling in that innings. When he got hit, I wasn't too concerned because things happen all the time in a game of cricket. You see players get hit a lot. I was hit a few times when I played. You think the only way you can get badly hurt is if you get hit on the temple. But this time, there was total panic from the word go, players running around, screaming.'

During the morning session, Waugh had run into Berry when the South Australian coach ventured up to the press box in the Bradman Stand.

'How's Hughesy going?' Waugh asked him, as told in Hughes' biography. 'He's not looking that good against the short ball.'

'He never does, but I'll put my house on him making a century today,' Berry replied.

Waugh gave Berry a strong indication Hughes was in line for a Test recall if Clarke didn't recover in time from his injury. Rod Marsh has since said the 'master plan' was for Hughes to eventually replace opener Chris Rogers in the Test side. It was just a matter of time.

Instead, Hughes wasn't fighting for a recall but his life. One man who had a haunting view of the incident was *Daily Telegraph* photographer Phil Hillyard, who was looking down the barrel of a telephoto lens. One of the best in the business, Hillyard covered most sports over a 20-year period, but cricket was different. He understood the game and instinctively knew where the ball was headed before many of his peers.

He knew what was on the line for Hughes that day — and what he had lost. When I speak to Hillyard now, I can hear the pain in his voice.

'Hardest thing I've covered in my career, and that includes the tsunami,' he says. 'The thing that stood out was Dave Warner, who wouldn't let go of him. When the [Medicab] buggy stopped in front of the Members, I ran around to take a photo and he said, "Mate, no, put the cameras down." Which we did. I was trying to photograph his compassion, but I understood.'

Tragic events are difficult to report. Few who cover sport could ever imagine a sporting match turning into these unnerving scenes of someone clinging to life.

Sport's supposed to be an escape from reality, not a reminder of its brittleness. Hillyard showed respectful restraint as Hughes' injury became the biggest story of the day. He filed a handful of images but none showing the point of impact.

Later that week, as Hillyard struggled to sleep, he penned a piece about Hughes that appeared in the *Sunday Telegraph*: 'After a cautious start, he played some incredible shots. It appeared a matter of time before I would be taking pictures of his century celebration. Through a 600mm lens you see it all. It's like you're part of the journey, peering into their inner thoughts, and I feel what they go through. I feel their low when they struggle. I feel their joy when they win. And I feel their pain right now.'

Clarke was in the shower at his home in Vaucluse when Hughes was struck. A glance at his mobile phone when he got out told him something was horribly wrong. He had dozens of missed calls from NSW general manager David Thompson, Malcolm Conn and others.

'He's been hit in the head, there's a helicopter on its way,' Conn advised.

Clarke froze. He dashed to his car and started making his way down New South Head Road towards the SCG.

'The helicopter is taking too long,' Conn reported. 'He's in an ambulance, he's headed to St Vincent's.'

It took 23 minutes for an ambulance to arrive after the first call for help. Orchard climbed into the back and sat next to Hughes as the vehicle made its way through traffic towards St Vincent's Hospital in nearby Darlinghurst. That's where Clarke was headed, too, as news started to ping across the country about the incident. Before long, Hughes' friends were aware of the severity of the situation. At the same time, the nation became deeply invested in his health, including many people who didn't follow cricket or barely knew his name.

For the next two days, a procession of the country's cricketers — some household names, some not — streamed into the hospital. It soon became apparent they weren't coming to see how Hughes was faring but to say goodbye. On Thursday, November 27, 2014, Hughes' life support was turned off, three days before his 26th birthday.

An emotional Australian team doctor Peter Brukner fronted a media conference to explain what had happened.

'This was a freakish accident because it was an injury to the neck that caused a haemorrhage in the brain,' Dr Brukner said. 'The condition is incredibly rare. It's called vertebral artery dissection leading to subarachnoid haemorrhage. If you look in the literature, there are only about 100 cases ever reported. He was not in pain before he passed and was surrounded by his family and close friends.'

The injury was so rare that St Vincent's had never seen a patient suffering from it before.

PEOPLE HANDLE GRIEF IN different ways. The night of Phillip Hughes' death, those who were closest to him sought comfort in the place where all this had started. The SCG had been locked down since the incident happened, but that hadn't stopped people flocking to its gates on Driver Avenue. Cricketers of all skills and all ages, and from all over the city, came to the ground to leave flowers and written tributes, including cricket bats, caps and gloves. News crews were present from sunrise until late at night. Hughes' death became a national obsession.

Soon after his passing, family, friends and former teammates gained access through the Paddington Lane gates and down the pathway to the ground before parking their cars behind the Noble Stand. The Trust had opened the dressing-room and Long Bar in the Members Pavilion as a safe place for Hughes' loved ones to gather, to grieve, to begin to process what had happened.

When they arrived, they glanced out to the middle and saw some flowers resting in the spot where Hughes had been struck, a thoughtful gesture from long-time SCG Media and Communications Co-ordinator Caron Lefever, who had come to know Hughes well, as she had with so many sportspeople, particularly Australian cricketers. The home dressing-room became a 'grieving room' where people could talk to psychologists linked to Cricket NSW and to the NSW team chaplain Simon Flinders. Some players wandered out to the middle, trying to make sense of it all. Mitchell Johnson had flown from Perth to say goodbye at St Vincent's, but when he arrived at the SCG the grief struck him, tears flowing. Mostly, though, people sat in silence, numb with heartache and disbelief. How could this have happened?

Few of the people at the SCG that night were thinking about playing cricket. The first Test in Brisbane was postponed, with the series against India reorganised so that it would commence with the Adelaide Test on December 9. It remained uncertain how many players would take the field, such was their grief. Before the Australian team headed to Adelaide, the players converged on Macksville High School for the funeral service on December 3. Prime Minister Tony Abbott, Opposition Leader Bill Shorten and cricket greats such as Shane Warne and Brian Lara were among the mourners.

Hughes' death deeply affected many people. A social media campaign urging people to 'put out your bats' on front porches and in front yards gathered momentum, and soon they lined streets across the country. The SCG continued to be a place for the public to grieve and pay respect. The funeral was broadcast on television, but more than 4000 people converged on the ground to watch it on the big screen after the Trust threw open the gates. For people who couldn't be in Macksville, this was an appropriate place for many to be.

As mourners streamed into the ground, they were greeted by a line of 63 bats, symbolising the score Hughes was on when he was struck. Each bat had been inscribed with a small vignette of Hughes' life, the last of them guiding fans to the wicket square. A small white picket fence surrounded the pitch. A large action photo of Hughes rested on an easel, and it was surrounded by the numerous flowers, bats and messages that had been left at the gates during the previous week. People sat down on the turf or in the stands, watching the vision on the big screen as a light breeze drifted across the ground. Among them were Roosters and Swans players, who'd stopped training to pay their respects. The pain, sorrow and love for Hughes was felt across the SCG that day. Clarke delivered one of the eulogies and explained how the ground and Hughes would be indelibly linked.

'I could see him swagger back to the other end, grin at the bowler, and call me through for a run with such a booming voice a bloke in the car park would hear it,' Clarke said. 'The heart of a man who lived his life for this wonderful game we play, and whose soul enriched not just our sport, but all of our lives. Is this what indigenous Australians believe about a person's spirit being connected with the land upon which they walk? If so, I know they are right about the SCG. His spirit has touched it and it will forever be a sacred ground for me. I can feel his presence there and I can see how he has touched so many people around the world.'

As Hughes' coffin was carried out of the hall to Elton John's *Don't Let the Sun Go Down on Me*, the congregation rose and applauded, as did those at the SCG. Thousands of mourners followed the hearse carrying Hughes' coffin through the quiet streets of Macksville. Normally, it was herds of cattle that stopped traffic on the Pacific Highway. Now it was a hometown hero, but in the most tragic of circumstances.

That afternoon and well into the night, cricketing greats stood shoulder to shoulder with locals at the Macksville RSL Club — the team Hughes had played cricket for as a boy — and shared stories about him. Clarke stood among them, Red Bull and vodka in hand, the poison of choice on big nights out when the pair were young and living out their sporting dreams.

'After the funeral, when I came back to Sydney, I went straight to the SCG and walked out onto the ground,' Clarke says. 'I stood at the end he got hit, trying to work it out. I'm not sure why I did it, but my body just took me out there. I don't think that will ever leave me.'

PHILLIP HUGHES WILL ALWAYS be a part of the SCG. The large bronze plaque affixed to the red brick wall outside the home team's dressing-room means there is a permanent reminder of him for every player who walks along that famous race. The face on the plaque captures Hughes well, right down to his trademark five o'clock shadow.

The bust was sculpted by Cunneen Signs, a Sydney company that had previously designed tributes to Sir Donald Bradman, Monty Noble and Dally Messenger at the SCG and Sydney Football Stadium. Normally, they take months to create; Cunneen made Hughes' plaque in two weeks so it would be ready for the New Year's Test at the SCG, which loomed as an emotional return to the ground for players, officials and spectators.

And the Hughes family. On the morning of January 6, 2015, two hours before play, they gathered in front of the plaque. It was the first time they'd seen it. With the exception of some ground staff and Channel Nine technicians, there was nobody else there.

The family stood in relative silence for about 15 minutes, each taking turns to touch the bust, before taking their place in a private suite. Written tributes from the public left outside the gates, then on the pitch in the middle of the ground at the memorial, had been placed in the large cupboard in the suite for the family to read. At one point, SCG Trust chairman Tony Shepherd visited the Hughes family and gave Greg Hughes honorary membership.

'It might be difficult to come back,' Shepherd told him, 'but the Hughes family will always be welcome here.'

Says Shepherd now: 'Phillip's death left a deep scar at the SCG. You just don't think this could happen in a game of cricket. He will never be forgotten at the SCG.'

Australia arrived in Sydney for the fourth and final Test of the series with the Border-Gavaskar Trophy already in their keeping — a remarkable effort from a side still coming to terms with the death of one of their own. Before the opening Test in Adelaide, Dave Warner had walked into the nets, faced deliveries for five minutes and then walked out.

'I shouldn't be here,' he told his teammates.

The following day, he blasted 145 in Australia's first innings. Steve Smith scored an unbeaten 162. The delay to the start of the series gave Clarke enough time to recover from his hamstring injury. He made 128 in Adelaide, but it came at a price, as he hurt his back when he was on 20 and then tore his hamstring off the bone while trying to pick up a ball with one hand while in the field. Australia won that Test by 48 runs and then the rescheduled Brisbane Test by four wickets. The Boxing Day Test at the MCG finished in a draw.

The fact the series had been decided didn't lessen the emotion in the days before the Test in Sydney. From the black armbands worn by each player, to the '408' painted on the outfield, to the emotional tributes from batsmen looking to the heavens whenever 50, 63 or 100 was reached, Hughes was never far from anyone's thoughts.

Smith, who was also close to Hughes, was selected as captain in Clarke's absence. He wasn't playing in the Shield match when Hughes was hurt, because he had suffered a quad injury, but he was near the ground when the accident happened and arrived soon after. Three days before the Sydney Test, he strode out to the middle, confronting all the uncomfortable thoughts running through his mind. 'A few people who were out there on the day the tragic incident happened have been dreading this moment a little bit,' Smith told reporters when he returned. 'We'll get a feel for how people will be and hopefully everyone will be OK.'

As for the plaque, Smith offered this: 'Hughesy was one of us, he was one of our good mates. Particularly this week, it's going to be great to be able to walk past that and see the little fella there to give us a bit of inspiration as we're going out on the field.'

As had been the case in Adelaide, Warner struggled in the SCG nets the day before the Test. 'It's not like I was scared of getting hit,' he says. 'It was just the unknown. It was like that for many of us. I also politely asked the curator if we didn't use that pitch for a Test, because it brought back so many emotions.'

Hughes was batting on pitch number seven when he was struck. Normally, Test matches at the SCG are played on pitches four, five and six, so it was unlikely to be used anyway. There was no suggestion that the condition of pitch seven played any part in the tragedy, but at the end of the summer it was dug up and returfed.

Warner was itching for a big score to honour his mate after Smith won the toss and elected to bat on a sparkling Sydney summer day. He touched the plaque as he walked along the race and then burst through the gates onto the field.

'It was hard,' he reflects. 'It was my first time back there [as a player] since it happened. I didn't train too much at all leading into that game. I was taken aback with how I reacted before I got out there: I didn't want to go out on the field and let any emotions come to me until I played on the day. That's where the mind takes over … you ride those emotions.'

If Warner had been struggling in the lead-up to the Test, those doubts had slipped away by the time he reached the crease, and he and fellow opener Chris Rogers put on 200 for the first wicket. The most poignant moment came when Warner turned a ball off his hip down to fine leg to take his score to 63. As the crowd applauded, Warner walked across to the patch of turf where Hughes had fallen unconscious just six weeks earlier, where Warner had cradled his stricken mate's head. He bent down and kissed the pitch. He put his palms together to pray, then rose, looked at the heavens, and wiped away the tears.

Warner reached 101 before popping up an easy catch to gully while facing off-spinner Ravi Ashwin.

'It's always going to be in the back of my mind and I'm always going to remember my little mate,' Warner said at the media conference at the end of play. 'I thought it through in my head, [how] to pay tribute to my mate, and how to do that was what I did today. Every time I play here, I'll definitely be doing that … I had a tear in my eye this morning when I walked out to warm up and I saw Greg in the stands and Megs. It's fantastic for them to be here. The hurt and the pain they've gone through, and how much it would have hurt them to come back today … it's just courageous for them to be here and I applaud them for making the effort to come down.'

Warner thinks back to that innings now and knows he carried lessons from it for the rest of his career. The following summer, he scored a century against the West Indies. The next summer, he made his century-in-a-session against Pakistan.

'The beauty of that game [against Pakistan] is that it showed when you're playing with a clear, free mind, it's incredible what the body is capable of doing,' he says. 'I didn't think I was going to get out. I didn't have a worry in the world. Whatever I saw in front of me, I just played. It's amazing how you can't get yourself into that [state]. It doesn't matter how much you "dig deep" or "focus". When your mind is clear, your body goes with it.'

The Test against India in 2015 almost finished in similar circumstances to the Test seven years earlier, with Australia needing three wickets late on the final day. Unfortunately, there were no miracles like the one spun by Clarke, who was sitting in the commentary box for Channel Nine. Smith, who scored 117 and 71 (from 70 balls), was named player of the match and series.

The series was over, but it took much longer for the pain to subside for the players. For some, it may never go. An inquest was held in October 2016, but it offered few answers. NSW coroner Michael Barnes found nobody was to blame for Hughes' death, but invited players to reflect on the 'unsavoury' practice of sledging as it undermined 'such a beautiful game'. Helmets have been altered and debate continues about the use of short-pitched bowling.

Phillip Hughes lives on in the memory of those who knew him and those who did not. No sport celebrates numbers like cricket and two Hughes numbers — 63 and 408 — will never be forgotten, especially when they come into alignment at the SCG. On November 27, 2020, for example, Australia played India in a one-day international and, at 4.08pm, play was stopped and a minute's applause rang out.

Of course the connection between the SCG and Hughes extends beyond numbers for Warner. He can *hear* Hughes each time he bats at the ground.

'Always,' he says. 'When we batted together, there would be these little things he'd say while walking out. Talking about his cows, what we're doing after the game, typical Hughesy stuff. He'd have his little grin on his face at the other end. Laughing between overs at me. "Why are you blocking that? You don't block anything."'

Clarke feels a connection with every ground he played at, particularly those where he scored runs and celebrated famous victories as a player and captain.

'But the SCG is different,' he says. 'It's always going to be different because of my connection with Hughesy. It's hard to put into words how a sporting ground can connect you to a friendship. Even when I drive past the SCG, when I'm on Anzac Parade, I see the light towers and my mind goes straight to him. It's still sad, but I remember so many great things that happened there. The SCG does that. It's the place where I had my highest of highs, my lowest of lows. There's sadness, but there's also great memories.'

That's what the SCG is to many of us. For many decades, people have been drawn to this special place, often sitting alongside family and friends, in grandstands old and new, casting a discerning eye over different sports and events. There's an undeniable spirit at the SCG that makes it feel like a living, breathing creature, with so many of its stories still unknown to the wider sporting community but etched in the minds of those who know them.

The great ground doesn't just connect us to sport, but also to those we care about the most. Year after year, SCG officials receive requests from members and the public to scatter the ashes of loved ones across the hallowed turf. The ashes of champion Western Suburbs rugby league halfback Keith Holman and the great fast bowler Ray Lindwall, who also played in a rugby league grand final for St George at the ground, are buried underneath their sandstone plaques on the Walk of Honour at the request of their families. Then there's the resourceful people who aren't fussed with red tape, casually walking to the boundary and emptying trouser pockets containing their beloved's remains.

The memory of Phillip Hughes will stay with us forever, through the images of him playing and of the grieving that occurred at the SCG and elsewhere in the days and weeks after his death, and through the plaque outside the home dressing-room that means so much to his family and friends. These stars who gave us enormous pleasure might be gone, but at least, as Alan Davidson assured us in the chapter that opens this book, memories last much longer than dreams.

Acknowledgments

The idea for this book came to me at a Bradman Foundation gala dinner at the SCG on October 29, 2014. Steve Waugh and Sachin Tendulkar were on stage after being inducted as Bradman Honourees. After Waugh relived his epic last-ball-of-the-day century, I texted Phil Heads, the SCG Trust's communications director, who was sitting in another part of the room: 'I need to write a book about the SCG.'

It's been a long, long process since then to arrive at the book you have in your hands today. A lot of people afforded me more patience than I deserved, especially Phil, who I thank for his advice, support and mostly for his friendship. Thank you also to Venues NSW chairman Tony Shepherd and his board, and chief executive Kerrie Mather, for their belief in the project. A big shout also to Caron Lefever and Sue Channells for their help, not just with this book but with many other requests I've made over many years.

This book would never have happened without the stamina and professionalism of Geoff Armstrong, a great author in his own right, but an even better editor and publisher who can spot a factual error from a thousand yards. His advice and additions have been invaluable. Thank you for everything you've done for me, Geoff.

I interviewed and consulted more than a hundred people for this book and thank everyone for their time. I also referred to countless books, newspapers and periodicals. Philip Derriman's *Grassy Pitches and Glory Years* was an invaluable resource in providing an overall feel for the ground's early years. Other books are referenced in the chapters and bibliography, but I'd like to especially acknowledge Peter Jenkins' *Wallaby Gold*, Tony Lockett's autobiography, *My Life*, Steve Waugh's *Never Say*

Die and Malcolm Knox and Peter Lalor's superb *Phillip Hughes: The Official Biography*.

One of the highlights of researching and writing this book was meeting St George heroes Johnny King and Eddie Lumsden near their homes in the Hunter Valley. Johnny provided rare footage of the famous 1963 grand final. Sadly, Eddie passed away in October 2019. A true gentleman. Thank you also to Ray Baartz for meeting with me in Newcastle and being so open about his career-ending and life-threatening injury.

I'd also like to thank, in no particular order, the late, great Greg Growden, the late, great Noel Kelly, Kathy McCabe, John Watson, Jeff Apter, Richard Colless, Kevin Sheedy, John Quayle, Robert 'Crash' Craddock, Shane Watson, Adrian McGregor, Stu Wilson, Malcolm Conn, Ray Gatt, John Taylor, David Gallop, Jim Tucker, Gary Lester, Ian Heads and David Gyngell, who all helped with information and setting up interviews.

As a sportswriter, I've been lucky enough to visit the best stadiums around the world, but I've never loved one more than the SCG. I got lucky with the first match I attended there: the one-dayer between Australia and West Indies on New Year's Day 1996, when Michael Bevan hit a match-winning four off the last ball of the night.

I had goosebumps then and the place still gives me goosebumps now. It's where I've witnessed so many special events, but none more important than raising a glass in the Long Bar in honour of my beautiful friend Rebecca Wilson after her passing, and carrying the coffin of former *Sydney Morning Herald* sports editor Rod Allen on my shoulder in front of the Members Pavilion to Elton John's *Rocket Man*.

To write about the SCG and its heroes, great and small, who have graced its hallowed turf is a true honour.

Andrew Webster
September 2021

Bibliography

Jeff Apter, *The Book of Daniel: from Silverchair to Dreams*; Allen & Unwin, Sydney, 2018

Paul Barry, *The Rise and Rise of Kerry Packer*; Bantam, Sydney, 2007

Richie Benaud, On Reflection; William Collins, London, 1984

Neil Cadigan, *Greats of Origin*; HarperSports, Sydney, 2011

Andrew Caro, *With a Straight Bat*; The Sales Machine, London, 1979

Alan Davidson, *Fifteen Paces*; Souvenir Press, London, 1963

Philip Derriman, *Grassy Pitches and Glory Years: Grand Visions of the Sydney Cricket Ground*; Playright Publishing, Sydney, 1998

Philip Derriman, *100 Tests: A Century of Test Match Cricket at the Sydney Cricket Ground*; Playright Publishing, Sydney, 2012

Neil Harvey, *My World of Cricket*; Hodder & Stoughton, London, 1963

Gideon Haigh, *The Cricket War: The Story of Kerry Packer's World Series Cricket*; Bloomsbury, London, 2017

Ian Heads, David Middleton and Geoff Armstrong, *From Where the Sun Rises: 100 years of the Sydney Roosters*; Playright Publishing, Sydney, 2007

Ian Heads, *True Blue: The Story of the NSW Rugby League*, Ironbark Press, Sydney, 1992

Max Howell, Lingyu Xie and Peter Horton, *Stan the Man: The Many Lives of Stan Pilecki*; Celebrity Books, Auckland, 1997

Peter Jenkins, *Wallaby Gold: 100 Years of Australian Test Rugby*; Random House, Sydney, 1999

Malcolm Knox and Peter Lalor, *Phillip Hughes: The Official Biography*; Macmillan, Sydney, 2015

Alan Lee, *A Pitch in Both Camps: England and World Series cricket in Australia 1978-79*; Stanley Paul, London, 1979

Gary Lester, *Clouds of Dust, Buckets of Blood: The Story of Western Suburbs DRLFC*; Playright Publishing, Sydney, 1995

Tony Lockett, *My Life*; Ironbark, Sydney, 1999

Adrian McGregor, *King Wally*; University of Qld Press, Brisbane, 1987

Malcolm McGregor, *Paul McLean*; University of Qld Press, Brisbane, 1985

Ray Martin, *Stories of My Life*; Random House, Sydney, 2010

Jeff Sayle, Chris Handy and John Lambie, *Well I'll be Ruggered!*; Ironbark Press, Sydney, 1993

Norman Tasker, *The Gladiators: Norm Provan and Arthur Summons on Rugby League's Most Iconic Moment*; Allen & Unwin, Sydney, 2013

Doug Walters, *Looking for Runs*; Pelham Books, London, 1971

Steve Waugh, *Never Say Die*; HarperSports, Sydney, 2003

Steve Waugh, *Out of My Comfort Zone*; Penguin, Melbourne 2005

Andrew Webster, *Supercoach: The Life and Times of Jack Gibson*; Allen & Unwin, Sydney, 2011

Mike Willesee, *Memoirs*; Macmillan, Sydney, 2017

Larry Writer, *Never Before, Never Again*; Stoke Hill Press, Sydney, 2016

Larry Writer, *Pitched Battle: in the frontline of the 1971 Springbok tour of Australia*; Scribe Publications, Melbourne, 2016

Photographs

Index